GLEANINGS FROM THE WAYSIDE

My Recollections as a Golf Architect

BY ALBERT WARREN TILLINGHAST

A.W. Tillinghast

Researched, compiled, designed and edited by
Richard C. Wolffe, Jr., Robert S. Trebus and Stuart F. Wolffe

**Dedicated to
The Tillinghast Association
www.tillinghast.net
and to
Liz, Dee, Suzy, Charlie, Christopher, Matthew, Rachel, Jack, Tami and Clare**

Library of Congress Control Number: 2001 131986

ISBN: 0-9651818-2-0

© Copyright 2001 by TreeWolf Productions. All rights reserved.
No part of this manuscript may be reproduced, stored in a retrieval system, or transcribed, in any form or by any means, electronic, mechanical, photocopying, recording, or otherwise, without the written permission of TreeWolf Productions, 9 Coleridge Road, Short Hills, NJ 07078.

Printed in the USA by Smith Lithograph Corporation, Rockville, Maryland on McCoy Paper (Potlach Corporation, Cloquet, MN) distributed by Frank Parsons Paper Company, Inc.

INTRODUCTION

IN OUR WORLD, nearly all works, great and small, are accomplished through teamwork. Great teams have great leaders, and just as important, they have great contributors. Certainly, the same applies to the great golf courses of the world—there was surely an architect of record, but there were also owners, consultants, bankers, lawyers, engineers, construction foremen, irrigation specialists, skilled shapers, construction laborers, and many more. Working together as a team they made it happen!

In a similar vein, this book is a product of teamwork. We collected the written work of one genius of a golf architect. And we had a team of resources to draw from—the Library of Congress, the World Golf Hall of Fame, the Ralph Miller Library and the USGA Golf House. But more importantly, from these great resource institutions we had the professional help of Karen Bednarski, Helen Dalrymple, Marge Dewey, Saundra Scheffer, Rand Jerris and Nancy Stulack.

We had many other great contributors of photographs, historical information and other support to make it happen. These included in no particular order, Ken Stofer, Dick Ringwood, Frank Hannigan, Geoffrey Cornish, David Fay, Rees Jones, Geoff Shackelford, Ben Crenshaw, Peter Dock, Craig Surdy, Kevin Purcel, Bruce Smith, Jim Walton, Charlie Kirkwood, Jeff Hymes, Lowell Schmidt, Bob Labbance, Mark Leslie, Pete Korba, Dave Korba, David Kamens, Steve Weisser, Dr. Phil Brown, Jr., Lou Chanin, Tom Hand, Doug Smith, Richard and Benita Wolffe, Dee Trebus, Susan Witmer Wolffe, Liz Wolffe, David Applegate, Warren Chancellor, Cilla Jackson, Brad Klein, Mike Bacica, J.W. Jones, Laura Puchalski, Joe Shorto, John Crow Miller, Bruce Matson, Dick Smith, Ed Venella, Jack Rutherford, Randy Rotchin, Butch Berry, Donald Luke, Tim Minahan, Tom Morris, Tony Pancake, Barclay Douglas, Maynard Garrison, Judy Comotto, Paul Spellman, Kevin Brown, Peter Trenham, Ron Forse, Jim Nagle, Gary Gaylean, Stephen Goodwin, Dr. Peter Rosenthal, Brian Siplo, Ernest Ransome III, Ran Morrissett and any others we inadvertently omitted.

Stuart F. Wolffe, Robert S. Trebus, Richard C. Wolffe, Jr.

Many thanks also to the PGA of America for its courtesy in reprinting several of Tillie's articles, which originally appeared in the *PGA Magazine*. The importance of the financial support of Charlie Smith and his company Smith Lithograph also made it happen.

This now concludes our Tillinghast trilogy. The first two works, *The Course Beautiful* and *Reminiscences of the Links,* were very satisfying. We hope you enjoy this finale.

Richard C. Wolffe, Jr.
Robert S. Trebus
Stuart F. Wolffe
Baltusrol Golf Club
Springfield, NJ

TABLE OF CONTENTS

INTRODUCTION	3
FOREWORD BY GEOFFREY S. CORNISH, A.S.G.C.A.	7
RECOLLECTIONS OF A GOLF ARCHITECT	9
1. MODERN GOLF CHATS	19
2. BUILDING GOLF COURSES IN THE SOUTH	21
3. THE CATAPULTERS OF SAN ANTONIO	24
4. AND THEY BUILT A COURSE BY THE TRINITY RIVER	27
5. OUT TULSA WAY	29
6. THE NECESSITY FOR A TALE OF WOE COMMITTEE	31
7. SPRING LAKE	33
8. CALIFORNIA COURSES	34
9. ROUGH GOING	37
10. OUR GREEN COMMITTEE PAGE	43
11. A HOLE IS JUST AS LONG AS IT PLAYS	56
12. BOUNDARY HOLES	58
13. DENSE SHRUBBERY	60
14. AN UNUSUAL DOUBLE DOG-LEG	62
15. A SHORT PITCHED SHOT	64
16. THE BOOMERANG HOLE—A GROUND SAVER	66
17. A WASTED HAZARD	68
18. THE OPEN AT WINGED FOOT	70
19. A NINE-HOLE COURSE ON 20 OR 30 ACRES	76
20. MAKING THE MOST OF THE TEE	78
21. TEEING GROUNDS FOR TWO-SHOTTERS	80
22. SANS SAND PITS	82
23. A DOUBLE GREEN	84
24. MINIATURE GOLF COURSES	86

25.	POPULAR TYPES OF GOLF HOLES	91
26.	AN EXCEPTION TO RULE	93
27.	BLIND HOLES	95
28	DOWN TO OLD MEXICO FOR GOLF	97
29.	WINTER GREENS	101
30.	SNAKE HOLES AND GOLF HOLES	102
31.	THE FIVE FARMS COURSE	105
32.	OUT OF THE ADIRONDACKS	110
33.	WAY DOWN AND WAY OUT	112
34.	WHAT THE P.G.A. COURSE SERVICE REALLY MEANS	116
35.	THE MASTERPIECE OF DONALD ROSS	118
36.	GLEANINGS FROM THE WAYSIDE	120
37.	FROM THE GULF TO PUGET SOUND	122
38.	THINGS I AM OBSERVING	127
39.	INTIMATE SURVEY OF OAKLAND HILLS	130
40.	WHEN TRAPS ARE FRIENDLY	133
41.	TEXAS GETTING BENT-MINDED	135
42.	THE UGLY DUCKLING OF THE COURSE	138
43.	NOW WHAT ABOUT TREES?	140
44.	OLD ANANIAS PAR	142
45.	THE GIMME GUYS	144
46.	THE LONG ONE-SHOTTER	146
47.	THE TINY TIMS OF GOLF	148
48.	MORE CONCERNING MR. PAR	150
AFTERWORD—FOLLOWING TILLIE'S TRACKS		152
BIBLIOGRAPHY AND PHOTO CREDITS		160

FOREWORD

"EVERY sunlit day composes a symphony beautiful to behold," wrote Canadian Arnold Haultain, when describing the playing fields of the game in his *Mystery of Golf*. Published in 1908 and reprinted in part in the *Atlantic Monthly*, his book was dismissed as fanciful. Had it appeared after Baltusrol, Winged Foot, San Francisco Golf Club, and other courses of the Golden Age had seen the light of "sunlit days," it could have been considered realistic.

Some say that golf is no more than a game involving a club, a ball and a very small hole. Indeed, golf can be exciting on featureless terrain. Yet, golf architect Rees Jones said, in a foreword to *Reminiscences of the Links*, "Golf is a game in which the player's opponent is the golf course." To this end, course architects have created unbelievably magnificent and exciting golf holes to provide exhilarating corridors from starting point to tiny hole and have arranged them in fascinating sequences.

A.W. Tillinghast's masterpieces, the first coming on line in 1911, continued through World War I and the Golden Age of course architecture and then into the Great Depression. They were landmarks in the evolution of the art form of golf course architecture. In less than half a century, according to British architect Fred Hawtree, course architecture evolved from "the primitive to the classic," or as we claim on this side of the pond, somewhat less modestly, "from 18 stakes on a Sunday afternoon to the most magnificent landscapes ever created by our species."

GEOFFREY S. CORNISH
Geoffrey S. Cornish is a noted golf course architect, golf historian and author. His accomplishments in his field are many. He is President of Cornish, Silva and Mungeam, Inc. and is the architect of record of over 200 golf courses in the United States, Canada and Europe. He co-authored The Golf Course, The Architects of Golf *and* Golf Course Design. *He is a past president of the American Society of Golf Course Architects, and also served as Chairman of the History Committee. For his achievements he was inducted into the Canadian Golf Hall of Fame.*

Tillinghast's career spanned much of this evolutionary period and his contributions to our art form were numerous. Tillie created scores of handsome courses, several ranking among the world's greatest, and was able to achieve reasonable finality in his productions—something that eludes most of us—because American golfers never cease to seek something better. He also understood that engineering and science were inherent to works of art and incorporated agronomic and engineering principles into his own creations.

Tillinghast used the site, not the drawing board, as his canvas. A determined artist, Tillie never allowed bull elks, chiggers, ticks and even poisonous snakes to deter him, when he suspected that nuances such as unusual wind effects and distant vistas could be found and worked into his masterpieces.

The world of golf is indebted to A. W. Tillinghast for both his masterful creations and his informative, prolific literary compositions. Creative and often eloquent, these writings focused on design, construction and maintenance of the playing fields of the game. We are now grateful to Richard C. Wolffe Jr., Robert S. Trebus and Stuart F. Wolffe for compiling and illustrating three beautiful volumes containing Tillie's abundant published works, hitherto scattered in libraries from San Diego to Boston, and from Vancouver to Miami. These can provide golfers now and far into the future with an understanding of the aims and objectives of our profession.

Wolffe, Trebus and Wolffe compiled *The Course Beautiful* in 1995 and *Reminiscences of the Links* in 1998. Now they have produced *Gleanings From the Wayside* to complete the trilogy. As a bonus, this third volume includes an afterword describing Tillie's consulting work for the Professional Golfer's Association of America in the dark days of the Great Depression, a period in his life that has hitherto proved elusive to scholars of course design. We are also impressed, and deeply so, by the illustrations and photographs, reproduced by state of the art technology, from faded photos dating to before World War I.

Scanning the literature of course architecture, one finds these quotables:

Golf architect Rees Jones in *Reminiscences of the Links*: "Tillinghast was pure genius."

Cornish and Whitten in *The Architects of Golf*, Harper Collins, 1992: "Known in his day as Tillie the Terror, he was an outstanding golf architect and one of the most colorful characters in the history of golf."

Ben Crenshaw in *Reminiscences of the Links:* "He was an individualist to say the least."

Geoff Shackelford in *The Golden Age of Golf Design,* Sleeping Bear Press, 1999: "The most fascinating character of the Golden Age."

Frank Hannigan in *Golf Journal*, May 1974: "He was a superb, not a good or very good, but a superb golf course architect."

Tillie was indeed a superb golf architect and a giant in the evolution of course design, an artist, an author of two books of fiction and a prolific writer on subjects relating to golf. Surely what Tillie wrought so brilliantly justifies what Haultain said long ago about symphonies and golf.

I speak for the American Society of Golf Course Architects, its President John LaFoy, the Society's Executive Secretary Paul Fullmer and its members when I say that this trilogy, now complete with *Gleanings from the Wayside*, is immensely valuable to us in the profession. It will help contemporary golf architects create their masterpieces and will assist them in finding a meaning in life's work. Wolffe, Trebus and Wolffe have indeed made it possible for designers and the public to comprehend Tillinghast's philosophy as he added new dimensions to our art form.

Geoffrey S. Cornish
Amherst, Massachusetts

CATALINA ISLAND, ONE OF TILLINGHAST'S STOPS DURING HIS TRAVELS

Recollections of a Golf Architect

THE VARIED happenings in many places during the periods when courses are staked out and constructed provide an almost inexhaustible fund of reminiscence. Few people who golf over finely-turfed courses give a thought concerning the original condition of the land or the patient labor (often hardships) which went hand in hand with the reclaiming of jungle, swamp, forest and rocky glade. My golf architecture recollections cover a period of years.

THE SIXTEENTH GREEN AT SAN ANTONIO

In 1915 it was my work to lay out the municipal golf course at San Antonio, Texas. A telegram from Mayor Brown of that city briefly stated that I had been selected to plan the course in Brackenridge Park. Now on the face of it, the work of laying out holes in a city park did not suggest any difficulties. But I was to run into some "tough" going and not a little adventure which were unexpected. In the first place that section of the now beautiful Brackenridge Park, where the municipal course of the present exists, was a track of something less than a hundred acres of absolutely undeveloped land. It was covered with a thick growth of mesquite and ouisache wood. There were huge pecan trees, which were spared whenever possible—and there were other things as well, such as wood-ticks, coyotes, wolves, rattlesnakes and "bad hombres." More on these later.

As the lines of the course were started, I discovered that it was necessary to cross directly through a natural deer park, which was probably a quarter of a mile in diameter. A stream of ten to fifteen feet wide ran through the enclosure which was surrounded by high wire fencing. A herd of elk roamed at large and it was the rutting season. The two bulls had fought for the herd and the victor good-naturedly strolled about surrounded by his admiring "lady" friends. The other bull sulked alone, "nursing his wrath to keep it warm." I never did like his looks and gave him a wide berth. This feeling seemed to be mutual, for several days later he suddenly charged me and only the warning cry of one of the workmen saved me. The bull elk was almost on top of me when I took a headfirst dive

THE COURSE IN BRACKENRIDGE PARK, SAN ANTONIO, TEXAS, ON THE FIFTEENTH GREEN

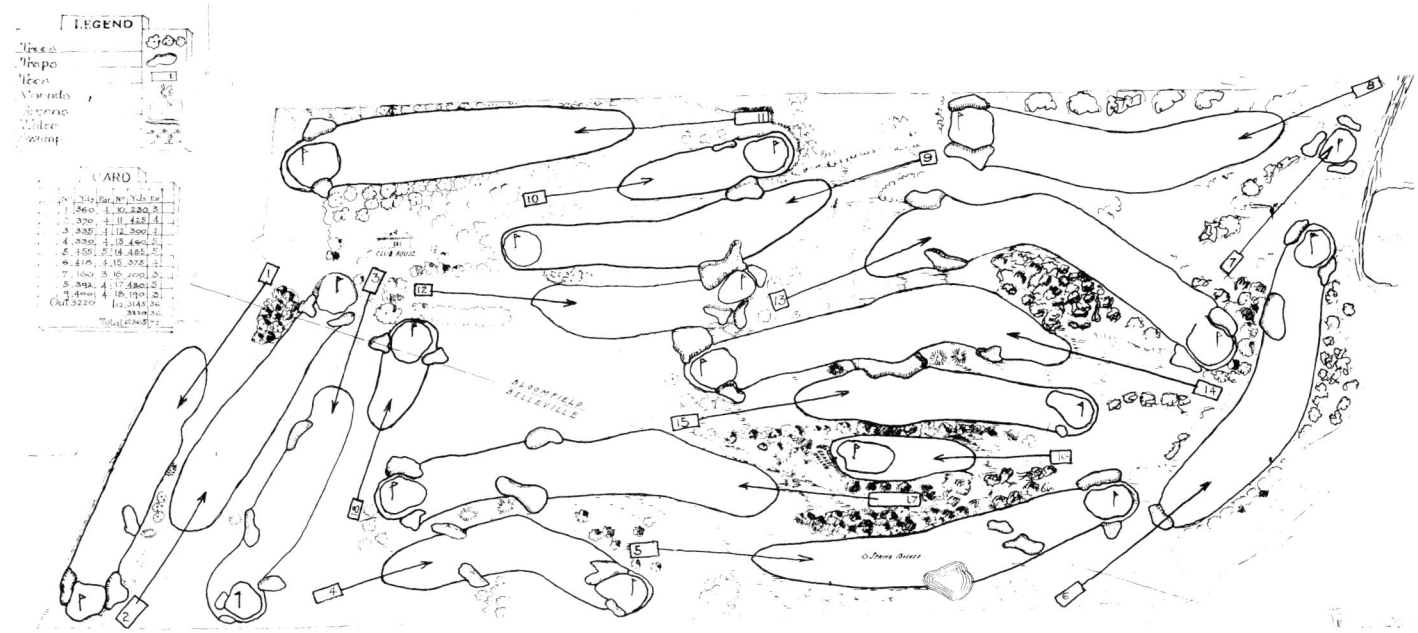

FOREST HILLS FIELD CLUB

over a thicket and the steep bank of the stream. But a dislocated shoulder was better than those horns.

The Southwest came to the fore in golf in a truly amazing way. The building of courses out there would astonish the visitor from other parts. In Oklahoma the spread of the game was marked. Work in this state, too, brings back many thoughts. In the course of work there it was my lot to be brought face to face with the race riots in Tulsa, when the white and black races fought in the streets of the city and over the bodies of the fallen all the way to the Frisco railroad tracks and beyond to the Negro section, which was burned to the ground for blocks. On another visit to Oklahoma it was necessary to travel daily an outlying road, which was at that time the favorite point for Hijackers. Fortunately, I was never molested, although frequently I traveled this road after nightfall. However, when I took my departure by train from a small railway station I had nearly all my money secreted inside my shoe. It was an unnecessary precaution, for I arrived fifteen minutes too late for the holdup.

My work throughout the South, particularly in Florida, brought with it many unusual incidents. A Negro by the name of Ed was in charge of the workmen and it was funny to hear him issue orders in a language peculiar to the locality. For instance, if there was a big log to be removed he would shout, "Gang de Gator," at which men would lift the log and await the next order of "Creep Turkle," when they would move away with it. It is obvious that "Gator" must have been passed down from the time when really big alligators were more common in that section than at present, and the reference to "Turkle" had its conception in the methodical movements of the big land turtles, or "gophers," as they call them there.

The East Coast provides another incident, which I think may bear telling. I had been in the vicinity of Jacksonville laying out a course, when I was retained by the City Counsel of Jacksonville to inspect and report on several properties which might be developed as a municipal course. The first tract visited with the committee of the council was known as the Sand Hills, a desolate area where was located the workhouse. I was taken to a rather dilapidated house on a slight

SEVENTEENTH AT ST. AUGUSTINE

elevation. A yellow sign on the door indicated that sometimes it was used as a pest house. Preferring another, and what seemed to me a less alarming point of view, I surveyed the Sand Hills from a corner which was waist high with bushes and rank weeds. As I stepped about there was now and again the breaking of something underfoot. Inquiry elicited the information that during the yellow fever plague in Jacksonville, sometime during the eighteen seventies, if my memory is not greatly at fault, hundreds of bodies had been buried in that corner; buried as well as possible at that time of disaster, each in a shallow trench. It is probable that my feet were breaking aged and rotted wooden grave markers only, but I fear that innocently enough the very bones of the dead were being trampled in that weed-grown corner of the Sand Hills.

On several occasions my work has taken me to Tennessee, not far from the notch of the Cumberlands, which John Fox, Jr. used as a setting for so many of his tales of the mountaineers. It had been my privilege to know the novelist before visiting the section, and an added pleasure to run across him there. It was shortly

THE MUNICIPAL COURSE AT JACKSONVILLE

before his death. He told me much about the country and the natives, but it was not until the following year that chance, offered the opportunity to witness a strange scene, which was worthy of Fox's pen. It happened that a young man, scarcely twenty, while under the influence of moonshine, had shot and killed a deputy sheriff. He was tried at the county seat, a town not far distant from the course we were building, and a rainy day gave me the chance to see the opening of the trial. The courthouse was undergoing repairs and as a consequence the court convened in a village schoolhouse. We sat at the children's desks, and it was difficult for some of the big fellows to get their legs under them. Many smoked corncob pipes and the smoke was dense. The prisoner lighted one cigarette after another. Nearly everyone was without a coat, even his honor the judge, for the day was sultry, and flies, and an occasional wasp, came flying through the open windows. Space forbids any details, but the sight of that prisoner on trial for his life, seated in front of a blackboard, which still bore the letters and figures of children's hands, and upon which he had

A VIEW OF THE EIGHTH PUTTING GREEN AT THE TULSA COUNTRY CLUB
During the play at the Oklahoma Amateur Championship.

scrawled probably the same letters only a few years since, is a picture which will remain long in memory.

It was in North Carolina that I encountered a thoroughly abject man. On this particular day it was a trifle cold, for as I recall it was during the month of February, and when it gets just good and snappy in Carolina it is almost impossible to get the men very far away from a fire. And so it was that my sole helper was one forlorn poor man. He was at one end of a hundred-foot chain and it was his business to walk ahead to the end of the chain, mark the spot so that I might pick it up, and so proceed. He had been marking the ground by giving the ground a few kicks with his heel and for a while all was well. Then the marks grew fainter and fainter until I called for him to do better. For a while he did, then the heel marks went faint again. A sharp rebuke brought him to a dead halt and he turned deliberately and slouched back to where I stood. The worm had turned. He said no word until he reached me and then he sadly lifted his foot and looked mutely at me. There was no heel on that shoe. Neither was there very much shoe for his bare, raw heel showed through all. Until his own heel wore out he had kept on trying his best to kick marks in the frosted ground. Then he said the only words I ever heard him utter, and he said it sadly as he looked at that raw heel, "Honest, mister, I ain't no hoe." He was believed and the situation relieved.

Winter work in the south, particularly the far south, is most desirable, but frequently the architect is called there in the middle of summer, and at that time he has to contend with much. Once in Florida when it was red hot I suffered intensely. Back among the pines the red bugs and chiggers were awful, and one had to go about constantly anointed with enough oil to make him smell like an old-fashioned parlor lamp. The mosquitoes were man-eaters. While riding a horse through the pines around the course I have felt those big fellows boring right through the cord riding-breeches, and there he would be, with his snickersnee all the way in and his tail sticking straight out like a rudder. In assassinating him one does not have to hurry for that mosquito is in there for keeps.

Some years ago I laid out a course in Virginia, and the heart of it ran directly through a fine watermelon patch; the month was July and the melons were prime. Imagine a gang of men doing their best work with that sight right in front of them. To relieve their sufferings, each evening we gathered thirty or forty fine melons and put them in a nearby branch to cool, and throughout the day from time to time a waterboy distributed chunks of the juicy to the men, as much as they wanted.

There is a certain element of danger which attends the converting of virgin land to the requirements of the modern golf course, but certainly no more than other professions know. The average citizen, walking the streets of any city, is open to more than the worker in open places. During the years I have given over to the planning of courses and the supervision of their construction, with thousands of workmen under observation during that period, I can recall but two fatalities. These men lost their lives when the dynamiting of rocks was in progress, and through their own disregard of danger. However, my own was nearly snuffed out once through no fault of anyone. The clearing of timber was being accomplished in a light sandy soil. The men were getting right down to the roots and allowing the trees to fall by their own weight. One huge pine had been rooted until only the tap remained. But the taproot was rotten and the tree fell directly at me. My back was turned, but as the

ON THE SEVENTEENTH GREEN AT SCARSDALE G.C.

big pine toppled the men shouted in such alarm that instinctively I threw myself flat on my face in the sand. The tree fell immediately over my prostrate form, and had it not been for a deformed trunk these gleanings would have never been written. In a trunk, otherwise straight as an arrow, there was a twist, and as luck would have it, this malformation was the part of the trunk which covered my body exactly as though it had been made to measure with only a few inches to spare all around. As it was, one jagged bough, which had been broken off close to the trunk, actually touched my back, but as lightly as a feather. Close call! Knock wood? You bet!

Naturally enough, particularly when the crew unfortunately happens to be comprised of mixed nationalities, there are brawls in the camps. In Westchester County, New York, a laborer deliberately shot a fellow countryman in the head. The victim was an old hand and a good one. These things are not pretty to see or contemplate, but they could happen on the street just as easily, for the vendetta is not particular.

To be sure minor hurts are numerous but pass almost unnoticed. Some rather nasty falls have been my lot, but my bones are intact for the most part. A rather laughable incident is recalled, although there were a number of men who, no doubt, failed to see any humor in it. A mixed gang of native and non-native laborers was clearing timber, and my previous exploration of this particular spot told of the presence of hornets, many hornets—more than conceivably inhabit one neck of woods. When the gang started in there I took to a convenient hillside to the windward. Every non-native came pelting out yelling with pain. With not a single exception the natives kept steadily on, stopping only to pick and brush the maddened insects off their faces and necks. If the hornets bothered these hombres with their stings there was never the bat of an eyelash to show the slightest pain.

IT WOULD BE HARD TO FIND A MORE BEAUTIFUL COURSE
Bluff Point, Lake Champlain.

Golf course building brings queer grist to the mill of labor: Italians, Negroes, Polish, Chinese, Mexicans, Indians—all sorts, and few of them really know what it is all about. They have to be taught in most instances. Imagine breaking in a gang of Mennonites or Dunkards. I never rightly knew which, but I do know that they spoke Pennsylvania Dutch exclusively, and every man Jack had whiskers down to his waist. One of them was reputed to be over eighty years of age, but he could put to shame many a younger man. Some years since, a course was building on Long Island, and as labor was scarce the committee had called in about fifteen Gypsies. I knew that one man's name was Mitchell and one day when I happened to want something done I called, "Mitchell, come over here!" Instantly the entire crowd answered the call. The name was tribal and common to all. At Newport, Rhode Island, many of the men are Portuguese. They are good workmen, too, for the most part. When we were building the course at Shawnee in 1910 the foreman of the Italians, an Italian himself, rejoiced in

BUCKWOOD INN AND EIGHTEENTH GREEN AT SHAWNEE

the name of Casey. Sometimes these Irish names have been taken because the original names are difficult to pronounce or to remember. But enough of workmen in general. The main thing is to see that they work.

Assistance in our work sometimes is hard to secure, and there is recalled an incident, which will go to prove that on occasions a kind of providence will help along. A few years back I was retained to make plans for the reconstruction of the course at Bluff Point, Lake Champlain. Already I had made a preliminary visit, and as my report was favored, instructions were given to prepare definite plans at once. It was very late in the fall and already the large resort hotel there was closed; indeed, the trains had discontinued stopping at Bluff Point for that season. The nearest point was Plattsburg, New York. My departure had been so hasty that I did not have time to summon my regular engineer, and really I was wondering what I would do. However, I took the chance of calling in some local surveyor. It so happened that the train slowed up for some other reason or another just as we came to the golf course, which was hard by the tracks. I seized the opportunity, threw out my bag and jumped off myself, for the speed of the train was not great. There was the course all around literally congested with engineers and transits. It happened that the engineering corps from the army training post at Plattsburg had selected this morning and this spot for practice. They might just as well practice on a golf course as anything else, and by this uncanny stroke of good fortune it was possible to return to New York that same night with all the data that was necessary.

The ideas of the general requirements of a golf course in remote sections sometimes are amusing to an extreme. On one occasion a gentleman came in to town, where I was engaged, just to talk of golf architecture as one brother worker with another. He was building a course in his hometown about twenty miles distant. He brought his plans with him and displayed them with considerable pride. He used up considerable territory in his scheme, starting out with a seven-hundred-and-fifty-yarder as hors d'oeuvre and finally winding up in a blaze of glory with a home hole of exactly a half mile in length. Apparently he regarded anything like a one-shot hole as utterly beneath contempt and the mere crossing of fairways was a minor consideration. That fellow surely was a glutton for distance, for if recollection is right, the nine holes had a total yardage close to the six thousand mark. I made no attempt to dissuade him; indeed, there was but small opportunity, for he did all of the talking. It was just as well, for probably any ideas of mine would have amused him and I must not forget that golf architecture is a serious profession.

In looking back over the making of many courses and recalling the incidents that are unusual, none is more interesting than finding oneself on historic ground, and it is almost with a spirit of reverence that these spots are made into golf holes. For example, at Ingelside, California, when the course of the San Francisco Golf Club was redesigned, I recall the story told me of a deep ravine, in which a famous duel was fought many years ago. It was how the duelists faced each other's pistol across the foot of the ravine, while hundreds of spectators from the city lined the hillsides. At Lewiston, New York, a short hole stretches across a ravine, along which was discernable a faint but unmistakable trench. In this, Continental soldiers were entrenched in battle with the British. In Westchester County, New York, both the Quaker Ridge and Winged Foot courses were laid over land which was one of the favored retreats of J. Fenimore Cooper, and in my own

BOBBY JONES AND CYRIL TOLLEY VERSUS JIM BARNES AND MIKE BRADY
Play in exhibition at Wykagyl C.C.

rambles in planning these courses thoughts of the author of the Leather Stockings novels came frequently to mind.

Shawnee, along the upper waters of the Delaware River in Pennsylvania, was built on the very site of the old village of the Minsi Indians of the Delaware nation. As excavations were made relics of these departed Americans constantly were brought to light—flint arrow heads, celts, stone hatchets and even pottery were unearthed. A wonderfully perfect pottery jar was turned up, but before it could be rescued a worker's pick had shattered it. Arrow and spear heads were not uncommon finds in many course building operations, and I am told that one of the finest specimens in existence was picked up by me during the building of Cedar Brook at Philadelphia. No doubt the builders of courses see and constantly think harder over these fragments of departed people than the players ever do.

As a matter of fact, architects are brought very close to nature in many ways, and even around the big cities, although in rough country there is much that the general citizen scarcely imagines. Within a hundred miles of Wall Street many deer are encountered, and during the winter of 1924, while examining a tract of golf country in South Jersey, three fine bucks were seen during one day. Fox, skunk, ground hogs, weasels, mink, muskrats, and on one occasion a black bear have made their homes within a few short years on what are now well-developed courses. During the work at Baltusrol in 1922 a man secured some remarkably fine flashlight photographs of night-prowling animals on the nearby wooded slopes.

The laborer, who is to be found in construction camps generally, is not the most cleanly person, but there was one who proved the exception to the rule. I met up with him while Essex County was under construction. Every day, and sometimes twice a day, that lad would go out to the stream, shed his clothes entirely and splash around for a good fifteen minutes. And this was in the dead of winter. Even though there was ice, he would go to it, enjoying it like a polar bear. He happened to come from the north of Italy, and was accustomed to dips in the glacial streams, and altogether a different breed from the laborer who, for the most part, comprise construction gangs.

When the golfer of today rolls up to his country club in a fine motor car, it is improbable that he give a single thought to the condition of that same road before the course was built. It must be remembered that usually the courses are located back from public roads, often miles away from main thoroughfares. In 1923 in the province of Quebec in the Laurentians, it was necessary for me to take a twenty-mile road twice a day and over a road which was absolutely cruel. It

BEAUTIFUL ELMS ON THE LAKEWOOD COURSE

was early in the winter, but before the snows, and consequently all the summer camps were closed. None but the native habitants was met with. On my first day there I noticed the apparent anxiety of the driver of our Ford to make an early start for the village. He drove like a mad man, and it would be difficult to imagine a rougher voyage. As it was, we passed absolutely no one on the road going in the opposite direction, and it is safe that none passed us going our way. But the seeming desolation of the country surprised me, although occasionally a head would appear at a window. Afterwards I found out that this was the one day in the year when, according to the habitant belief, the dead left their graves and, burrowing like moles, did something or other subterraneanly—possibly visited each other. But that driver was taking no chances, particularly after dusk. Yet in a year or two that same awful road became as fine as any state highway, and led to a country club.

Sometimes in getting back to a prospective site for a golf course the way is little more than a trail through the woods, where even a Ford cannot go, and then it is a case of riding shank's mare. In 1923 at Lakewood, near Cleveland, Ohio, there was a country dirt road, which ran for probably a half-mile back from the main thoroughfare. After a storm it was absolutely impassable for any sort of car. A year later in December, I rode over this same road, paved entirely for a distance of two miles, I should say, until it connected two roads. There was no reason in the world for paving but for the fact that a new country club opened there during that past summer.

In 1907 a sleigh took me over a distance of twenty miles, and it is my candid belief that we did not pass a score of houses after the first five miles. With the mercury showing eighteen below zero and a rough road it was tough sledding. Today that entire country has been opened up because a golf course was built back there in the woods. You could not wish for a better road, and houses? Plenty! These references to roads in these recollections are intended only to indicate the great power which a golf course displays in opening up almost unheard of corners of the land.

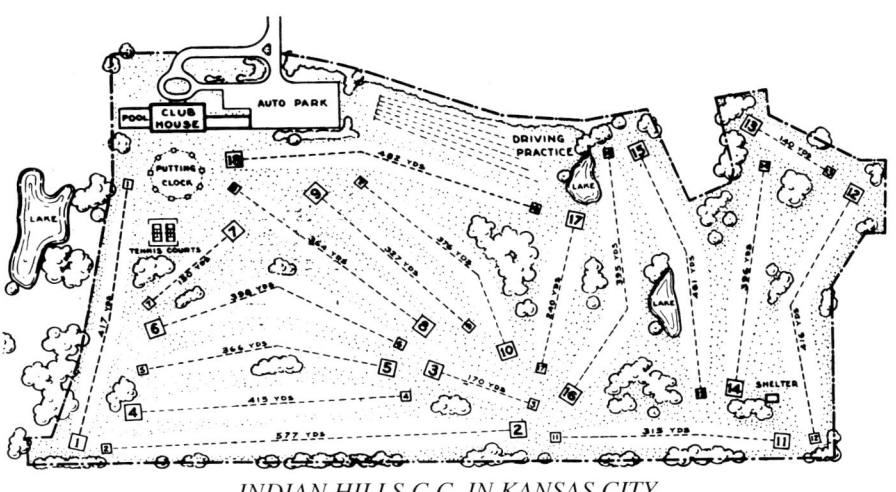
INDIAN HILLS C.C. IN KANSAS CITY

Frequently the natives resent the invasion of the golf pioneer. It has been necessary on more that one occasion to fight off or take refuge from vicious dogs which have been "sicked" on. Once an irate farmer emptied a thirty-thirty at myself and the engineer at a range of only five hundred yards, and he made us take cover, too. He was a renter, and knew that we were there for no good, as he took no interest whatever in the Royal and Ancient. At another time, at a place I shall not name for obvious reasons, I was made the object of a personal night attack simply because I was retained by a company whose interest in opening up a certain tract was deemed antagonistic to others. I will only say that it was in the far South. Fortunately, this antipathy to the spread of golf disappeared rapidly. In all parts of the country the game found ways there to stay. During the summer of 1923 I had the privilege of laying out a course about twenty-five miles out of Chicago. One day I was talking to the farmer who sold his property to the club. He was an elderly man, and apparently used to following the plough all his life.

"I suppose you will take up golf when the course is opened," I said half jokingly.

"You never can tell," he replied, and he was not joking at all.

That is right. You never can tell!

A.W. Tillinghast

Harrington Park, New Jersey

THE SITE OF THE INDIAN HILLS CLUBHOUSE
The original stake of the first teeing ground is in the foreground.

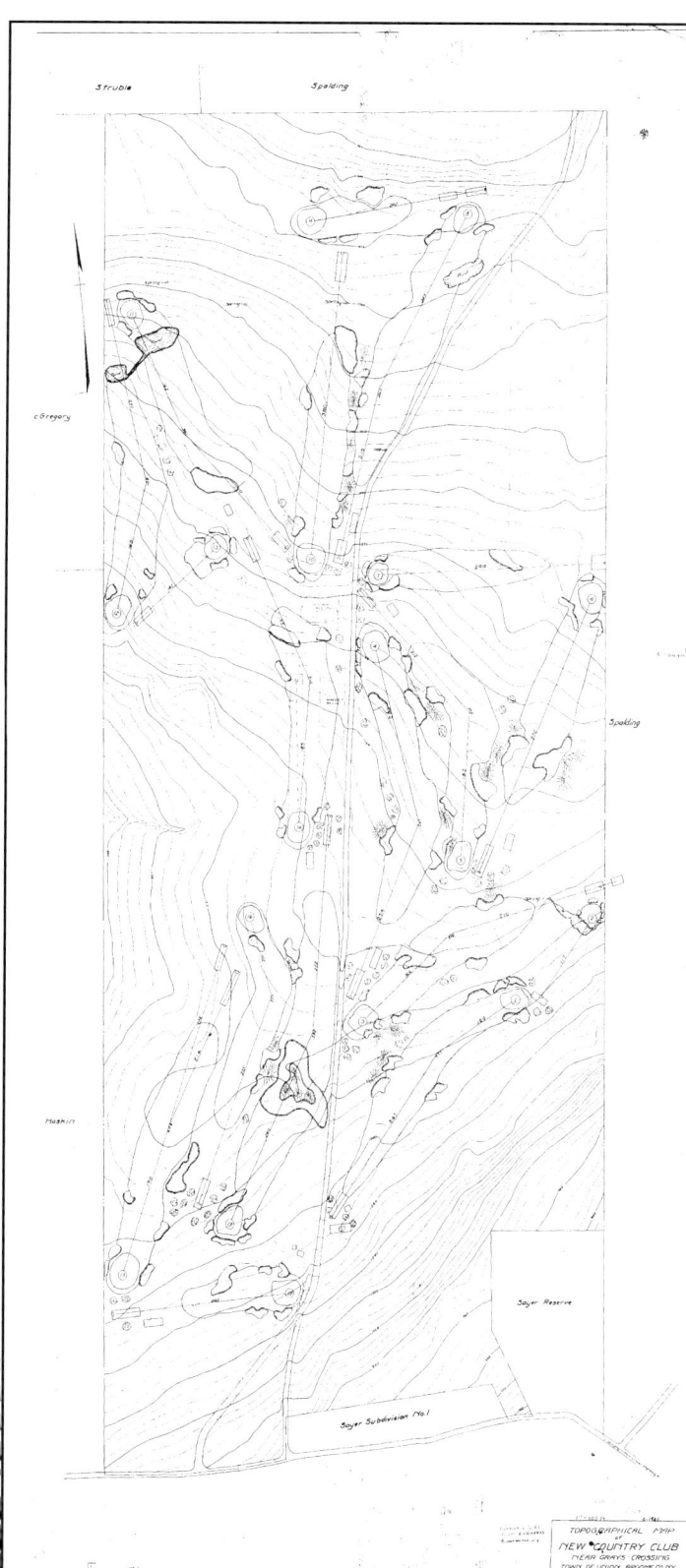
TOPOGRAPHICAL MAP OF A NEW COURSE
Binghampton C.C.

A FINE DOGLEG HOLE
On the Essex County C.C. course.

THE SUBURBON C.C. CLUBHOUSE
As seen from the first fairway

AN ELECTIVE CARRY IS AN OPTION
The sixth at Pine Valley.

The Punker's Lament

DON'T build us any bunkers;
Don't dig us any pits;
We're a legion of golf punkers;
Hazards scare us into fits.
We much prefer a fairway
Of the bowling alley type,
Like falling down a stairway
As we slice or pull or swipe.

Our course was built by Willie Ken
'Way back' in ninety-two;
Since then it's been once altered, when
We cut the vistas through.
If water hazards trap us,
We pick out by local rule;
The ditch, likewise, on Number Five,
Also the Home Hole pool.

Have I not seen the National?
The Garden City, too?
Their plans are most irrational,
Not like our River View.
Pine Valley is another Hell,
Designed by that mad Colt,
With dogleg propositions, well,
The place gave me a jolt.

You may talk about your places
Where a golfer has to play,
And to your very faces
"It isn't golf," I say,
You can't tell me that it is fair
To make one hit the ball.
You dig your hazards everywhere—
My shots are sure to fall.

If I should chance to miss a shot
I can't get home, you say;
Now, that's what I call 'bloomin' rot,
Look here! It's golf, I play—
The golf that Punkers like to see,
And I can prove it, too,
If some day you will go with me
To our dear River View.

1 — Modern Golf Chats

HAVE you ever seen a plowboy come to town, all-dressed up in a suit of clothes which had been marked "Nobby" in the window of a Cross Roads General Store? He looked all right at the Cross Roads, but his appearance was ridiculous among people who wore up-to-date clothing. America was becoming dotted with ready-made golf courses of the Cross Roads style, until a few enterprising men visited real courses and, realizing the absurdity of their own links, started in the work of tearing down and rebuilding.

Today the Cross Roads golf course is something of a curiosity. It may seem curious that early American golf courses were laid out on such puny scales and along such unintelligent lines. The game was biff and bang, with little else to think of; no problems to solve. But after all it is not so much to be wondered at. Our early players were faddists whose conceptions of golf were exceedingly crude. How could they be expected to appreciate the finer points of the game as did those in the old country, where golf had been played for so many years?

It is not necessary to attempt a description of those early American courses, with their featureless greens, mathematically correct and symmetrical bunkers and the ridiculous little bandbox teeing grounds. They are of the past, but they served their purpose. The golf courses which we Americans are constructing today are very different, and so carefully are they built, after a thoughtful preparation of plans, that some of our productions are not surpassed even in the old home of golf.

This Texas course presents an admirable example of the elbow type. Graded carries of the mesquite confront the player, but a beautifully undulating green presents its longest face to the second shot of the courageous driver. The dotted lines show how the timid player may avoid any trouble from the teeing-ground, but after doing so it is likely that he again will elect to play safely, taking three to get home rather than attempt an even more hazardous shot than which faced him at the start.

For a long time the greatest obstacle in the way of modern courses in America was the opposition of the mediocre player. He fancied that any attempt to stiffen the courses must make them so difficult that the play would be beyond his powers. But now he realizes that the modern golf architect is keeping him and his limitations in mind all the while he is cunningly planning problems which require the expert to display his greatest skill in negotiating holes in par figures. We are planning and building not to penalize very poor strokes, but rather those which are nearly good. If our holes are of proper distances as dictated by natural conditions the duffer who misses a stroke cannot be figured as a serious factor, so why add to his discomfiture?

"But how may this be accomplished?" is a most natural question for you to ask. Let me attempt a simple and brief explanation, for in the limited space of these tabloid articles, elaborate analysis is impossible. Instead of relying on hazards which extend directly across the line of play we are building them diagonally. It is obvious that these diagonal hazard lines present a much longer carry at one end than at the other, and all carries between the two points vary. In the placement of the short carry we consider the light hitter, and as he stands prepared to play at such a hazard, he is to be the judge of the distance which he may successfully attempt. After a while, as he finds his game improving, it is natural that he becomes more ambitious, and he attempts greater things which he knows will be adequately rewarded, for the hazards guarding the approaches to the green are placed in such a manner as to grade the benefits of length and accuracy. In brief, every player gets exactly what may be coming to him and it is not necessary for anyone to bite off more than he can swallow.

The old-fashioned cross bunker always leers at the player with a "You must." The modern diagonal hazard shows even a more ferocious face at one end as it says to the scratch man, "You should." But all along the line to the short end it is saying, "You may."

The accompanying sketch of a one shot hole, which the writer recently laid out on the municipal golf course of San Antonio, Texas, illustrates the diagonal carry. Here the courageous drive finds the green, but there are other carries of the river which prove a hardship to none.

In subsequent articles I shall attempt further explanations of why modern golf construction is taking care of every class of player.

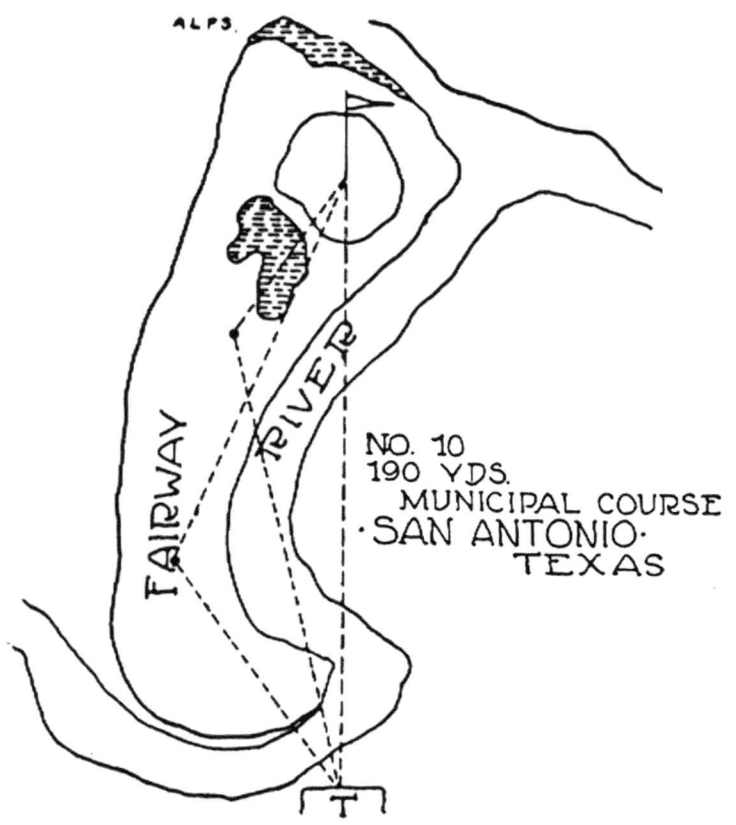

BASSETTS CREEK IS THE CHALLENGE ON THE PAR 5 TENTH AT GOLDEN VALLEY C.C.
This creek provided numerous opportunities for elective play, as it meanders through the golf course on its way to the Mississippi River.

2   Building Golf Courses In The South

IT IS quite possible to estimate the number of golf courses which were constructed in America during 1916. To observe that they were many is sufficient. But without a doubt the South and Southwest contributed more than any other section; and possibly personal experience as a golf course architect in these parts during these times may enable me to speak of the situation there with some little understanding.

The native Southerner wants to play over a good course himself, and recently there has been manifested a determination to create courses of distinction. To a great extent the present activity may be attributed to a realization of the fact that the thousands of northern tourists who visit the South during the winter months will not tarry where they cannot golf.

THE LILLIPUT LINKS AT ATLANTIC BEACH, FLORIDA
This nine holes approach and putting course was planned in August 1915 and opened before Christmas Day of that year.

The City of Jacksonville, Florida, never considered a municipal course until this fact was driven home in no unmistakable manner. They never knew that the city was the natural Gateway through which visitors must enter and depart from Florida, and hosts of them break their journeys at this point.

"But why do they not stay here longer?" was the question which the Jacksonville business man asked himself, and he began to investigate. He found that the pilgrims had as their destinations, golf resorts, and then Jacksonville concluded that semi-public courses must be provided in order to transform the visitor of a night to one whose stay would extend through days. There was everything to attract except satisfactory golf.

So might be enumerated many other points in the South which are touched by tourists, and quick to realize the necessities of the occasion, the up-to-the-minute men in these places are building golf courses. And they are insistent upon modernity, too, for no longer are they content with the extremely primitive types which once existed throughout the country.

As an illustration of the South's progressive methods, let us turn to Atlantic Beach, not twenty miles from the City of Jacksonville. At this place there existed a bungalow colony and a large modern hotel, and in the summer of 1915 it was decided that a golf course was necessary. I was called there in August of that year and after putting in three days in riding over an unbroken tract of palmetto and working over charts, sufficient work was outlined for the large force of laborers, who were called in that same week. They camped on the ground, and the amount of work which they accomplished was prodigious.

It must be remembered that nearly everywhere one puts his foot in Florida he is walking on palmetto, each springing from a gigantic root frequently four and five feet long, and much thicker than a man's arm. Thousands on thousands of these roots have to be grubbed, and this is easier said than done. There is a knack in getting them out and I have watched a powerful man, who was a new hand at the work, struggle with one root for an hour, while at his side was a little old man who had removed seven or eight in the same length of time. However, these palmetto roots are not without their uses, and several years before on the West Coast of Florida I hit upon an idea of assembling them on various parts of the fairway and covering them with sand. In this fashion an imitation of rugged dunes was accomplished, which not only relieved the flat country of monotony, but proved an easy way of disposing of the roots. As a rule you cannot dig deep pits in Florida, for water is encountered close to the surface, and in creating hazards, it is necessary to build up. It is comparatively easy to create artificial water hazards.

THE TENTH GREEN AT ATLANTIC BEACH, FLORIDA
The entire eighteen holes opened for play in 1915.

The native grasses spread very quickly, and after the ground is once cleared and prepared it does not take very long before a very satisfactory fairway is produced. The photograph of the tenth green at Atlantic Beach shows exactly how this part of the course appeared in August of 1915. That they were playing golf over this same country a year later proves how quickly a course may be prepared.

LIKE A MIRROR OF THIS BEAUTIFUL LAKE
Which must be carried on the second shot of the first hole at the San Jose Country Club.

Another photograph of the Lilliput Links at Atlantic Beach, reveals a well knit turf and smooth putting greens, which were not developed prior to August, and by the way, this miniature approaching and putting course, close by the hotel, proves very popular with the ladies and children, and even among the best golfers as well.

In laying out a course which is to be turfed with Bermuda, the architect has to remember that his distances may not be so great as those on northern links, for a ball gets but little run, and a course of six thousand yards in those parts would demand as much vigorous play as one three or four hundred yards longer over northern turf. And speaking of turf brings the thought of greens. There has existed differences of opinion regarding the ideal southern green, whether it should be of grass or sand. Undoubtedly the native grasses which have been used for greens in the South do not provide a very satisfactory turf over which to putt, and for the most part, the inhabitants declare that the finer grasses cannot be produced and maintained in that climate. This timeworn theory has been proven erroneous, for in some places fine greens have been developed. But, for that matter, good grass may be grown anywhere, provided proper preparation be made and intelligence devoted to its development—and incidentally, that amply sufficient funds be provided.

I like turfed greens where the shots may be played boldly up to the hole but where we have to conceive of the shots striking short of the greens and rolling onto the billiard table like patches of sand, the game savours strongly of skittles.

In the early days of golf construction the usual procedure was to confine the work to the meadowlands and open, but nowadays whole forests and jungles are cut through by fairways. Particularly is this true in the South, and I have recollections of Davista where I was turned loose in a mass of tropical vegetation which was so dense as to seem almost impenetrable. The last of the clearing was accomplished in the winter of 1915, and they were playing golf there a year later.

The photograph taken in October 1915 on the site of the municipal golf course of San Antonio, Texas, shows a section immediately in front of the thirteenth green, but scores of laborers made short work of the tangle.

THE THIRTEENTH AT BRACKENRIDGE
The green is reached by an approach over this point.

While the early clearing of the San Antonio jungle was going on, the work was not proceeding fast enough and after a conference with Mayor Brown and Park Commissioner Ray Lambert, it was decided that an additional force of fifty men for ten days would be necessary. "Very well, we will have them for you in the morning! Do you want to come along and see us get them tonight?" I did. The force at Brackenridge was composed of city prisoners. That night the raids on cockpits and crap games provided the necessary fifty. Not forty-nine or fifty-one, mind you, exactly fifty—and all huskies. It was noticeable, too, that during the raids all the big, strong bucks were placed under arrest while the little fellows somehow or other managed to make their escapes after only halfhearted attempts to pursue. Before leaving that old city one of the shanghaied hombres that was gathered in to order that night gave me a mark of his esteem which will remain with me always. In an effort to escape the guards, which for no reason at all I unwisely attempted to frustrate, he neatly broke my nose with the hickory handle he had carefully removed from a grub-hook.

The convicts were put to work, and one day we had a very exciting time when two of them escaped from their guards, never to be seen again. With one eye ever on the lookout for freedom, the convict laborer is not nearly so efficient as the free man, but nevertheless, the prisoners are mighty handy to fall back on when the city has work to do.

To those professionals who play over the Brackenridge course in the big Texas Open Tournament, it may be interesting to say that when the sixth green was built it was necessary to dig out a den of lobo wolves, a mother and her young. That one visit to San Antonio provided much to turn over in the mind in after years.

But not alone to the far South is confined the wave of golf construction and reconstruction. In all of the states new courses are being planned and developed, and for the most part there seems to be a determination to have these courses built along modern lines. To be sure there are some who have yet to be educated to the requirements of the game and players of today. In their eyes any collection of holes constitutes a golf course but they will learn their lesson eventually when they realize that golfers of the present are critical and discriminating, refusing to accept a new course which presents the antiquated features of days gone by. But fortunately the South is realizing that really fine courses may be their portion and that they intend having them augurs well for the future of the game in that section.

3 THE CATAPULTERS OF SAN ANTONIO

THE FALL of 1915 saw me in "San Antone," in old Texas, with its Alamo and other ancient Spanish Missions and the distinctly lingering atmosphere of the pioneer days. But it was not to saunter to quaint corners that took me there. My mission was to lay out the Municipal Golf Course in Brackenridge Park, and the site of the course certainly was no park. Through a half-jungle of mesquite and huisache we blazed the way for future championships. There were rattlesnakes aplenty, but distinctly more obnoxious were the chiggers and Texas wood ticks. Individually and collectively they were mean hombres.

As mentioned earlier, in clearing one green we had to evict an old mother wolf and her litter, and during the days to follow I not only had my shoulder dislocated by a charging bull, but my nose broken by a grub-hook handle, wielded by a big Mexican convict laborer, who desired to hie him hence. I wish to this day that I had not tried to thwart his "hieing" ambitions.

Altogether many adventures were crowded into two weeks and old San Antone furnished a fertile field for recollections. For example, the necessity for a night raid of the Mexican cockpits and gambling shacks to gather in an even fifty prisoners. What else could Mayor Brown do? The city depended on convict labor, the hoosegow was under-patronized and we had to have fifty men to hack away the dense scrub-growth over the city's future golf course.

But above all else and most green of all, is the memory of my day with the Catapulters. On a Saturday night, a very pleasant Texan called on me at

THE BRACKENRIDGE CLUBHOUSE

A RUSTIC BRIDGE AT BRACKENRIDGE PARK

THIS IS THE OUTLOOK THAT CONFRONTS THE PLAYER
From the ninth tee on the Brackenridge Park course, opportunities for trouble are abundant.

the Menger Hotel to invite me, particularly, to be the guest of himself and friends on the following day. He explained that they played golf and had formed a club for this highly laudable purpose. This rather surprised me as the only golf club that I knew of there was the San Antonio Country Club, where Frank Lewis was an executive. My visitor only informed me that his club, rejoicing in the name of "The Catapult," had only been playing golf for a short time, and further added that they were not very good at it.

So it came to pass that Sunday forenoon found me traveling in his Ford to an unknown destination, but which happened to be directly across the main road that skirted our golf work at Brackenridge. The clubhouse was a saloon of one, Ed Beers, and the course was "laid-out" over an adjoining acre of adobe. There were eight holes only in view, and without fear

BILL MEHLHORN STUDYING A FOUR-FOOT PUTT
On the seventy-second hole of the big San Antonio open tournament. Failure to hole this putt cost him first prize, since he was left tied with Walter Hagen and lost in the playoff.

BILL MEHLHORN, JACK O'BRIEN AND WALTER HAGEN
These were the three principals in the championship; the runner-up, tournament manager and the winner, respectively.

of contradiction I assert that this was the very first of the countless Tom Thumbs, Tiny Tims, and What Have You midget courses that were to infest the land years later.

The first hole presented an abandoned street watering cart which might be played over or under, as the urge had it, and each of the others were similarly devised. One offered the wreck of a Ford as an obstacle. Only eight holes have been mentioned. The ninth was inside the saloon and was approached through the window, whose entire frame bore the wounds of many futile shots. But one had to loft in to get in, which all succeeded in doing eventually.

It appears that originally the Catapulters had banded together to pitch horseshoes, which they did for some time until one man stopped the show. He was a left-hander, whom we may call Andy for no better reason than that the passing years have fogged his real name. Well, Andy got to be so deadly that he literally road herd on the others. They all were discouraged. They could not even work out any handicapping scheme, even to the filling of Andy with keg beer. With or without it, he was supreme—the undisputed champion.

Then a conference of all. Andy excluded, and it was decided that the only way to trim the champ was to switch decks on him. Consequently, it was determined that a game, which none of them had ever played, be the future pastime of the club, and golf was the name of the game. Their sole information was gleaned from a Spalding's Guide, and soon clubs were picked up, a bargain lot of old niblicks and putters, without a single left-handed stick among them. Yet, on this Sunday the Catapulters were deep in despair, despite the handicap of starboard clubs. Andy had discovered a way to loft and sink them by the simple expedient of turning a putter and knocking the ball around with the back of the blade.

He was so resourceful that when, for example, a side-tilted picnic table might block his direct way, Andy would sight an empty beer keg, off line. Hitting this with rare accuracy his ball would carom off to exactly the right spot close by the hole. Andy made his own doglegs, the lines of which were many and devious. He was a champion.

Some seven or eight years later I had another call to Texas and stopped in at San Antonio. I looked in vain for the old saloon.

THE CARRY TO THE SEVENTEENTH FAIRWAY
On the municipal links at San Antonio, Texas.

In its place stood a spick-and-span house, bright in white and green paint and showing a splendid swinging sign which bore the legend: "Ye Golf Inn." I entered (to make inquires only). There stood Ed Beers in knickerbockers.

"Yes all the boys are fine." At the moment they were all across the road playing the Municipal Course.

"Yep, Andy was over there, too, skinning them alive." Still champion!

FAIRWAY BUNKERS ON THE EIGHTH AT BRACKENRIDGE

4 AND THEY BUILT A COURSE BY THE TRINITY RIVER

IT WAS in the year 1920 that a few of the outstanding golfers in Texas concluded that they would like to play over a more testing course than was their custom. Most prominent of these were Cameron Buxton, Charles Dexter, Louis Jacoby, Collett Munger, and H.L. Edwards, all of Dallas. True they were all members of the country club of that city, which possessed an enjoyable but not overly stiff course. Later, George Rotan, and other leading players from other parts of Texas came into the fold as the new course of Brook Hollow developed.

AIRPLANE VIEW OF BROOK HOLLOW G.C., 1926

Cameron Buxton, who came originally from North Carolina, was a close friend of the late George Crump, whose conception of Pine Valley was the direct result of a similar situation. As most golfers know, this great course was planned to give the best golfers of the Philadelphia district testing play which their individual courses utterly lacked. Buxton had been one of George Crump's most enthusiastic coworkers at Pine Valley during the years he lived in the North and before he finally followed his business into Texas. "We need a Texas Pine Valley," he often declared and encouraged by those with whom he played, he threw himself wholeheartedly into the project. Equally enthusiastic was Dexter, and finally a tract of land, hard by the Trinity River, was discovered after many tracts had been examined and rejected. The condition of blow-sand there seemed to promise a better turf structure than the heavy and tight "dobe" variety, so common in those parts.

CHARLES L. DEXTER
One of the pioneers of Brook Hollow, and the USGA.

So here it was that these pioneers of Brook Hollow concentrated on proper layout and modern construction. Although complete plans for eighteen holes were drawn, only nine were finished and played during 1922, but the fall of the next year found the eighteen completed. Every effort was directed to the course itself and any thought of an elaborate clubhouse never came to mind. Brook Hollow was from the start, and still is, a golf club rather than a country club. The course itself has proved to be an exceptional test of the power and versatility of the golfer. The greens contour to place great premium on

CAMERON B. BUXTON IN 1920
As the course was being staked through the thickets.

the placement of tee-shots. The light sandy soil, typical of the land immediately along the Trinity River, provided a well-knit Bermuda grass fairway just as soon as the plants matured and spread. The variety of turf is essential to the climatic conditions of Texas and altogether is quite satisfactory.

The year 1934 witnessed the course withstanding successfully the attacks of the greatest amateurs of the Mid-West. The Trans-Mississippi Championship was played there and a great field participated including Lawson Little, Johnny Goodman, Johnny Dawson, and Gus Moreland. The latter needed 159 in the medal round and did not qualify.

Moreland was not enjoying his usual robust physical condition and to this may be attributed his failure to conquer the course on this occasion, for he knows every yard of it. However, the visiting notables found that more than a casual acquaintance with the varying problems was not enough to keep them in the running and a fine Texas golfer, Leland Hamman, of Waco, won the championship.

This tournament found Brook Hollow in grand condition and no one managed to menace par figures, so it would seem that the hopes of the founders and builders of this really fine course have been amply realized. The one great pity of this being that "Cam" Buxton did not live to see it all.

165 YARDS TO CARRY THE POND AT NUMBER EIGHT AT BROOK HOLLOW G.C.

5   OUT TULSA WAY

MY ATTENTION was attracted by a solitary man who had been swinging an iron for an hour, and was still swinging it, in fact, out on a flat on the hillside. Far across the slight valley was a caddie retrieving ball after ball, and he was not even working up a sweat for he seldom had to move far out of his tracks. On this hillside was spread a pocket handkerchief, the target at which the iron shots from the other side of the valley were being directed, and the balls fell about this small square of white with monotonous regularity. It was what anyone would call smart shooting at a two-hundred-yard range.

It was out in Oklahoma on the old course at Tulsa around 1920. I had just arrived from Dallas, Texas, where I had planned the Brook Hollow course, and my visit here was for the purpose of rearranging the Tulsa layout. During my survey on the previous day I had observed this solitary figure swinging his iron against the skyline, but until now, on nearer view, the deadly precision of the marksman (for he was indeed just that) had escaped me. His ammunition consisted of probably fifty balls for each volley kicked up the dust pretty close around the distant handkerchief. If it happened that two or three successive shots did stray a bit wide of the mark, the distant figure displayed every symptom of utter disgust.

"Who is that bird over there?" I asked my guide, who told me that it was the club's young pro and further added that this practice was of almost daily occurrence, adding, "He must have knocked a couple million golf balls over at the rag." So I made it my business at the first opportunity to look over this patiently persevering sharpshooter, at closer range. He was a rangy lad, well set up and powerful. "Name's Mehlhorn," he explained, "Bill Mehlhorn." And so it came to pass that I witnessed the early training, out Tulsa way, of a man who was destined to develop into one of the great shotmakers of our country, a truly sturdy golfer.

"WILD BILL" MEHLHORN
A fine golfer, who, unfortunately, has never been entirely appreciated. His great shots have yet to click at the right time.

I have often wondered if "Wild Bill" harbored visions of supreme greatness, as day after day as a mere broth of a boy, he whaled those screaming irons across that Oklahoma vale, and I think that certainly he did. Surely he had every reason to do so. That he never reached the great heights to which his undoubted shotmaking ability should have taken him seems to me one of the tragedies of golf. Possibly he was not lucky enough to get all the breaks that help to make sustained success and pave the path to supremacy.

It is likely that Mehlhorn was never entirely understood. He had a big heart, generous and without envy of those who have dusted him off in the golf race to the summits. Maybe, too (and I think it extremely probable), he was sensitive and took to heart many things which would roll off the thicker hides of others, and his rugged exterior would seem to belie any such trait in his makeup.

Out there in Oklahoma, I believed that I was seeing a great golfer in the making, and I still harbor the suspicion that time yet may prove this to be a truth. And, if it may help him any, I would like Bill

Mehlhorn to know that there are many, many golfers in America who will be happy indeed when he does come to his own in a big way.

At this time oil was "coming-in" and Oklahoma was riding high, wide and handsome. Strangers swapped oil-leases in Pullman smokers and the lowly Osage Indian suddenly waxed affluent, riding about in automobiles of ancient vintage, which had been restored to an alarming degree of grandeur by liberal coats of vivid paint. The more noise the motor made the better the Indians liked it.

A little later, I revisited Tulsa to lay out the Oakhurst course. The tract was a quarter-section, one hundred and sixty acres, and I required almost a year before clear title could be obtained. It was necessary to secure the signatures (or marks) of quite a few Indians, each owning some small portion of the one hundred and sixty acres. This hampered the work considerably, for shyster lawyers made a bit here and there by hiding the desired Osages away and holding out for bonuses. Soon a new law remedied this evil.

But this was not the only handicap that hindered me. A bit of hazard always lends interest, and the state laws which permit cattle to graze at large seemed to have brought every mean bull to that particular quarter-section. But even so, they did not prevent the work from lagging. I confess a lurking fear of this gentry, probably dating back to a day when I managed to weather a treacherous attack of a mean bull, but suffering a dislocated shoulder. Among the undesirables, which made our particular quarter-section their stamping ground, was one with liver and white decorations. His countenance was extremely disagreeable and his whole demeanor hostile. Undoubtedly he disliked me exceedingly. Every time I see a tiled floor of this combination my thoughts fly back to him. That liver-colored brute actually stalked me for the entire week of the course planning, always seeking points for sneaking attacks. Certainly I never did find golf holes under such duress, one eye on the terrain and the other on my tormentor. That he did not muss me up more may be traced to a suddenly-acquired agility, but probably quite as much to his failing sight. Yes, he was old, and ornery. I hope that bull got the mumps or something else equally annoying.

JAMES KENNEDY HAD TO HOLE THIS SHOT TO TIE BILL MEHLHORN
In the Oklahoma Open at the Tulsa Country Club.

BETWEEN ROUNDS AT THE PGA CHAMPIONSHIP
Walter Hagen and Bill Mehlhorn watch William Creavy tune-up his putting stroke on the practice green.

Editor's note: *Although a contender in many major tournaments, "Wild Bill" Mehlhorn's best finish in a major was second in the 1925 P.G.A. to Walter Hagen.*

6 The Necessity For A Tale Of Woe Committee

SOME TIME ago, during the progress of a tournament, one of the contestants thus expressed himself in the clubhouse: "I think it would be an excellent idea if at every tournament the club would erect a small tent close by the home green and then appoint a committee of three to occupy it in relays. As an act of mercy each should be stone deaf. Their only duty would consist of sitting there patiently, with countenance expressing extreme sympathy, while the players who desired to review their matches told of their tribulations. At the finish of the narrative they should simply say, 'Tough luck,' and administer the chloroform."

"All matches should be met by an envoy. 'Any remarks, gentlemen?' Upon the affirmative reply the player should immediately be conducted to the tent of Committee on Post Mortems."

The suggestion could be directly attributed to the previous half hour. He had been buttonholed by one who had just lost a 20-hole match. Every one of those 20 holes had been reviewed by the unfortunate golfer. (I say unfortunate because in nine cases out of ten, fortune has smiled only on the other fellow.) Our friend had been patient; he could not be rude, but he had been undeniably bored. The situation is a very common one. One has only to stop for a moment in the club or locker rooms during a tournament and from all sides he hears plaintive excuses, dismal as the wails and laments of the keener at a wake.

The followers of golf generally desire to know only results. When a contestant enters a clubhouse after his match someone is rather sure to say, "Well how did it go?" He may be a very solicitous friend, yet in reality he only wants to know who won and the margin of the score. The harrowing details of a match seldom interest anyone other than the player himself. It is a very safe rule to suppress the incidents unless they are really requested.

A.W. TILLINGHAST

Misery loves company, and there is no denial of the fact that it does make a chap feel better when he is able to pour the story of his sorrow into willing ears; but, after all, is it not better to accept defeat like a stoic and wait for another day?

Nearly every excuse which we ever hear really discounts the performance of the adversary. It may not be intended for there are no more generous sportsmen in the world than golfers as a rule, but still the excuse carries with it the unfortunate insinuation that the other fellow was lucky to get away with it. Harry Vardon once said that he had never beaten a well man in his life.

Excuse finds many servants—the weather, physical condition, a broken favorite club, an incompetent caddie, new shoes, a sore finger, the pro's bungling repair, the condition of the course (very general), the wind, the pair ahead, the pair following- but why continue? Their name is legion. I must admit that often the excuses might be legitimate, but for all they are best unsaid. I do not mean to be Pharisaical, for I fear that many times I have wearied some patient friend, and to all such I express my contrite apologies, but, like an old dog, I grow wiser.

I do not wish my readers to infer that I object to the review of our matches afterward. It is a genuine delight to foregather with our golfing friends and rake through the embers of past days, playing our games over again through the pipe smoke. The round table of golfers is an institution which will never die. It is the comment at the time that had best be laid away in camphor. If the medicine is bitter, shut your teeth hard and smile. Admit to yourself that the other fellow outplayed you (usually the best golf wins); make up your mind that he won't do it when you meet again and then go after him.

I think that I am very safe in asserting that the one word "yellow" explains more lost matches than any other. It is the yellow funk that caused that pull into the rough, or that topped ball which found the pit in the crisis. It gripped when you stood over your ball; you were afraid that you would do it, and consequently you did. It was the yellow that prompted you to blow up on that two-foot putt on the home green. Was it altogether luck when your opponent sunk that 20-footer? Honestly, he had the courage to be up and a steady nerve when he started that ball straight for the cup.

I am free to confess that I have never seen a golfer in my life who at sometime or other did not exhibit the yellow. Of course, some seldom show a sign of it, while others always carry a full cargo. One can get it out of the system just as he can correct the slice in his drive, but excuses will never do it. Just admit to yourself that your game was a bit yellow—that is half the battle. Then fight it and keep right on fighting it. The courage which enabled you to recognize it will eventually prove your salvation and help your game.

The reference to excuses reminds me of one of the most remarkable illustrations imaginable. Several years ago two very prominent players were fighting it out in a tournament. One always experienced great difficulty in playing if anyone chanced to move. As they were preparing to drive off for one hole near the finish of the match a solitary golfer was discovered playing ahead on the same hole. As he had no standing, the players very properly shouted "Fore." The player turned, stepped aside and signaled them to drive through. He was 200 yards from the tee. The subject of my narrative hashed his drive and in his irritation exclaimed, "That fool man is responsible for that." "Why he never moved a muscle," replied the other, in amazement. The retort was remarkable, "I know darned well he didn't, but I thought he was going to."

A SPRING SETTING OF RARE APPEAL ON THE PROPERTY OF POXONO C.C.

7 SPRING LAKE

OF ALL reconstructed holes the eighteenth at Spring Lake probably has been as much discussed as any and many criticisms have been leveled at it. While this hole as it now stands is a par 4, those who criticize it are players who would require 5 were there not a bunker along the line, and it is the big sand pit, which makes into the fairway from the left, to which they object. Our sketch illustrates the hole, which is of drive and mid-iron length.

Originally it was very ordinary, indeed. The fairway was wide open and the second was absolutely blind to a green just beyond a small stream in the gully which extends in front of the new green. This new green stands forth prominently on the brow of a hillock, and a tremendous amount of fill in the back was necessary to make it stand up well to hold the shot. The great pit extends from the left to the very center of the fairway and it offers a varying carry for the drive. To gain the fairway on the left beyond the pit the drive must carry 175 yards, and the second to the green is open and not particularly difficult. But if the player declines to attempt any carry of the pit, he has an open way around on the right but from this side of the green is hidden by trees. Naturally the play from this side calls for an extra stroke as indicated by the dotted lines.

Now there are some that contend that the pit should not extend quite so far into the fairway; that a short straight drive should have to contend with no obstacle. If this contention is true then I hold that there is no finesse in golf. The gully in front of the green could scarcely be carried with any second of the short driver and were the pit not there as it is, there would be many hard-hit half-topped drives finding spots on the fairway from which the green could be reached. Surely this pit does not interfere with even the most humble player getting home easily with his third, and it only makes it necessary for the seeker after par figures to hit his shots and not "get away with murder."

This happens to be the only criticism of the new hole, which, by the way, has many defenders. The new green is a marked improvement and brings the final play in full view of the clubhouse. But the point which I would emphasize is that the critics of the pit are those who would not reach the green in two shots in any event.

The green committeeman of every club constantly is harassed by objections to features, which introduce strategic play, generally by players whose games are not affected in the least. So long as your holes make it necessary for the par man to play hard, sound strokes do not worry. The others will appreciate these same features when they find themselves getting an occasional win, and many halved holes with cracks who come to grief.

THE EIGHTEENTH GREEN AT THE SPRING LAKE G.C.

8 CALIFORNIA COURSES

IT IS the winter of 1920, the time of the year when the courses for the most part are being swept by winter blasts. It surely will be right and proper to confine our page to committees which are particularly active. So this page will be given over solely to a few remarks concerning California Courses, particularly as the subject is fresh in my mind (these lines are being written in Arizona).

Prior to 1920, the visitor to the Pacific Coast expected to find only sand greens and the tiny, boxed, hard clay tees of primitive design (they scarcely are large enough to be dignified with the term teeing-grounds), and these are what he did play to and from. There seemed to be justification for them, for the development and maintenance of grass, which has to hold up under constant play throughout the year, is no light task. Watering, during the dry summer, particularly is costly, and it has to be done most diligently.

California realized the necessity of producing better teeing-grounds, putting greens of distinct types, and superior courses generally. Many of the more important clubs undertook the work of reconstruction in most vigorous fashion. They once believed that players would be satisfied with the monotonously flat, sanded greens, and certainly a well kept green of this material is preferable to a very poor quality of turf. I know of one club which developed turfed greens in the southern part of the state and this is the experience of the committee there: While the new greens came on, temporary grassed greens were prepared from the fairway, close by the sanded greens, and the players could take their choice. The great majority played the temporary, turfed greens in preference.

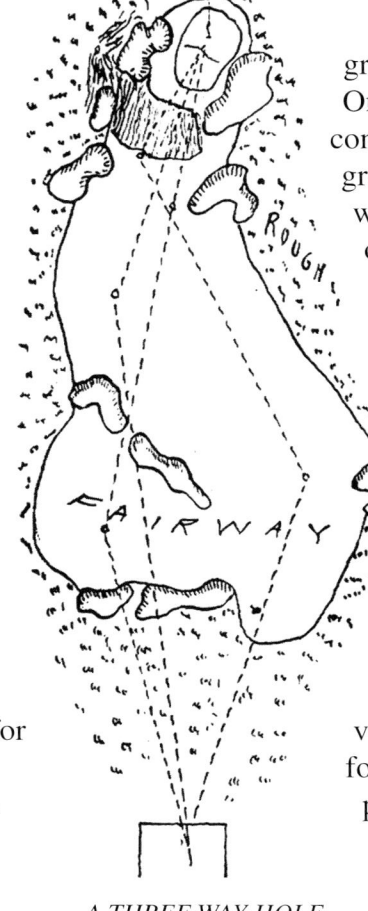

A THREE WAY HOLE
Constructed on the course of the San Francisco G.C. at Ingleside California.

One of the best known organizations constructed and maintained finely turfed greens designed after the fashion of those which are to be found on the great courses of the Middle West, East and Great Britain. Undoubtedly the large, turfed teeing-grounds were introduced slowly but surely.

Without a doubt California would have developed more great players if there were no such thing as a clay teeing-ground on any of her courses. There exists the general tendency to slap the ball from the hard surface and this is bound to make trouble with the execution of sound shots, particularly the irons. As a rule, too, the fairways were very wide and the bunkering of the courses for the most part did not compel the careful placing of shots to the extent that it should. But there are many rarely fine holes in the state, some of the most impressive natural holes one could wish for; and some grand golf country, too.

The fact that some truly excellent turf has been developed in their putting greens proves that it may be produced and nourished generally. The soil varies considerably from light, porous sand to the well known adobe, which retains moisture for a long time but cracks considerably when dry. Naturally each variety demands widely differing treatments, but in sections miles apart they have been successful in creating good seed beds for putting green turf by the always true method of introducing proper soil, prepared after an intelligent analysis of conditions.

A sample of one of the new holes built in California is suggested by the sketch, which differs from the

ONLY A WELL-PLAYED SECOND WILL CARRY THE NATURAL CHASM ON THE NINTH AT PEBBLE BEACH

actual work in minor details. The green is undulating, with a pronounced flare working into the right front entrance. It is built up by scooping back the soil from in front, thus making a natural-looking dip and causing the green itself to stand up well from rather flat and featureless surroundings. The contours and placement of hazards render the green almost unassailable with a long shot from the right. It shows its best face to the second shot, a long iron or brassie coming directly in after the drive has made the long carry of the elbowing pits on the left. This, of course, is the true way to get par figures if there is power enough and courage back of the shots. Then there is the way around to the right, but this safe route gives the player absolutely no encouragement of getting home with any kind of a second, and consequently he is forced to play to the left before getting into the green with the third.

But there still is the third choice. By placing a very accurate and controlled drive to the left, to the portion of the fairway which lies between the pits, the clear way to the green is opened up, but it will take a tremendously long second to get home or into the swell in front. The sketch shows by dotted lines, the three routes, and it is a matter of choice to be guided by a knowledge of the player's powers.

This is a fair sample of some of the new golf building along the Pacific Coast. When one stands on a California course, he almost invariably is impressed with a magnificent panorama. The country seems so very big, everything is on such a gigantic scale that it makes itself felt as well as seen. The trees seem bigger than those usually encountered, and they are. The mountains loom high and they extend far. How is it possible to put pawky things in the very heart of such surroundings?

DEL MONTE LODGE HAS A FINE VIEW OF THE LINKS

Apparently there are many native grasses like sedge, which are excellent for the purpose of making artificial mound work look natural, rugged and dunelike, and this is exactly the treatment that some of the California courses need. True, much of the golf

THE SEVENTEENTH AT PEBBLE BEACH IS GUARDED ON TWO SIDES BY THE PACIFIC OCEAN

PEBBLE BEACH'S EIGHTH GREEN IS GUARDED BY A YAWNING CHASM

country has nothing to ask from the hand of the builder of courses. It would be a pity to mar some wonderfully natural holes by attempting any artifice to improve. There are certain holes, which I have in mind that are all satisfying exactly as nature designed them. But there are many very flat areas which must be used and bold mound work is necessary, and it must be very daring in conception and unusually impressive. As I have said, the country is too big for pawky things.

ONE OF THE FEW INLAND HOLES
On the course at Pebble Beach.

9 ROUGH GOING

ROCKS ARE NOT IMPASSABLE OBSTACLES IN THE CONSTRUCTION OF FAIRWAYS
As the work at the Scarsdale club shows.

IT IS NOT the object of this article to exalt the work of the golf architect or the builder of courses, but rather to guide construction committees to waste places where attractive holes may be built, even though the tract may have appeared useless, even quite impossible, in the eyes of the layman. Lido, certainly one of the best courses in America, was constructed on low, mosquito-infested marshland that was reclaimed by filling with sand dredged from the ocean bed. Pine Valley was built on property which was covered with pines and the scrub common to that particular New Jersey section. A great portion of Essex County was cut through the forests of the Orange Hills, and the removing of timber was an important factor at Somerset Hills, Quaker Ridge, Winged Foot, Scarsdale, and hundreds of other courses.

The seven new holes at Scarsdale were constructed entirely through a wooded, rocky section and represent an extremely formidable undertaking, and one which seemed quite impossible to many. Cuts were made through the woods, rocks were dynamited and in some instances covered with turf, fairways twisted and dog-legged to avoid huge boulders whose removal would

LOOKING OUT ON THE SUSQUEHANNA RIVER—FROM THE PUTTING GREEN AT BINGHAMTON C.C.

have involved unnecessary expense. But after the rough clearing was finished and the fairways and greens graded, often by using the stones from walls and from the property generally, a very charming collection of holes was added to the course, taking the place of others of antiquated design which were arduous to play.

Scarsdale is used as an illustration because the original course represented golf construction of other days. A score or more years ago sites for American golf courses often were selected along violent slopes. These were called "sporty," but generally speaking, the hill holes offered little other than a test of a man's ability to rival an Alpine goat. Consequently, it must not be assumed that in directing attention to the use of waste places the selection of unusually hilly ground is intended—far from it.

This recalls the examination of property for the new course near Binghamton, New York. Three types of properties were submitted to the architect. Some of the tracts were flat and low lying along the river; good farm land but not at all suited for golf. Then there were the side hills which were rejected at once. The ultimate selection was an ample area on a pronounced plateau which was nicely undulating without making stiff climbs necessary, for it was considerably better to get the players from the main roads of the low country to the club house on the highland in motor cars rather than making it necessary for them to do their climbing afoot after the play started.

The clearing of wooded property is not difficult or expensive, particularly in the South and Southwest. The Municipal Course of San Antonio, Texas, was built on land which was well wooded, and although it was necessary to sacrifice some fine pecan trees, yet there were sufficient remaining to make the course very beautiful. Today public golfers of that city are finding it easy going over land that once was well nigh impassable in places and infested with rattlesnakes—which have entirely disappeared with other objectionable features. The accompanying photograph of Texas construction shows the eighteenth fairway of the new Alamo Country Club. Not only was this particular hole laid through huisache and mesquite but a great portion of the course was as well. This was waste land gently sloping from wooded ridges to barren arroyos.

Although the work of clearing was considerable, it did not begin to compare with the difficulties which are presented in rocky country.

In the old days the property which was selected for golf purposes usually was farm land which had been under cultivation, and little thought was given to getting into rough country which possessed fine golf and scenic values. It was easier to follow the fields, usually along public roads where ground was valuable for residential purposes, a development which must inevitably follow close on the heels of the country club. Roads must be of easy grade, and usually immediately adjoining, the land is cleaner and more level than that which lies back, and which is not so desirable for farming or residence. Yet the back-lying country, which is rougher, invariably is more acceptable to the golf architect. It is true that the cost of preparing these areas is more than it would be necessary over the more open meadow land, but it will be found that the cost for clearing and construction will not be nearly so great as the actual value of the property along the thoroughfares.

Sometime since, a club in northern New York desired to reconstruct its course which had been there for some years. The club house was immediately on the main road, which skirted a considerable part of the course. It was not property which offered any appeal or inspiration, and the committee was considerably surprised when the architect went rambling off from the open country into some forests and rough land beyond, some of which was swampy and rocky. However, the new property was acquired and with no great difficulty the swamps were drained and the rock obliterated. An entirely new layout of holes followed, and today the club possess a very charming course, superior in every way to the old one. Although the club house occupies the same position by the road side, the value of the old course for residential purposes has more than equaled the purchase of the back-lying rocky country and the construction of the new course.

THE TASK OF CLEARING
A Texas fairway is a he-man's job.

When various lands are under consideration by a construction committee, it is but natural that they should incline to the easier going and take to property which seems to lend itself to quicker and less expensive construction rather than another which obviously would require more clearing and more expensive construction. But, there is a tendency on the part of a layman to overestimate the difficulties which the rougher country seems to present; as a matter of fact, wood clearing is not so costly as many imagine, and usually the soil yields exceedingly good turf because of the quantity of leaf mold which has accumulated during many years.

As an example of the actual cost of constructing one of the best known modern courses in the country, figures show that one property under consideration embraced approximately one hundred fifty acres—enough for eighteen holes and club house grounds. It was hard by a main thoroughfare and the cost would have been two thousand dollars an acre. True, the country was open and the soil of good quality; possibly seventy-five thousand dollars would have been quite sufficient for the construction of a thoroughly satisfactory course. The probable cost of the property with course amounted to approximately three hundred and seventy-five thousand dollars.

However, the club eventually was induced to purchase another property which was more removed from the highway, although the clubhouse was located close to it, and this back-lying tract was purchased for seven hundred dollars an acre. About two hundred acres were bought at a cost of one hundred and forty thousand dollars, and although the actual construction of this rougher section amounted to one hundred and twenty thousand dollars, there was a saving of one hundred and fifteen thousand dollars, and a far better course was produced. These figures apply to the cost of property near one of the large cities, which will account for the high price of the land, but parallel cases might be related in sections where golf land was much cheaper.

It might be of interest to the reader to know that the cheapest land for golf development that I have ever known in the years I have been in the profession was eight dollars an acre. I have never known of a thoroughly modern course of eighteen holes to be constructed for less than fifty thousand dollars. This was the construction cost of one of the most famous courses in the country, which had an unusual location and which lent itself readily to all of the ideals of the builder of courses, both in design and construction. In this instance the country was very open, entirely free from stones and with almost a natural drainage.

It must not be inferred that when wooded land is to be cleared that there is a wanton destruction of fine trees. The fairways are studied carefully when they are staked in order to preserve as many fine trees as possible. Most of the small trees are uprooted by the use of tractors. This very valuable assistant in golf construction is called into service, too, when larger trees are to be "pulled," but in some instances a small quantity of dynamite is generally used to loosen the roots and permit a good quantity of dirt to fall back into the hole after the roots have left it. Certainly the excessive use of explosives in "blowing" trees is to be avoided, for the stump holes are made much larger than necessary and frequently splendid trees standing nearby, and

THE PARTIAL AND ARTISTIC CLUBHOUSE OF THE ALAMO (OAK HILLS) C.C.

A TREE BEING DYNAMITED TO MAKE WAY FOR A GREEN

which are desirable, are injured.

The reference to rocky country calls to mind the professional visit made into the Province of Quebec, where the writer planned a course in the heart of the Laurentians. The section is some sixty miles north of Montreal, on the very edge of the "Big Woods," and in the heart of a beautiful lake country. After leaving the Canadian Pacific Railway, a ten-mile journey into the back country was necessary. My impression as the car covered the miles was not promising, for on all sides large rocks and boulders showed themselves, and the small farms had been tilled by the inhabitants after fatiguing, patient work in the clearing of stones. Mountains showed hard faces of rock through the timber, with every indication of iron ore in sufficient quantities to affect the compass somewhat.

HUGE PECAN TREES SHADE THE GREENS
On San Antonio's Brackenridge Park.

When Lac L'Archigan was reached the terrain was very pleasing, with particularly fine contours, but the great rocks seemed to be everywhere. However, the tract which had been selected for the course was comparatively free of the rocks, which evidently had been removed by the farmers. The soil showed a fine sandy loam, over gravel, with a clay hardpan bottom. As a matter of fact, investigation showed that the rocks generally were only on the surface and plowing was not at all difficult. Only two holes stretched over rocky country, and the treatment of this may be of interest.

It so happens that the course finds its way gradually from the club house site to higher levels, so gradually that no stiff climbing is made necessary. The two holes in question cover this

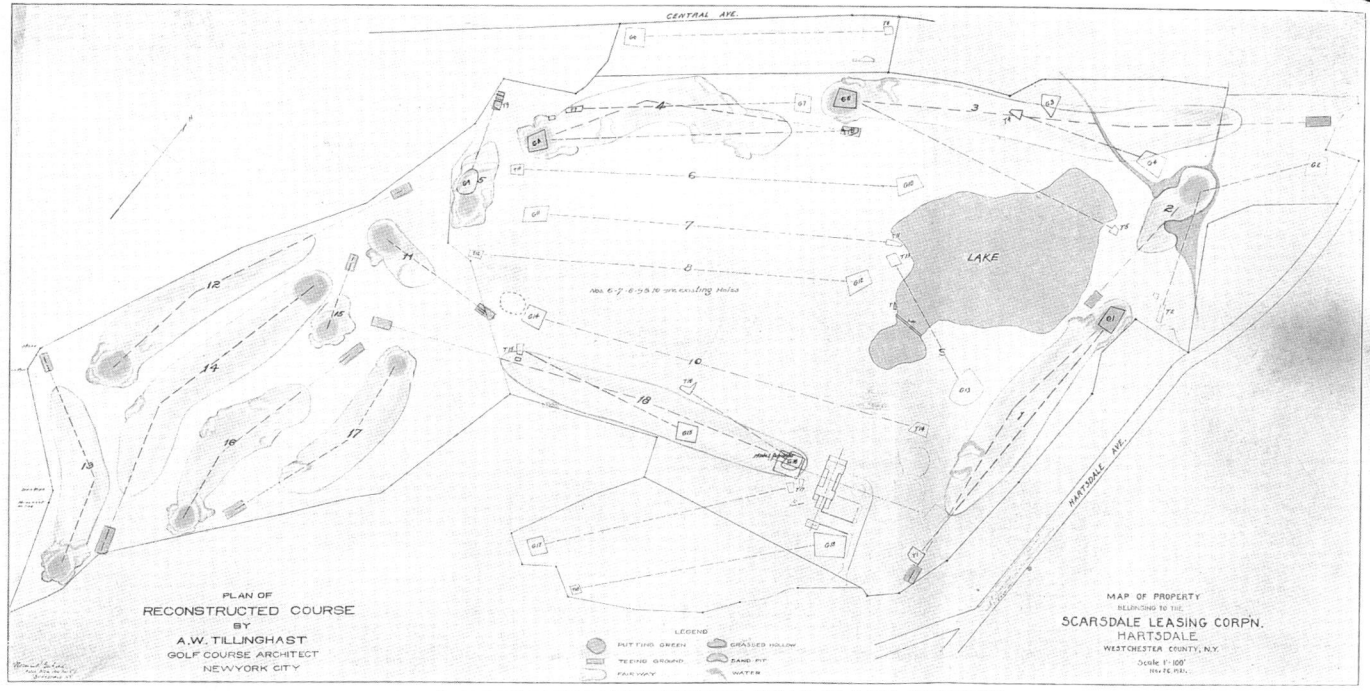
PLAN OF THE RECONSTRUCTED SCARSDALE COURSE

gradual ascent; the rocks were slipped down the slopes to the gentle gullies at the bottoms, where they were covered with soil; this operation made away with the rocks and reduced the grades which otherwise would have to be taken by the players.

It must not be inferred that the motive of this article is to force golf construction in very rough sections where the cost of construction will be excessive. If clear ground may be found, obviously it is more desirable to take the easier method, but I am endeavoring to direct attention to the waste places which so frequently are overlooked because of the false assumption that they are impossible. Practically nothing is impossible in the way of golf construction, but certainly the development of exceedingly rough country is unwise unless actually driven into it, as was the case at Scarsdale.

To illustrate the point, let me refer to a case which came under my observation several years ago. The course in question had been laid out in the days when "Sporty" courses seemed to be the vogue, and it represented an unfortunate selection of property, a bad collection of distances and mediocre construction. The club anticipated the purchase of adjoining property which presented practically the same terrain as the other. The old course could have been improved, but a million dollars never would have made a pleasing collection of holes there. The committee was advised very candidly to abandon all thoughts of improvement and to seek other land in the same vicinity, where an entirely satisfactory and modern course could be produced at far less cost then would be necessary in tinkering with the old one. They resented the suggestion and immediately proceeded to throw away a considerable amount of money on the old course, until evidently their eyes were opened to the folly of it, and they took the original advice to select other property.

THE MAKING OF SCARSDALE

10 Our Green Committee Page

IT IS ASTONISHING how often we run across the compound word, Green Committee, spelled in the plural Greens. Seldom do the more notable clubs make the mistake. It is not Greens Committee and here is the reason. The entire course is called The Green and inasmuch as the committee has charge of the course in its entirety, not the Putting Greens only, it is the Green Committee. We refer correctly to the Greenkeeper, he whose duty it is to attend to the turf of the whole course, fairway and putting greens together. Frequently on score cards and bulletins the word is misspelled.

In the days when Bogey was considered as a standard, a legitimate drive was conceived to be about 160 yards. This was in the time of the gutta percha ball. After the introduction of the rubber core, it was assumed that a good drive should cover 200 yards under normal conditions. Soon Bogey became obsolete and a new standard—Par—was considered. With longer flying balls coming into the hands of golfers, Par figures became more exacting. The United States Golf Association fixed the length of a Par drive at 225 yards and afterwards increased the distance to 240. Now we may figure as we will with the pencil, yet the fact remains that it is impossible to accurately fix a limit on a long drive. We may have a hole which measures 250 yards and some long hitters will be sparing their wood or getting home with iron. The modern golf architect has been forced to recognize the ever-increasing lengths of the shots and build accordingly.

The very rough sketch shows a recent type which will permit the "sloggers" to let into their drives with all they possess, with the certain knowledge that they will be rewarded. A hole similar to this is to be found on the new course of Essex County Country Club although it differs somewhat from the sketch.

Let us assume that the hole measures close to 300 yards, a very satisfying drive for anyone. For most players it is a two-shotter. If the long carry of 180 yards is made over the pit to the fairway on the Flat B, which slopes slightly up to the green, a fairly easy running approach remains. If the shorter carry to the fairway on Flat A is taken, a difficult pitch has to be made. So much for the hole as a short two-shotter. But a very long drive to Fairway B will get the green, for it will be helped by the slope, which extends

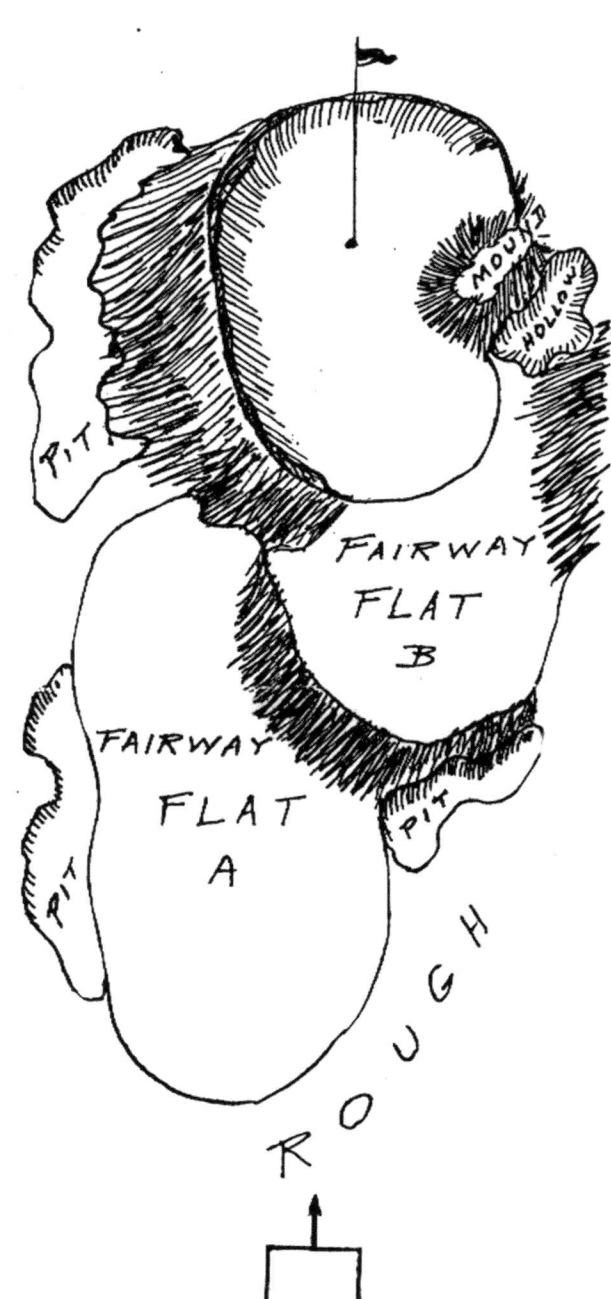

along the right. But it will be observed that such a drive must be not only long but exceedingly accurate as well, in order that it may strike exactly right to gain the run to the entrance of the green which opens to it. The placement of side pits and hollows is obvious. The construction of the natural-looking mound to the right of the green, and sloping gently to it, lends considerable variety.

HERE is an old saying: "Patch by patch is good housewifery, but patch on patch is plain beggary." Let committees who are remodeling their courses keep this in mind. It is well enough to attempt only what your resources will permit, but let every detail be a well-considered part of the completed whole. Even though the work is done like patchwork it can be made neat and satisfying. But slovenly work, which has to be done over, is very like "patch on patch."

On a well-known seaside course, a number of new pits have been dug. On the face of it this statement will carry wonder to the close observer, for digging carries with it thoughts of shovels. And shovels have been used to dig straight-sided, pawky pits. At the best they are horribly artificial in appearance, and aside from their usefulness, appearance counts for a great deal. Certainly we want to make our artificial creations resemble nature as closely as possible. Scoops, dragged by horses, already have proved their efficiency and economy in many places. With them we can create excavations and fills with slopes which are rugged and pleasingly harmonious. On seaside courses it is very easy to scoop out pits which are worthy of the name. Here is a windswept section where nature scoops out and deposits on a lavish scale. Can man imitate the great broad, rugged dunes with shovels? It is almost like trying to kill an elephant with bird-shot.

On many courses the turf is in unusually bad condition. In some sections they blame it on winterkill and nearly everywhere some excuse rather than the true one is advanced. Getting right down to the truth we will find that the turf has been neglected either through ignorance or lack of the usual funds. Some clubs have been forced to cut their usual appropriation for, with many members in the service, their dues are sadly missed as much as they. But soil needs food, and if it does not get it, there is sure to be a lean and hungry look come over the turf. It is well enough for those clubs which have the funds to go ahead with improvements, but even among the smaller organizations, where the resources are sorely taxed, great effort should be made to keep the turf from going back. It is not necessary always to spend great sums of money to do this.

THE THIRTEENTH GREEN ON THE ESSEX COUNTY C.C.

Bent grass makes the finest and truest of golf turf and certainly the approaches should be turfed much better than the fairway and only slightly inferior to the green itself. Not only is the quality of the approach frequently neglected but its contour, and its character, quite ignored.

In another article, I asserted that the character of the green represented the value of any golf hole. Now let me add that the character of the approach to the green is of almost equal importance and in some instances it dominates. Very often an unusually fine natural approach is the dominant, and the hole is constructed in two directions from this obvious feature, the green itself being wholly artificial in its design, which is made to fit in naturally and blend with the approach. Of course, the approach may be considered properly only in the study of holes other than one-shotters for irons. Truly enough these short holes probably present impressive green surroundings but these constitute pitfalls for erring shots. The real approach is that stretch in front of the greens which are reached with the longer shots. The greater the shot the more it is necessary to give thought to the contour of the approach and the quality of its turf, that truly hit shots receive a just reward without unmerited punishment resulting from erratic ground surface.

Probably nothing in golf breeds more discussion, condemnation and approval as a new pit. No doubt the committee has given the exact location of a new pit a great deal of thought, and it is possible that a golf architect has been consulted. Yet, when that new hazard is built, nearly every player has something to say about it. This is natural. Some of the thoughtful players will analyze its location and construction, but for the most part, the members will pass judgment upon it with only their own play in mind and praise or damn it after thinking of their personal good or bad luck at this particular point.

Pits are dug to serve as hazards and at the same time to lend their contours to a pleasing harmony with the surrounding ground. First of all, their value as hazards must be considered. Do they catch and punish wayward shots? Some pits will trap and hold any ball that enters their maw. Others will hold a goodly proportion, but there are some, so faulty in design and location, that a ball is trapped on rare occasions only. Of course it stands to reason that a very shallow pit will catch less shots than one which is deeper, but sometimes a deep pit is so badly designed that it is not so effective as a shallower one which has been properly built.

I have prepared four sketches representing the sections of sand pits. Regard Figure C for a moment, and it will be apparent that it is not a good type because the side, from which a ball should enter, is higher that the far side. Any hard-hit topped shot would be unlikely to be trapped by such as this, and yet we see this type very frequently. Figure B shows a pit dug into the slight rise in the ground, which is a most desirable place and pits so dug are not only effective but pleasing to the eye.

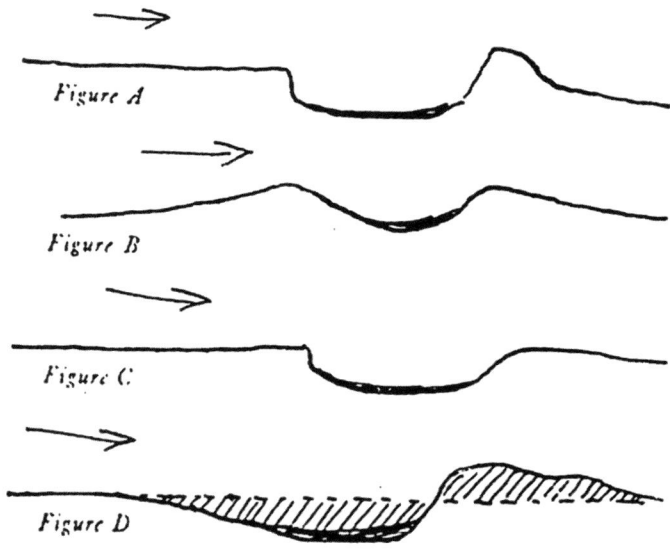

To many, the digging of a pit means nothing more than the excavation which is to hold sand and the convenient dumping place for the earth which has been removed. Usually in past years, this dumping place was on the far side of the mathematically correct and symmetrical hole, and the mound was very precise, too. Fig. A attempts to illustrate this old dig-and-dump method. The mounds were (and are) hideous, often barren of vegetation, because the topsoil is under all.

Figure D illustrates the better method of digging a pit in level ground. The shaded parts representing the earth which has been removed from the pit proper and, afterward, distributed broadly beyond in such a natural manner as to give the hazard the appearance of having been dug into a slope when, in reality, the suggestion of slope has been created beyond the hole. This deception is helped by gradually depressing the entrance to the pit. Now I know that this may seem absurdly simple to some who have given golf construction an amount of study, but everywhere so many crude and inefficient pits are to be seen that we must infer that many committees are in need of elementary instruction and kindergarten suggestion.

Hazards dug on the tops of hillocks and long undulations are wasted generally. Put them at the base rather than on the top, where a ball can only find them by lofting directly into them. The delight of the golf architect is noting depressions where balls will be thrown naturally from surrounding undulations. After all, bunker building is only common sense.

In facing bunkers, great care must be exercised in keeping the slopes not so upright as to permit balls getting in an unplayable position under the face. The bottoms of the slopes should let the ball roll well away from the face into the sand, where the player may have an open shot at it. The tops of the faces may well overhang a trifle. This will keep many running balls from getting free.

WHENEVER any work of importance is attempted, the first question naturally is: "How much will it cost?" This is particularly hard to answer, particularly when the first building of a course is being considered. It stands to reason that men who are doing golf construction work can come rather close to the actual cost after careful estimate, but it is not easy. I know of one club that recently built a new course. A well known turf-expert was asked to submit an estimate for building the course to the plans of the architect. Naturally this included the establishment of turf with the best available materials. After carefully figuring, he estimated that the work would require an outlay of $45,000. Another was consulted by the club and he told them that it all could easily be done for $25,000. Naturally the latter got the work, although the constructor was not footing the bills himself but rather working under salary. Before the work was completed and the course ready for-play the club had spent more than $50,000 and it is doubtful if the turf and general construction are as good as it would have been under the development of the first man.

When extensive work is contemplated it is far

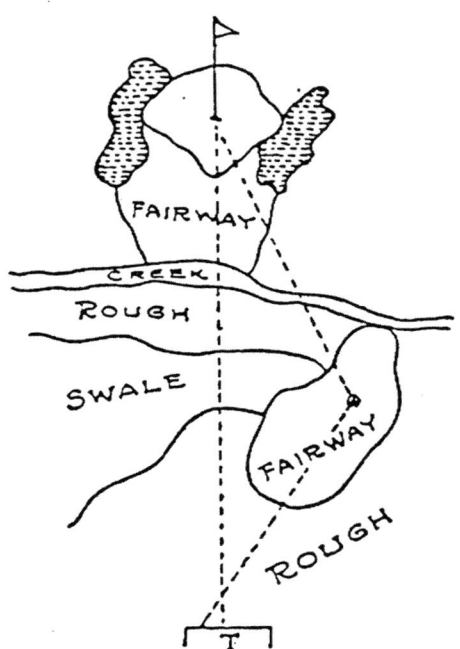

200 YARD HOLE
·ST. DAVIDS·

This fan-shaped green offers a greater premium to an absolutely straight shot than appears in the sketch, for undulations on the two front sides are likely to throw into the pits. Here we find another example of a segregated fairway, introduced for the player who finds the carry of the creek beyond his powers.

better and cheaper in the end to call in an expert of reliability and repute, and trust to him. He has a reputation to sustain and he will be just as eager to get the best results as the club will be to have them.

Surely there are many pitfalls into which the committee, which has not great experience, may tumble. Take seed for instance. Every golfer knows that there is a great difference between true golf turf and lawn grass but how many green committees really know good seed when they buy it? I actually know of one dealer who was getting a good price for a very inferior grade of certain seed. He knew perfectly well that the seed which he offered was not of the highest grade but he defended himself before another dealer with the airy observation that his seed was good enough, and no one who bought it was well informed enough to distinguish the difference. Of course there is no defense for chicanery such as this but I cite the case to illustrate the necessity of relying on reputable advice.

A COMPARATIVELY simple and economical scheme for the improvement of a hole is illustrated by the rough sketch on the following page. It shows the development of a section of the fourteenth at Shawnee, one which was previously never bunkered.

The hole measures 440 yards and it was permitted to be very wide open until the turf "found itself." The rough Alpinization or mound work has been the only guard to the green, and the second shots which cleared it represented a carry of about 400 yards from the back teeing ground. The long hitters got home in two, but those who were conservative played short of the Alps and found themselves with an easy approach to a large, wide open green.

Having planned the course originally, a working model for the redevelopment of the hole was prepared. Let us look at the sketch for a moment. It shows how many holes may be improved to make the players think a bit.

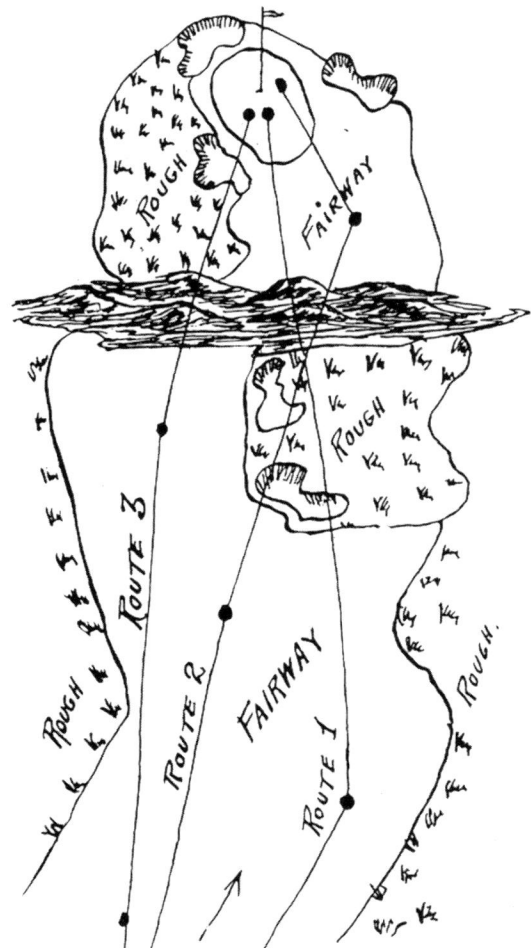

A large section of the fairway in front of the Alps has been converted to rough in which two pits have been placed. Those who wish to play short now must place their shots with accuracy in the fairway on the left, but after doing so they find that the approach to the green is not open. It has to carry another area of rough and hazard beyond. The green shows its best face to shots coming in from the right and thus the drive which is long and placed on the right of the fairway is rewarded. The sketch indicates three routes which might be taken by players of high and low degree, but it is obvious that it is impossible to play short without leaving a well guarded approach.

In sandy soil a great pit might well take the place of the Alpinization. It is likely that this illustration may be suggestive of an improvement to the many two-shot holes which are quite featureless.

Another word concerning holes of drive and brassey length. It is to be assumed that they have been trapped with the sole thought of making it necessary for the scratch man to play two irreproachable shots before gaining the green. But if weather conditions place the green beyond the range of two well hit balls, the hole immediately has lost its value and becomes a nondescript three-shotter. This cannot be condoned. At least three teeing grounds must be provided to permit moving the markers forward in times of adverse winds or sodden turf. A two-shot hole must play as such, no matter what the yardage may be.

The photographs on these pages show the competitive play of the ladies in the 1919 National Championship at Shawnee.

NOS. 1, 2 AND 3 SHOW MISS STIRLING'S FULL SWING
Nos. 4, 5 and 6 are Miss Peacock, Mrs. Vanderbeck and Mrs. Gavin, respectively.

CROSSING THE BINNIEKILL, AN ARM OF THE DELAWARE THAT MAKES AN ISLAND OF THE SHAWNEE COURSE

THE TENTH HOLE IS THE LONGEST AT SHAWNEE AND FOLLOWS THE DELAWARE

MRS. W. A. GAVIN TRYING TO COAX A PUTT TO DROP ON THE PUNCHBOWL TWELFTH GREEN

MRS. R. H. BARLOW AND MRS. C. H. VANDERBECK ON THE SEVENTEENTH

THE BUCKWOOD INN AND EIGHTEENTH GREEN, MISS STIRLING AND MISS VANDERBECK ON THE GREEN

MISS STIRLING RECEIVING THE MEDAL
From Sterling E. Edmunds, Vice President of the USGA.

C. C. WORTHINGTON AND HIS THREE SONS
Ed, Reg and Ross.

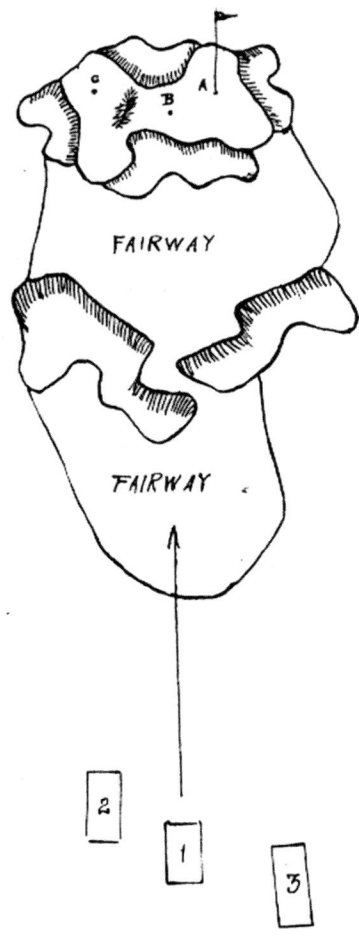

EARLIER I expressed regret over the diminishing number of drive and pitch holes. It is well enough to stretch out the distances of long two-shotters (the modern long-flying balls have made this necessary); but often, in striving for distance, committees seem to overlook the rare qualities of an occasional hole which demands a checked pitch to a closely guarded green. The sketch on this page illustrates such a hole, one measuring 340 yards. The varying carries over the pits from the three teeing grounds are not difficult to imagine, and the very irregularly shaped green permits the placing of the cup in such spots as to absolutely fix the route of the proper drive. Of course the green is raised well in the back and slopes gradually to the front, affording a surface which will hold a correctly played mashie pitch. In the left center a rather prominent though gradually sloped undulation appears.

The cup, in this instance, has been cut well over on the right, opening up to the pitch from a drive which has been placed on that side of the fairway and well hit over the diagonal hazard. Had the cup been cut at point C rather than at A, a similar drive would demand a very awkward second shot, but a ball played over on the left would be well rewarded. Naturally the direction and velocity of the wind must dictate the selection of the teeing ground and the placement of the cup. Playing this hole with the wind dead against, the cup might well be cut at point B. To be sure, the pitch to this spot would be exacting but the player would have the head-wind to help him. It is not much of a trick to stop a mashie or iron into the wind. Only a correct estimate of the strength of the stroke is necessary.

NOT long ago I was looking over a book, an old publication, in which the author had collected numbers of "bulls." To Ireland many "bulls," or blunders, are traced, but the little book told of many from other sections. There was one in particular, which suggests a topic for this page. Sir Walter Scott places one of his characters on the west coast of Scotland, looking eastward over the sea. Now it is a matter of record that Sir Walter had a knowledge of golf, and possibly this deterred him from allowing his hero to face into the west.

Certainly one of the greatest bulls in course construction is the planning of holes which have to be played directly into the sun. There was a course in Texas which had to be rebuilt because most of the holes of the homeward journey made it necessary for the players to shoot squarely into the afternoon sun. Orientation should be one of the first thoughts when selecting ground for a course and in laying it out. Anyone who knows tennis would not think of building a court facing east and west. But seemingly not so much attention is paid to golf holes, and as a consequence many otherwise fine golf holes are unenjoyable simply because they are "blinders."

ALTHOUGH golfers generally are aware that gently undulating country is most desirable, there is a tendency to select ground that is too hilly. The next photograph shows an ideal tract in Tennessee, where the Country Club of Kingsport constructed a course which should prove rarely distinctive. The land drains naturally to lower levels on all sides and the fairway is filled with the gradual, gentle slopes that may be cut easily because of their generous proportions. Let us have too, just enough woodland to vary the monotony of green fields, partially shaded nooks for a teeing ground or putting green, or a grove around which a fairway may twist. Let us have some constant water course, no matter how small. With a little ingenuity it may be made to lend itself to the making of a lake. And this reference is not an idle one. There are many ugly little water courses which may be the means of transforming a course to a thing of beauty and a better test of golf, which now wind sluggishly across the course, little better than tantalizing hiding places for stray balls. A photograph rather flattens the landscape. The lens of the camera does not show the picture quite as does the retina of the eye, but possibly this bit from Tennessee may show the suggestion of the ideal inland golf country.

NOT so very long ago a gentleman suggested a new box for tee sand. It was to be made of cement, molded to an appropriate design. Such a box certainly would be well nigh indestructible, but its great weight must make it a permanent fixture, and here is its weakness. Teeing grounds should be changed frequently. We no longer depend upon the pawky little terraced bandboxes which were so common only a few years back. Every variation of the wind should determine the placement of the discs or the selection of one of several teeing grounds. Sand boxes should be sufficiently light as to render the work of shifting easily within the powers of one man.

A little sketch may prove useful as a suggestion to correct a frequently encountered fault. While the mistake is general, I have in mind a particular hole, the green flanked by a water course in a grove. It is a long two shotter and the chief fault is to be found in the hazard immediately back of the line of play. If you will take the trouble to analyze the shots which come up to most greens, you may be astonished to note the overwhelming percentage of short ones. For every ball which runs a bit beyond the hole there will be three or four timid, short ones. Golf preaches the doctrine of being up. With this in mind we scarcely can reconcile ourselves to the punishment of a shot, straight on the pin, which is a bit too brave, especially if the shot is a brassey or cleek.

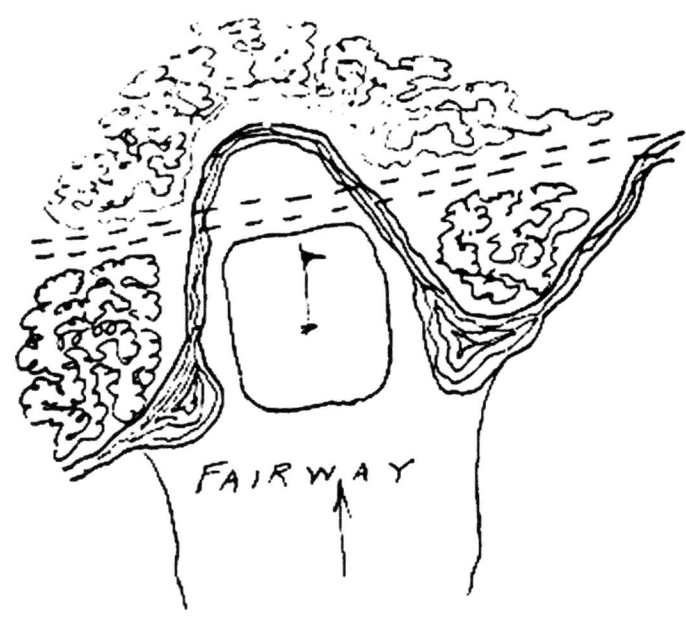

The dotted lines show the present course of the water hazard, which punishes a slightly over played straight shot fully as much as one off the line. The work of diverting the water to a new channel is not great and a much fairer hole would result.

ONE of the greatest contributions of the golf architect to modern courses is the frequent introduction of a twisting and irregularly shaped fairway. Such holes are designated generally by the terms dogleg and elbow. The application is obvious but usually the terms are regarded as being synonymous. This indiscriminate reference is apt to prove confusing and it has always been my custom to make this distinction.

THE COURSE AT KINGSPORT, TENNESSEE, IN THE MAKING

A dogleg hole—One which presents a fairway, bending around an encroachment from either side but sufficiently distant from the teeing ground to be beyond the possibility of being carried by a drive. In brief, some encroachment which forces the play around it.

An elbow hole—One which offers a similar encroachment but within the carrying range of a well-hit drive.

Some of the best holes in America are either dog-legged or elbowed, and they well illustrate the varying characteristics of the encroaching areas—hillocks, trees, water, sandy stretches, rough, quarry holes and even boundary lines. One of the most famous holes of the days of the gutta-percha ball, the Station Master's Garden at St. Andrews, Scotland, furnishes an example of adjoining property extending into a line of play. Here a well-hit drive crossed an angle of the yard occupied by Forgan's sheds and the second shot to the green was comparatively simple. Naturally the timid players declined to attempt it and elected to play safely around.

TO illustrate the two types I have prepared sketches. That marked A is a typical elbow hole with little to feature it other than the elbow on the left. Three lines of play are indicated and it is not difficult to see the great advantage which follows the successful carry.

Sketch B represents a dogleg hole where the play is forced around to the right. In this instance a drive which has not covered two hundred and twenty-five yards will not open up to the green to any sort of second shot, and one which covers two hundred and forty very properly rewards the sturdy driver with a more open shot to the green. For longer holes, which are considered as three-shotters, there might be a combination of the elbow and dogleg features. The double dogleg has already been described in previous articles.

While the dogleg and elbow holes may be manufactured from the whole cloth, they usually are the common sense developments of natural conditions and consequently they frequently prove to be great ground savers. For example, we may have woods fringing the land on one side, and by cutting it for a teeing ground and in again at a point probably four hundred yards further along for a green, we have a picturesque and thoroughly satisfying hole without

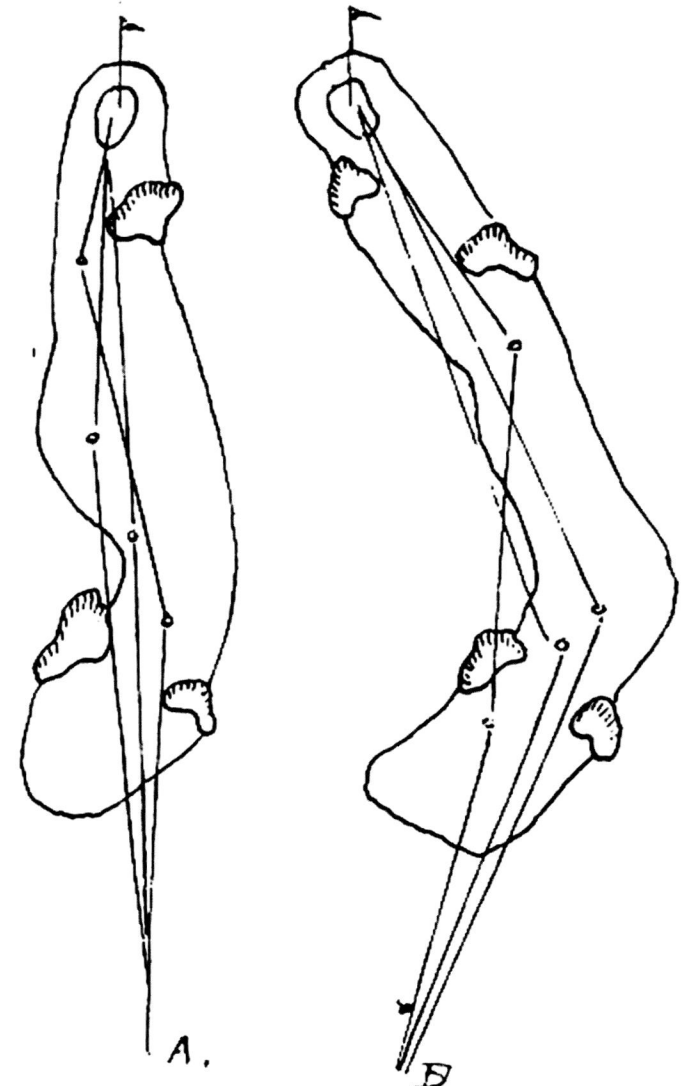

using a great deal of meadow land and without cutting much timber. But the greatest value of holes of these types is the elimination of deadly parallels. The most troublesome tracts of land with which the builder of courses has to deal are those which are contained in the four sides of a parallelogram. Unless there is an unusually large acreage the designer of the course is hard-put to avoid parallel holes. By twisting the fairways he is able to overcome the evil to a great extend. But aside from all else the dogleg hole offers one of the best tests of the golfers' shots than any other type of two-shot holes.

THERE still is another variety—the Cape, and possibly the name is not familiar to some of the readers of this page, although the type is encountered often. Here there exists some encroachment which makes into the fairway just before the green is reached, and it demands that the drive be well hit and placed with accuracy before the green opens up to the second shot. Several holes planned by Charles B. Macdonald are fine examples of this feature. Another well-known Cape hole is the seventh at Shawnee, one of the plainest yet most exacting holes on the course.

MANY courses have been constructed over ground that has been partially or wholly covered by trees and scrub growth. Generally, such conditions are encountered inland but sometimes they are to be found not far removed from the sea. Spring Lake furnishes an example and here the fairway often extends through an avenue of trees. Pine Valley may be designated as a seaside course although it is some miles from the Atlantic Ocean, but it is close enough for the classification, particularly when we consider the character of the sandy soil. This great course was built on land which was covered entirely with thousands of Pines, scrubs and a goodly number of big trees.

Nothing can be more offensive to the nature lover or so monotonous to the golfer than avenues of fairway between straight and precise lines of woods, yet in many instances the builders of courses have hewed with mathematical precision. Let us glance at our sketch for a moment and consider that the dotted lines represent the edges of woods, extending straight along the sides of the fairway. It strikes one that it is remarkably stupid for anyone to display such a lack of artistry, but horrible examples are to be found everywhere. "But," the practical golfer may observe, "why strive for that which is pleasing to the eye? It is golf which is to be considered first of all."

Certainly we must agree with the latter part of this comment. We must think of the demand of the game first, last and all the time, and not once may the desire to please the eye sacrifice the merits of the hole. But if a little extra thought will enable us to construct soundly, yet artistically, there can be no complaint.

Now let us go a step further and see if we cannot improve our hole by casting loose from formal lines. If we can do this, surely the most critical golfer must approve. In the sketch, I have endeavored to show a plan of clearing a fairway through woods and the heavy lines, running in and about the dotted ones, showing the irregular edges of the woods. If large and imposing trees may be brought boldly before the eye from their former wooded seclusion, so much the better. It will be noticed that, in producing this effect there has been considerably less felling of timber than is necessary along the dotted lines. The fairway widens at the end of the drive, closing in between shots and again gradually to the teeing ground.

However, I wish to call attention to the pockets A and B. Where marked by the first letter, the fairway eats into the trees and furnishes a resting place for a sliced ball. A similar treatment at B takes care of the pulled drive. At these places our irregular lines of woods make it less probable that erring shots will enter among the trees, which usually result in exasperating searches. But these mistakes, while not cruelly punished, exact their penalties nevertheless, for the trees in front extend out into the direct line of desired play.

I know of two courses where at present the plans call for the planting of trees at certain points to relieve the monotony of straight wood-lines and to add to the value of the holes. All of this might have been avoided by a little thought when the course was constructed originally. It is far easier to remove a tree than to replace it.

ON hilly courses it is difficult to prevent wash along the slopes before the turf knits. The fairway has been seeded and along comes a heavy rain. The water finds its way through the top soil, strikes the adamant clay subsoil, and away slides all that is valuable. The farmer has to contend with this quite as much as the green committeeman and some interesting experiments of the former are well worthy of consideration and trial. The enormous waste of fertile land that is taking place in some sections by torrential washings may be prevented, it appears, by breaking a downward passage for the storm-water through an underlying crust-hardpan. Left unchecked, a wash speedily develops into a gully. Dynamite has been used successfully to correct the evil. In blasting the wash, charges (each consisting of one half-cartridge of red-cross farm-powder) were placed every 15 feet to a depth of about 30 inches. These were tamped tight and exploded with cap and fuse. Two rows of charges, one on either side, were placed parallel to and along the entire length of the wash, about 6 feet back from it. They were so arranged that the charge on one side was not opposite that on the other. Additional charges were placed every 30 feet in the wash itself, and at and above the source of the wash. Where the washes crossed a terrace, the charges were placed every 15 feet for a considerable distance at right angles and along the back of the terrace, where the water would naturally settle. The blasts were attempted for the purpose of breaking through the hardpan so that the water would wash through it to the pervious stratum below instead of being obliged to run off on the surface. In brief a vertical drainage was desired.

The experiments have proved successful, and not only has the blasting broken up the ground for satisfactory drainage but, by careful comparison, the yields of crops on ground so treated has been considerably greater than those in nearby land where the dynamite was not used.

THE history of green committees generally is very like the adage of the new broom. The newly appointed chairman is likely to sweep very clean. In order to make a showing an entirely new policy is pursued. Naturally this unhappy condition is encountered mostly among the smaller organizations that can least afford it. The older clubs have learned their lesson of sticking everlastingly at it. Usually a newly appointed chairman is one of the old committee who has been quite in accord with the policies of his predecessor. The development of any hole is only a series of steps along a path which has been thoroughly considered. This may be said of turf building, too.

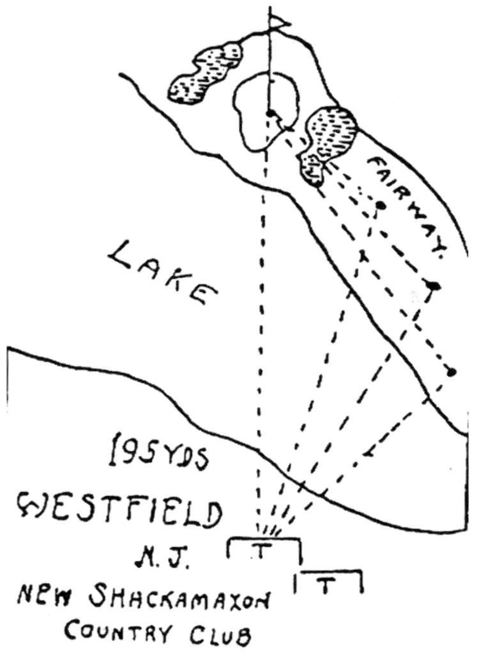

Yet how often do we find atrocious holes which might have been good if too many tinkers had not spoiled them. There are many ways of trapping any hole. Certainly one scheme must be better and more logical than others, but even an ordinary plan, if carried through to completion, is infinitely preferable to ever-changing policies and compromises.

The hole illustrated is No. 17, and it presents a brave stroke across water if the green is to be reached from the teeing ground. The sketch shows that there are shorter carries of the rather formidable hazard, but it is scarcely likely that par figures will find their way to the card of any who does not take the neck-or-nothing route.

Not long ago two golfers observed a very overdressed person, but it was not because he was overdressed which attracted attention to his raiment so much as the great variety of his bad taste. He was decorated rather than clothed.

"Good heavens!" muttered one of the golfers, "there goes the seventh hole at _____!"

Many of the thoroughly bad holes in the country have been decorated and not clothed rationally. Mr. Smith, who was chairman in 1912, was responsible for the building of the hole, and Smith's ideas may have been all right. But in 1913 Mr. Jones was appointed green committee chairman and right away he starts in changing Smith's hole. Two years later Mr. Brown covers up much of the work of his predecessors and adds a bit of his own, and in 1917 the poor old hole is wearing Smith's shoes, the trousers of Mr. Jones, Brown's coat, and various snappy haberdashery supplied by several others.

All of which brings us to the conclusion that if the hole is not satisfactory it is well to give a thought to its complete change rather than decorating it to hide its faults.

GREEN committees should not be thin-skinned and sensitive. Not long ago a club in the Middle West called in a prominent authority for an opinion of the course. It is to be assumed that they recognized the shortcomings of the links in a general way, but when a close analysis of the holes was followed by an honest report, the expert was paid his fee and told to depart in peace. As a matter of fact his findings hurt the pride of the committee. They did not relish a frank statement of facts, for some of the holes, truly trivial affairs with nothing to recommend but much to damn them, had been laid out by the players in a hit or miss manner. They were distinctly bad. Undoubtedly the committee realizes that they heard the truth from the expert they had called in, but the truth hurt.

Yet, after all, they had not paid for blarney. Had the honest opinion of the golf architect been reserved or ambiguous the club would not have received that for which they had paid. A man visits a doctor, not to hear pleasant things but to ask for advice and take it.

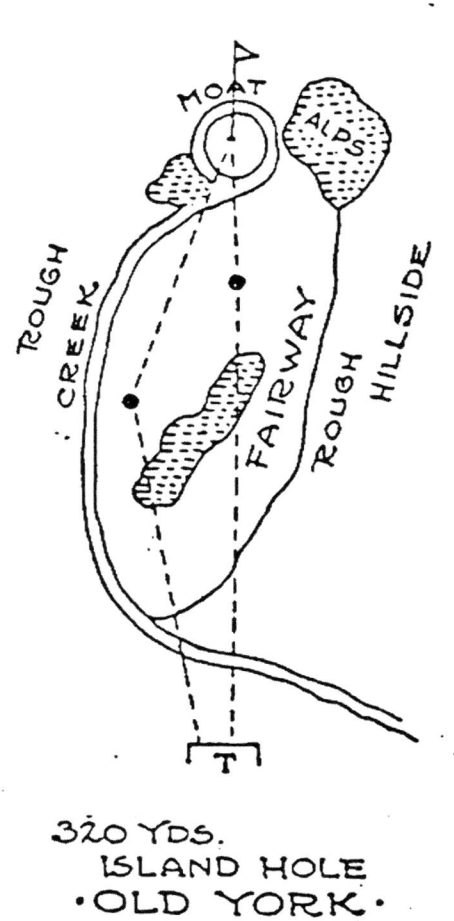

The feature of the hole represented by this plan is the large pit extending diagonally across the fairway. It is evident that the player who successfully negotiates the longest carry over this hazard leaves himself only a mashie pitch to the green. However, there are shorter carries to be attempted, each followed by a more risky approach. This plan was prepared for the remodeling of the Old York course. Originally the Island Green was open to a mashie shot from the teeing ground over the Alps.

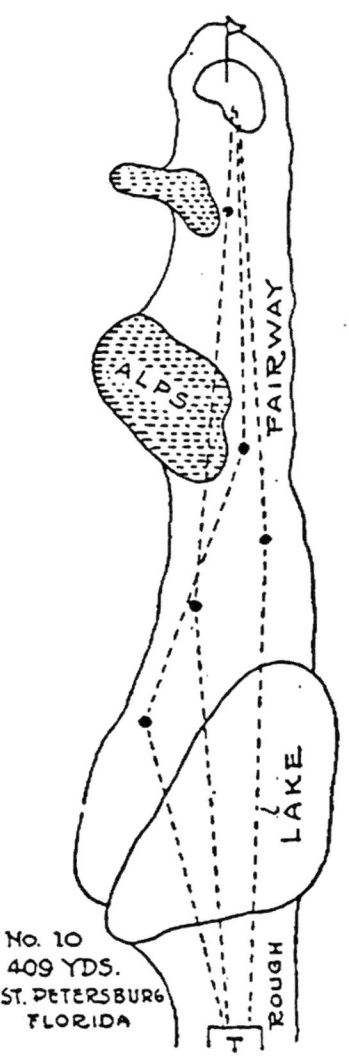

This St. Petersburg hole shows the reward for the long carry of the lake with the length of the green presenting itself to a second shot. However, the carries of the water are graded and the player may bite off only as much as he can digest.

11 A Hole Is Just As Long As It Plays

IF YOU TAKE the trouble to analyze the various holes of the courses in general, you will discover that the brassey and cleek* are not called on nearly to the extent of former days before the very resilient balls were perfected. Indeed, the cracks seldom resort to them for second shots on the majority of courses, and the duffers do so more frequently, of course; but even they usually drag them forth to pick up the distance lost after a poor drive. The reason for this is obvious. Long two-shot holes, for the most part, are not long enough. If they are planned properly, the player who can follow up a long drive with an almost equally long brassey or cleek will get home, and weather conditions should not be permitted to interfere with these demands of the long two-shot hole. Extra teeing grounds insure the preservation of the true value of any hole. But it is of the length of holes of this type under normal conditions, that these few lines are devoted.

Undoubtedly, too much attention has been paid to the yardages fixed for the purpose of figuring par. For example, 240 yards supposedly represents the length of the par figure drive, and many holes are laid with a slavish adherence to this distance. To be sure, most every thoughtful designer of a hole recognizes the fact that this rule must be affected by the slope of the fairway, an uphill drive naturally calling for considerably more power than one over favoring ground. I recall one hole in South Carolina, where the actual measurement is a trifle more than three hundred yards, but so far below the teeing ground is the green that any well-hit drive reaches it, and a crack can get home with a raking mid-iron.

Now let us assume that we allow ourselves to be influenced entirely by arbitrary figures, without a thought of the old adage that "a hole is just as long as it plays," or bearing in mind that the latest brands of golf balls are adding considerable distance to the shots of experts and duffers alike. If the figures rule our plans, the extreme distance of any normal two-shotter could not exceed 450 or 460 yards if we assume that the second shot is slightly under the length of the drive. The extreme distance of par four holes, according to the USGA. figures, is less. If you will watch the best players shooting their seconds to holes of this length, you will observe that they use mid-irons unless bucking a stiff head-wind. And, as a matter of fact, most of the so-called long two-shot holes are little more than 400 yards. So far as figures go, I am of the opinion that we must consider lengths from 460 to 480 yards before a true type is produced.

And in placing hazards for the long two shotters, we may not conceive a scheme for bunkering the three-shot hole until the yardage of 500 yards is exceeded.

It has been nearly ten years since I had the pleasure of planning the course at Shawnee. There were laid three holes of between 440 and 460 yards. They were regarded as exceedingly long two-shotters. Before a true fairway turf was secured, principally through the use of the first used three-cutters in gang arrangement, these holes were played by the golfers in general with two wooden shots, and the cracks were getting home with jiggers* for their seconds. In recent open tournaments, with finely turfed fairway which yields to remarkable run to the drives, the pros get these greens easily with irons on their second shots.

Naturally the average player will protest that we think only of the very long players when we plan holes. As a matter of fact the limitations of the golfers in general are considered at all times, particularly in placing hazards with elective carries. Certainly the very long hole cannot be closely bunkered. The distance makes it unnecessary, and even the duffer will find no great hazards. But we do want to call upon the

*Editor's note: *a brassy is equivalent to a two-wood, and a cleek a one-iron, and a jigger a 2-iron.*

par figure player to hit two of his best before he marks up a 4 on the long two-shot hole, and we would like to see the brassey and cleek called upon more frequently.

Our sketch shows roughly the plan for one of the new holes on the North Hempstead course on Long Island. The hole, as it now stands, is the second, a very short one of less than 100 yards. The green is by the side of the lake, which figures only if the mashie shot is pulled. The new plan calls for a very irregular shaped green and an unusually wide teeing ground to allow various angles of play. The new hole will be longer, the placement of the cup regulating the distance between 110 and 135 yards. It is possible to cut the hole in such a spot to call for an accurate pitch over water, or in other places where the water hazard is less in evidence.

A short time since, I was called to look over a course where the greens had suffered considerably from winterkill. The greens, like many others in various sections, were made with the attempt to produce undulations. The result was a complete failure to show any natural contour, and the matter of surface drainage had been overlooked completely.

A LIGHT TRACTOR WITH THE TRIPLE GANG-CUTTER
Tractors, by the year 1919, come in use on golf courses to a greater extent than formerly. Shackamaxon has used one constantly for two years, and it has been found a great saver of time and money. Before long the tractor-drawn gang-cutter displaced many horses.

Between the "humps" (which were scalped by cutter-blades) there existed little basins which could serve no other purpose than that of holding water. If a green is hollow at all, there must be an outlet and, above all, the artificial contours must be natural in appearance. Gentle slopes are vital. They not only appeal to the eyes of discriminating players but to the man who pushes a cutter over them.

ON THE EIGHTEENTH GREEN AT THE METROPOLITAN OPEN AT SHACKAMAXON
Johnny Farrell putting, George Voigt and Harry Cooper are left center. The famous island green, the ninth, is in the upper left.

12   BOUNDARY HOLES

HOLES closely paralleling boundary lines frequently are necessary. They never are desirable for reasons which every player knows. In the building of courses today every effort is made to keep as far away from the boundaries as possible, but there are times when it cannot be done. The shape of the tract of land often makes it necessary to swing holes close to the property limits. In most the advantage gained by placing the drive over on the right-hand side of the fairway in the direction of the boundary. From this point the second shot to the green is comparatively easy. Danger has been courted and a reward for the brave effort is provided. The sketch also illustrates how a hole may be swung slightly away from the boundary rather than absolutely parallel with it. Sometimes we encounter several holes

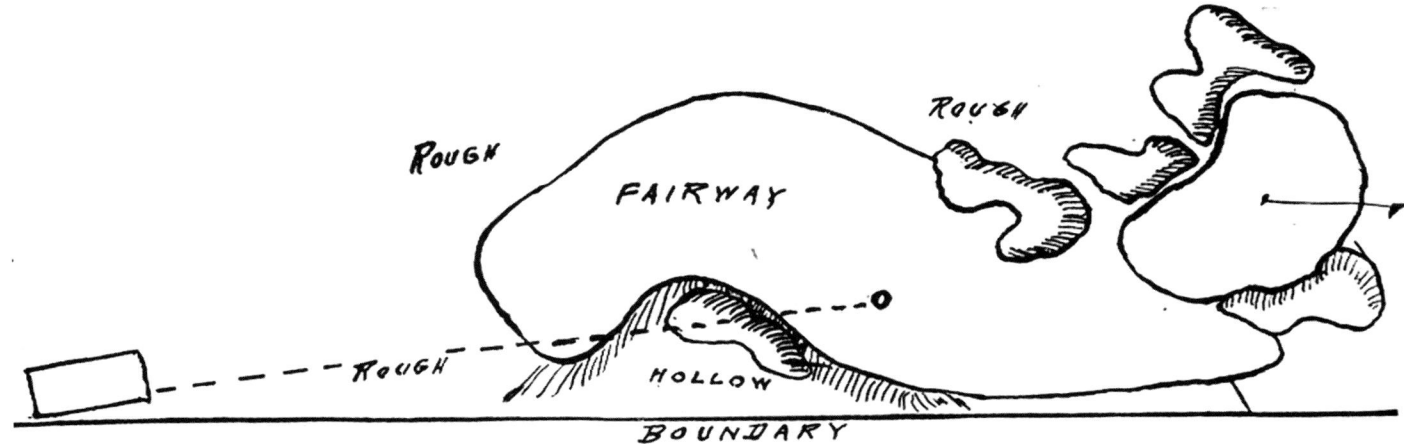

instances we find these holes running absolutely parallel to the boundary, when a little thought could have made the arrangement less monotonous.

The attempt to place teeing grounds in places where there will be the least likelihood of slicing or pulling out of bounds often is misdirected. A little thought will convince us that the closer a teeing ground is placed to the boundary the less will be the tendency to play out of bounds, for the play is thrown away from the line rather than directly along it or maybe toward it, as it is when the teeing ground is located as far away from the line as it may be.

However, when it is necessary to hug a boundary, an effort to make the boundary help the hole should be made. It is a mental hazard, and every player really fears a boundary quite as much as any hazard on the course. So if he is courageous enough to place his shot close along the danger line there should be an adequate reward for the effort. The sketch illustrates the point far better than any words of mine. It shows in succession along a boundary. This certainly is most undesirable and monotonous, and particularly bad because shots of the same sort are called for. It is best to divide the boundary holes so that the slices and pulls are equalized. The question of whether the boundary on the left is preferable to one on the right is open to debate. Personally, I rather incline to the belief that it is better to punish the slicer but, on the other hand, it must be remembered that sliced balls are far more numerous than pulls, and consequently the prominence of the boundary is made greater.

When boundaries exist, green committees sometimes neglect a point which is very important: the keeping of a fair-sized strip of rough between the fairway and the boundary line. This does not have to be rank but just long enough to hold a ball which is not running with great speed. It is manifestly unfair to dish out the same punishment to the ball which is only slightly wayward and one which is to-hell-and-gone. The strip of semi rough will help the condition greatly, and its size will be dictated by the local conditions. From ten to fifteen feet of it usually is sufficient.

Another point which the committees should consider carefully is the clear definition of the boundary line. There should be no shadow of doubt as to whether a ball is in or out. Often rail fences are used to mark the property line, and the crooked rails make it difficult to determine a close question. Posts and wire are better, but frequently the posts lean from their original positions and the wire bends and sags. One of the easiest, and at the same time economical, methods is the plowing of a furrow, which lasts for several seasons and always absolutely indicates the boundary line. If the ball is in the furrow it is out of bounds, and consequently no impossible lie is presented because of the existence of the furrow. This scheme has been tried in many places and most satisfactorily.

Every effort to prevent a ball from running out of bounds should be made, particularly at spots where the ground breaks sharply toward the line. It is far better to catch moderately running balls in sand pits or grass hollows than to give them a free patch to trickle over. This is particularly true when a hole demands that the shot to the green must be played directly toward a boundary line which is not far away. The rear of such a green should be so constructed as to catch and hold in grass hollows a ball which is overplayed to no great degree. For the most part golfers are seldom up with their shots. Fully seventy-five percent of shots fall short of their objective. Golfers ever are striding to "be up," and it is a mistake to punish unjustly when the efforts gets up a bit too far.

Every now and again we find that committees have deemed it wise to manufacture boundaries on the course itself. A section is staked off and the area is regarded as "out of bounds." Such artificial boundaries, however, have little to recommend in them.

THE TELEGRAPH BOUNDS THE RIGHT SIDE ON THE FIRST
Hermitage C.C., Richmond, Virginia.

A BOUNDARY ROAD, LEFT, ON THE SECOND
Five Farms course, Baltimore C.C.

15 A Short Pitched Shot

IN MY SKETCHES there have been shown various schemes for the guarding of greens. Recently there was a reference to the necessity of closely bunkering such greens as were designed to receive pitched shots. I think that there can be no sensible argument against this. Certainly a short, pitched shot should be sufficiently controlled to find placement on a comparatively limited area and to hold there, provided there has been imparted sufficient under-spin. Such a green appears in the sketch on this page, but it is the teeing ground to which especial attention is suggested.

Let us assume that this hole measures only one hundred and ten yards in length. This may seem very short to many, but I believe that a controlled pitch of no greater distance than this calls for one of the most skillfully executed of all strokes known to the golfer. It is the wrist shot, played with rare precision, yet with great crispness. Were the hole much longer, the length would permit a full shot with a lofted iron, and such a shot is far more easily executed. So much for length of this particular hole, although the same teeing ground would serve equally well on a hole of greater length.

It will be observed that the teeing ground is built in the shape of a fan's curved edge, which preserves the same distance to the green no matter where the plates may be set. But the great width makes it possible to change the character of the shot completely at the discretion of the committee or the caretaker. Naturally the direction and velocity of the wind would absolutely dictate the placement of the tee plates and the position of the cup in the green itself. Then, too, the caliber of the players would have much to do with it. The very irregular outline of the putting green and the positions of the guarding pits make it possible to present a most exacting shot to the pin, or a comparatively easy one, with others grading between.

Provided there is sufficient room, such a teeing ground might well be one hundred yards in width. The wider it is, the greater variety is made possible. The arrows on the sketch illustrate the course of three different shots to the cup placed in the center of the green. Obviously the cutting of the hole in other parts of the green will make any of these shots considerably more difficult. I think that a study of the sketch will bring with it a conviction of the infinite variety which such a generous, fan-shaped teeing ground will make possible.

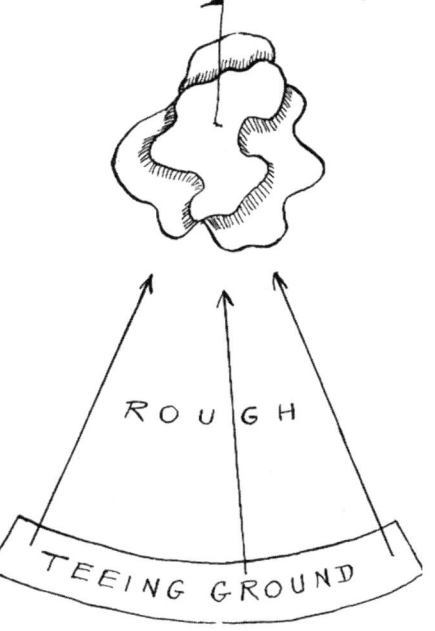

On any hole of this short length there is no fairway. It is rough from teeing ground to green, and the pits should be pretentious. The only correct shot on such a hole is one which pitches to the green and holds. The wrist shot must be mastered before it may be played with confidence. The guarding pits should be in full view from the teeing ground and of such proportions and character as to make the player fear the consequences if he falls short or wide, or if his pitch does not hold.

"But such an extensive teeing ground will require a deal of attention," you may say; "the cutting with a hand mower will be considerable."

There is no reason why a hand machine should be used at all. If the teeing ground is constructed properly and graded very gently, if grading be necessary, it will be quite possible to cut the grass with any fairway machine. It is important that the teeing grounds, from which players use their irons, be unusually large, for the wear is greater than on those from which wood is brought into play. The plates must be moved each day to allow the turf, scarred and cut by properly hit irons, to rest and heal.

THE TWELFTH AT SOMERSET HILLS
110 yards and only the most accurately pitched shot will give the player his three.

16 THE BOOMERANG HOLE— A GROUND SAVER

OFTEN there is the danger of trespassing into the freakish when the planning of a thoroughly original hole is attempted, but so long as the shots called for are sound and fit well together, there need be no great reluctance to depart from the conventional types. Indeed, it is safe to assert that far more interesting golf would be the result if conventions were not followed so slavishly.

Certainly there is little excuse for weird holes which are played to best advantage with trick shots or little dabs into basins or onto hummocks whose presence is known only to those who are very familiar with every detail of the fairway or green. Golf is not a game of trick strokes. But no hole should be open to the criticism of being a freak if it demands thoughtful and accurate play. This, then, may be taken as a defense of the hole illustrated on this page. If the appellation, "The Boomerang," fits, it will do as well as any other. Briefly, it calls for play out and back, to and from "Robin Hood's barn," to a green which is not a great distance from the teeing ground, yet quite closed to play "as the crow flies." It really is an exaggerated dogleg of extreme type. Let us regard it for a moment to determine its "whys and wherefores."

From teeing ground A, three drives are indicated; No. 1 being 185; No. 2, 215; and No. 3, 250 yards over a fairway which is skirted by woods on the right. It is obvious that there may be variations of this obstruction on the right. It might be the making-in of water or a pronounced hillock. In either case the same result would be obtained by the construction of the putting green contours and the guarding pits. However, in this particular instance, we have woods which effectually close off any play direct from teeing ground to green.

The shots to the green now swing back at a sharp angle (that is, provided at least 185 yards have been covered with the drive). Otherwise a safety shot, a wasted stroke, must be taken before the green is in range of sight. It is true that the longer the drive, the greater distance remains for the second shot, but it may be observed that the placement of the drive bears a distinct relationship to the hazard arrangement at the end of the second shot.

A hole such as this would not be resorted to frequently, but it works out very well as a ground saver. It must be remembered that it is vital that an impenetrable barrier extends between teeing ground and the green "as the crow flies."

Any truly great golf hole either possesses some outstanding natural feature or a striking artificial feature which has been constructed cunningly in close imitation of nature. Generally artificial hazards, which are worthy of the name, are placed correctly. The fact that they have to be constructed, frequently at great cost, makes it necessary that great care be taken in planning and placing them, and consequently they figure in the play to a considerable extent. But it is astonishing to observe the many examples of wasted natural features, the ignoring of the value of water courses, hillocks, dips and swales, when intelligent thought would put to good use their obvious merits. Practically like flowers that are

> born to blush unseen
> and waste their fragrance on the
> desert air

hundreds of magnificent, natural hazards show pitiful, shamed faces as though imploring some recognition of their worth, ashamed because they are seldom visited by good players but know only the curses of "Dubs."

Not so long ago I was called to visit a certain course to make suggestions for its further betterment, and it was genuine delight to spend that day with the chairman of the green committee, because he was one who gives real thought to every feature of his course. From time to time, when calling attention to some pit, he would remark, "And that one gets quite a few customers too."

Now I liked that way of putting it, for it seemed like the satisfaction of the merchant who has been successful in having his wares appreciated by discriminating patrons. There is a vast difference between the junk of the peddler, which gets the sucker or "Hick" trade because it is of the job-lot variety, and the dignified offerings of established houses, where quality is to be had.

Any decent golfer would just about as soon be seen making his Christmas purchases in a Bowery pawn shop as to be caught bunkered in some of the so-called hazards into which one only can get by scalping his ball or kicking it. Yet those same hazards would be great if located elsewhere on the same hole. In other words, many holes are built backwards so far as the value of a fine natural hazard is concerned, for it figures only at the beginning of a shot rather than near the finish of one. Sometimes it seems as though the location of "sporty" teeing grounds had been the thought of the builders of the links rather than the selection of greens and their surroundings.

One of the greatest holes in America, in my opinion, was constructed with very little labor or expense. A simple arrangement made it possible to play the hole the reverse way, with a teeing ground placed on the old featureless green and with the new putting green close by the former teeing ground. In this way a great excavation has to be considered when playing the second shot to the green, whereas this feature formerly was immediately in front of the teeing ground and of absolutely no use. True, it did trap a topped drive, adding greatly to the humiliation and distress of the poor player who would not have been able to get home with his second in any event, but we do not wish to add to the tribulations of the habitual three-figures men. Any sort of a drive used to carry it, and the crack players never even deigned to notice it at all. There it was, absolutely lost in plain view. In the future it will rank with the most notable hazards of golf. In the next chapter I will have more to say on this subject, with a sketch to illustrate the points I have endeavored to emphasize.

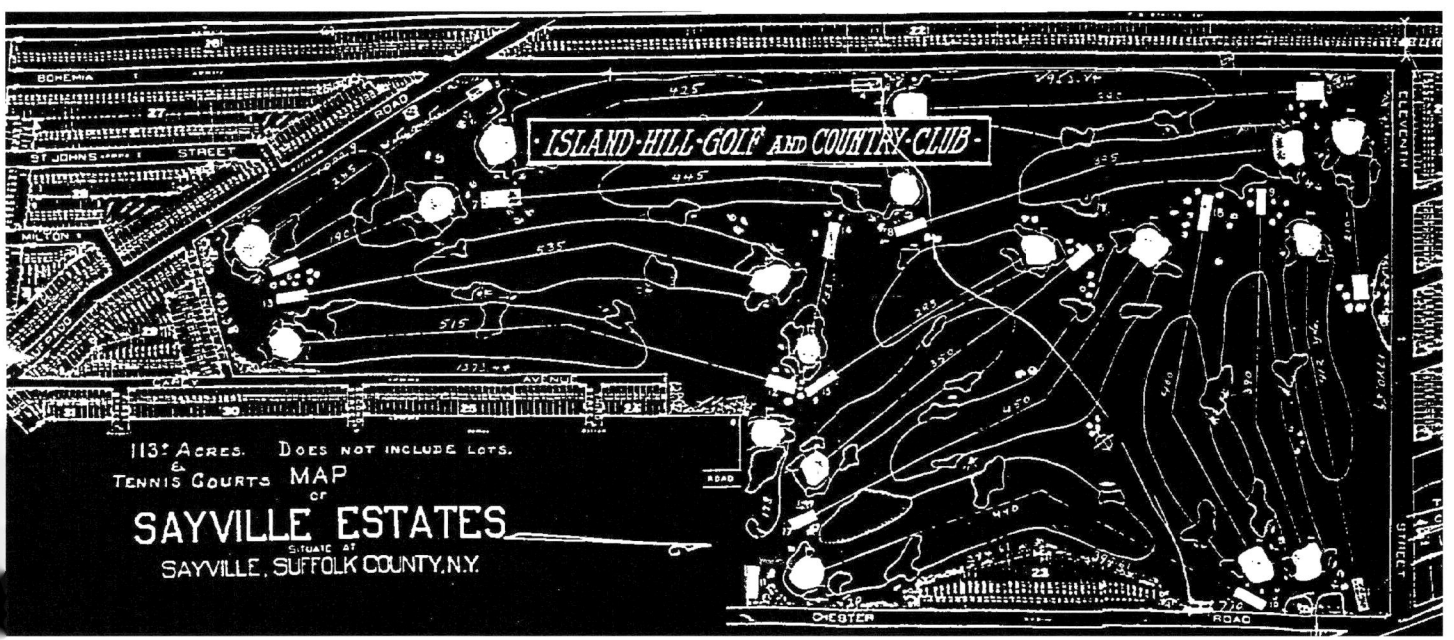

17 A WASTED HAZARD

AT THE START let us define a wasted hazard, one which is misplaced to the Nth degree. Any hole dug on a golf course is rather likely sooner or later to trap a ball. If it is placed properly we may very rightly regard it as a hazard; otherwise, it is a pitfall and unworthy of consideration. Consequently I insist that any so-called hazard which traps only a half-missed or an atrociously wild shot is wasted. Hazards should not be placed to add to the irritations and tribulations of the duffer or even the moderately bad player. If distances of the holes are sound and the approaches to the greens and greens themselves are trapped intelligently, there is no necessity of thinking about holes in the ground into which the scalped ball of the dub may squirm, thereby encouraging the further defacement of a once valuable golf ball and utterly destroying the peace of mind of a usually serene and placid golfing lady or gentleman, who could not get down in par figures unless they miraculously sunk a full brassey.

Not long since, in the far West, I was called to reconstruct a certain course and there I saw some glaring examples of misplaced bunkers. Not only on one hole but on hole after hole there were mounds and little traps immediately in front of the teeing grounds at distances varying from thirty to seventy yards, while beyond the fairway was wide open for the slicer or hooker to do pretty much as he liked. Those traps had cost money to build, yet even the average player could scarcely excuse himself if he drove into any one of them. They were wasted except for the purpose of making the course ridiculous. Happily we encounter few such glaring examples of waste in these days of modern course building. But even on some courses of comparatively recent construction there are wasted hazards, neglected opportunities, particularly in the treatment of promising natural features.

Usually the mistake may be traced easily to the attempt to provide an imposing teeing ground, which is most laudable provided the green and its approaches are equally impressive. It is the end of shots where our features should be brought into the play, not at the very beginning. But only too often is the cart put before the horse, and driving off from a beautifully situated teeing ground, which gives promise of an interesting hole, we find the green disappointing and actually featureless.

There used to be a comic, who appeared in the vaudeville theatres, and his grotesque entrance used to be greeted with gales of laughter for he wore his exceedingly ample garments in reversed fashion. The tails of his coat were in the front and down his back extended the bosom of his shirt, cravat, etc. Some of the golf holes around the country rather remind one of this clown.

To illustrate the point I have roughly sketched the plan of a hole, which probably will need a few words of explanation in addition to the drawing. The shaded area represents the former teeing ground, which was situated high up on the brink of a deep excavation, probably an abandoned quarry hole. It was no great trick to drive out well beyond this, which was a hazard only to the extent which the mind would dictate. Only a badly topped tee-shot could get in it. The remainder of the hole was very ordinary indeed, with a green which was half-blind to the second and, besides being featureless, it sloped slightly away from the shot.

Obviously the hole had been built backwards and the notable natural hazard was wasted. In the reconstruction scheme the reversal of this hole was not at all difficult, and the new teeing ground will take the place of the former green. All of the old fairway will be used, and it only required the turfing of a natural putting green beyond and to the right of the great excavation to produce one of the best holes of drive-and-iron length to be encountered anywhere. To be sure, a stretch of fairway had to be developed leading up to the new green, which is in open sight to the shot home. The putting green itself is unusually large to permit the placement of the cup in many spots in order to add variety to the second shot and to make the hole harder or easier as conditions may warrant.

This hole will cause the cracks to extend themselves in playing across the old quarry or nipping off just a bit of it to secure par figures, but the sketch shows also the safe way which should not prove bothersome to even the humblest of players, although they may require at least one more stroke. By this simple method a wasted hazard was reclaimed at little cost.

How often do you see water holes which are marred with the same error? You may find the later lapping up to the very edge of the teeing ground, while beyond, probably only an iron shot distance away, lies the green with unobstructed fairway leading to it. Fully ninety per cent of the shots whiz over the water as though it never existed, and the hazard is wasted, save only to add to the terrors of the terrified. Do not infer that I advocate the elimination of hell from the pit. Far from it! You have got to put some fear into the hearts of golfers if they are to prove brave, stalwart players. Let our hazards punish well the failures of those who battle for ultimate success after the "nothing ventured, nothing gained" idea. That is what our true hazards are for. But let us use discretion in the placement of our pits, thinking much before coming to conclusions, and strive ever to remember that golf is a game of finesse as well as of brawn. To this end I believe in carries which are elective rather than compulsory, with adequate rewards for each effort that is better than another. But this thought furnishes material for many other chapters.

We may conceive of a course which might be perfectly flat in front of every teeing ground (not a desirable condition to be sure) and, provided the holes are of good lengths and the greens featured, a fine test of the game would be found. But no course, no matter how well trapped for the drives, or no matter how satisfying the distances may be, can ever be anything but ordinary if the shots to the various greens do not have to contend with outstanding features. You will not waste your hazards, either natural or artificially natural.

NOTHING TO WASTE
It's sink or dance on Baltusrol Lower's fourth.

ROSEMAN TRACTOR MOWER—AT WESTMORELAND
Comprising a light tractor to which are attached five cutting units, giving a cutting surface of 115 inches. Lightness and extreme simplicity make this a thoroughly practical machine, always ready for the hardest work. The large driving wheels are a feature and give very easy running on uneven ground.

18   The Open At Winged Foot

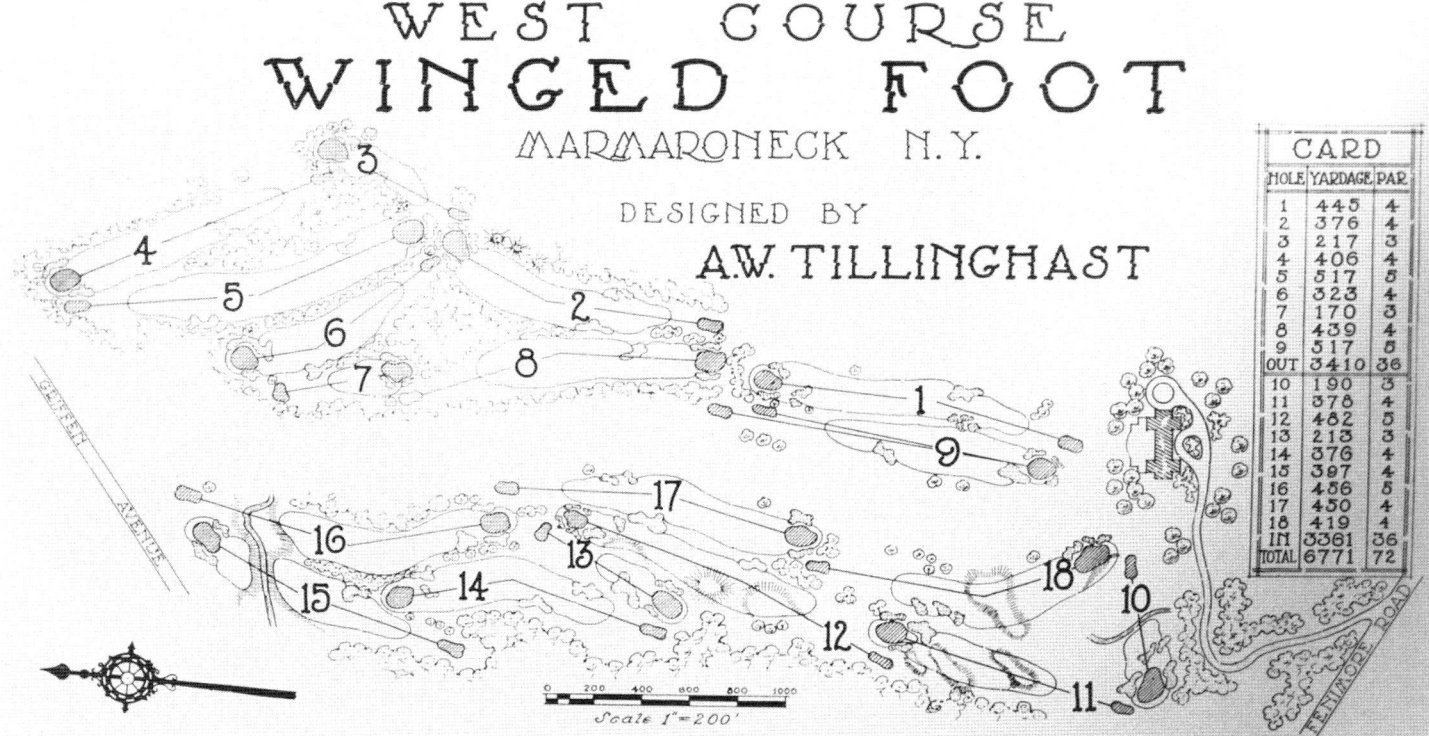

IN THE FALL of 1921 the organization of the Winged Foot Golf Club was launched by a coterie of the New York Athletic Club, headed by C. C. Nobles, who became the club's first president. It was my good fortune to be retained to select a site and design the thirty-six holes, generally directing the construction. I well recall the only order I ever received from these gentleman. It was brief and easily understood: "Give us a Man's sized course." After that time no one who creates golf courses ever worked with freer hands. But always was there the admonition, "Man sized," and as the various holes came to live they were of a sturdy breed.

In a nutshell this generally describes the course of the 1929 Open Championship of the United States, and in my opinion the winner can only be a man who hits them far and true and who can stand the gaff from start to finish. The contouring of the greens places great premium on the placement of the drives but never is there the necessity of facing a prodigious carry of the sink or swim sort. In fact every hole, barring the one-shotters, seems quite innocent and without guile from the teeing ground. It is only the knowledge that the next shot must be played with rifle accuracy that brings the realization that the drive must be placed. The holes are like men, all rather similar from foot to neck, but with greens showing the same varying character as human faces. There will be this difference from Muirfield, the host of the 1929 British Open—if the shots home are wide of the green centers the boys will be using niblicks rather than putters. Certainly the wind will not be nearly such a factor at Winged Foot as at Muirfield, but I believe the winning score will be three strokes higher over the American course, where bird figures will be less frequent. With such holes as the Babes in the Wood (7th). The Pulpit (10th), and the White Mule (13th), each a par 3, "Birdies" will be scarcer than ordinarily at the one-shotters.

Since Winged Foot was opened in 1922 there have been no changes, and no course ever received a national championship with less preparation. Aside

THE DAY WINGED FOOT WAS OPENED
President C. C. Nobles who drove the first ball, and
A. W. Tillinghast, architect of both courses, at the first tee.

from the recent addition of less than a half dozen pits, the original West course will be played and the average yardage of a trifle under sixty eight hundred will be the route without any attempt to stretch out the length to the extreme limits of the large teeing grounds just to make the scoring high. Nor will the holes be cut in canny corners of the greens to make putting tricky. Miss Winged Foot will put on no new ribbons or furbelows to beguile those who woo her during the Open, but just the everyday calico dress with her face washed up for the party.

Predictions may be out of place but I have been asked to give my own views. The course suits that rare shot-maker Leo Diegel to the ground, and if he is in form he seems to be the man to beat if he can beat himself first. Then there is Walter Hagen, of course. What a wonder that lad is! I have seen him play Winged Foot and he masters its difficulties well. Johnny Farrell knows it well and must be given serious consideration—and, of course, Bobby Jones. It would seem that the winner must break through this great quartet. Four consistent 74s must place close to the top in my opinion. With the boys getting around courses in such miraculously low figures these days the lowest round for the eighteen may possibly break 70, but it won't be done often—if at all. My engineer has measured the championship course carefully and the distances as shown on the map are from the center of teeing ground to green center in each instance.

Each hole may be longer or shorter according to wind and weather conditions. In my analysis of the holes, which follows, my estimates of the clubs which may be used are based on the class of this field and normal weather conditions.

No. 1: 445 yards. This hole, Genesis, had best be played from the right center of the fairway after the drive, probably with a 4 iron.

THIS GREEN MUST BE BOLDLY APPROACHED
Or the first terrace leaves the ball short.

No. 2: 376 yards. Elm. A long drive down the left of the fairway will open the green to an open approach. A pushed drive to the right makes the green exceedingly difficult to hold.

No. 3: 217 yards. This Pinnacle hole shows a good open green to a long iron or spoon. However a slight swell in front may deceive the player to the belief that a shorter club will reach.

No. 4: 406 yards. Sound View. An open hole but the three level green (depression in the center) places a premium on length from the tee and a careful approach.

SIDE VIEW OF THE FOURTH GREEN

No. 5: 517 yards. Long Lane. It is possible for the long hitters to get home here in two, but is likely that the brassie will be necessary to get the second one up. This second shot wants to be played from the right center of the fairway.

No. 6: 323 yards. A long drive down the left opens the green to a pitch, but it is not easy to hold from the right.

No. 7: 170 yards. The Innocent Babes in the Woods. The green is elevated slightly and the dip in front is deceptive. A high drifting 4 or 5 iron probably will be the choice of the pros.

CLOSE-UP OF THE SEVENTH GREEN

No. 8: 439 yards. Far up on the left of the fairway leaves the green nicely open to a 2 iron. As usual, off the carpet on either side will find fairly exacting rough but not poisonous. A pushed drive here is bad news.

No. 9: 517 yards. The Meadow hole. A drive and brassie may reach but not often. However, the second must be played with rare judgment and not from the right of the fairway. The green opens to the approach from the left.

No. 10: 190 yards. Bog between tee and green, waste land on right and woods on left. Just off the left front of the green there is a hummock which must be considered in playing a long drift with iron. This hole is called the Pulpit.

No. 11: 378 yards. Billows. The very undulating character of the fairway suggested the name. I believe this hole will yield more birdies than any other. A drive wee out on the right center will usually swing to the left center for the pitch to the green.

A VISTA WITH THE TENTH GREEN IN DISTANCE

No. 12: 482 yards. Cape. Three distinct hummocks make into the left of the fairway, from which side the green is not visible. The drive should be placed to the right as well as the second.

A WIDE EXPANSE OF SAND
Guarding the approach to the twelfth green.

No. 13: 213 yards. The old White Mule hole I regard as a particularly worthy one. A high drifting shot from spoon or long iron may do, but the true shot home pulls up into the green.

No. 14: 376 yards. Shamrock. Just a drive out on the right and a pitch to the elevated green. Look for birdies here.

No. 15: 397 yards. The Pyramid. A pulled or a pushed drive makes home on the second a forlorn hope. The iron to the green is across a valley and brook. The green is built up in impressive fashion and calls for great accuracy.

No. 16: 456 yards. Hell's Bells. The greatest disaster here is a pulled drive, for the tee-shot has to be played to the right-center if the green is to be gained with the second. The terrain does not help the shots to run here, and it is likely that the selection for

BEYOND THE BUNKER IS THE FIFTEENTH GREEN

the second will be a 2 or possibly 1 iron. A pit on the right approach to the green will bear watching.

No. 17: 450 yards. A slight elbow but the tee-shot had best be a trifle to the left of center. A 3 iron will suffice for the second if the drive is a good one.

No. 18: 419 yards. Revelations at last. Certainly one of the most attractive greens of them all, requiring a drive placed on the right followed by a high drifting iron to the elevation of the cup. A pulled tee-shot brings trouble.

From the foregoing resumé and a study of the plan it should be obvious that the key to low scoring over Winged Foot is the consistent play at hard-hit, accurate seconds to the greens and, incidentally the constant driving out far enough to get home under control. It may be remarked that this same course, while difficult for the rank and file of golfers to complete in low figures, is not a terrifying effort for the players of moderate ability, who are playing their thirds to the greens under the same conditions as the super golfers of the Open are facing with their seconds. Really I do not look for any dark horse to flash under the wire first at Winged Foot. Many of them who have been burning up less exacting courses throughout the country, but who have not been accustomed to the necessity of playing very tight second shots, will be under very trying pressure here. The Open at Winged Foot should show a particularly wide margin between the low and high scores as the sheep are separated from the goats.

The strain of Winged Foot is mental rather than physical for the absence of hills makes play not arduous. The terrain is pleasantly undulating and incidentally it is a good gallery course. May all the boys perform with credit to themselves, and may the best man win!

JONES DRIVING FROM THE TENTH TEE
First round of the payoff. Espinosa and Findlay Douglas, President of the USGA, are on Jones' left.

LEO DIEGEL AT THE FINISH OF HIS DRIVE
From the ninth tee in the final round. Diegel's play was alternately brilliant and ragged in spots.

A NEW USE FOR THE BAMBOO HOLES
Enthusiastic young ladies of the right weight secured preferred positions by standing on the poles.

THE GALLERY ON THE MARCH, A HURRIED SPRINT FROM THE NINTH GREEN TO THE TENTH TEE
In the closing round of the championship.

BOBBY JONES SINKS AN IMPOSSIBLE PUTT TO TIE ESPINOSA ON THE EIGHTEENTH

Editor's Note: *Bobby Jones won this 1929 U.S. Open in a playoff after tying Al Espinosa with a four round total of 294. This overall score was two shots above Walter Hagen's 1929 British Open winning score of 292 at Muirfield. Mr. Tillinghast correctly picked the winner, who was only one off in his predicted score.*

THE CHAMPIONSHIP CUP
Presented to Robert Tyre Jones, Jr. by
USGA President, Findlay S. Douglas.

WHEN GENE SARAZEN LOOKED LIKE A WINNER
Golf writers stuck close to him for news. Linde
Fowler with his periscope is on the right.

PREPARED FOR EMERGENCIES
Johnny Farrell carried his own
refreshments.

TOSSING FOR THE HONOR OF THE PLAYOFF
USGA President, Findlay S. Douglas, tosses the coin. Espinosa
wins the toss and the first hole, starting off with a 4 to Jones' 6.

WINGED FOOT PRESIDENT
Hands Johnny Farrell the check
for the best dressed golfer in
the field.

THE SECRET'S OUT
This is how scores were
known. George Kilmer
phoned them in.

SOME OF THE 125 MARSHALS
Receiving final instructions from the chief marshal.
The long bamboo poles were used to line up the
gallery, replacing the customary rope.

19 A NINE-HOLE COURSE ON 20 OR 30 ACRES

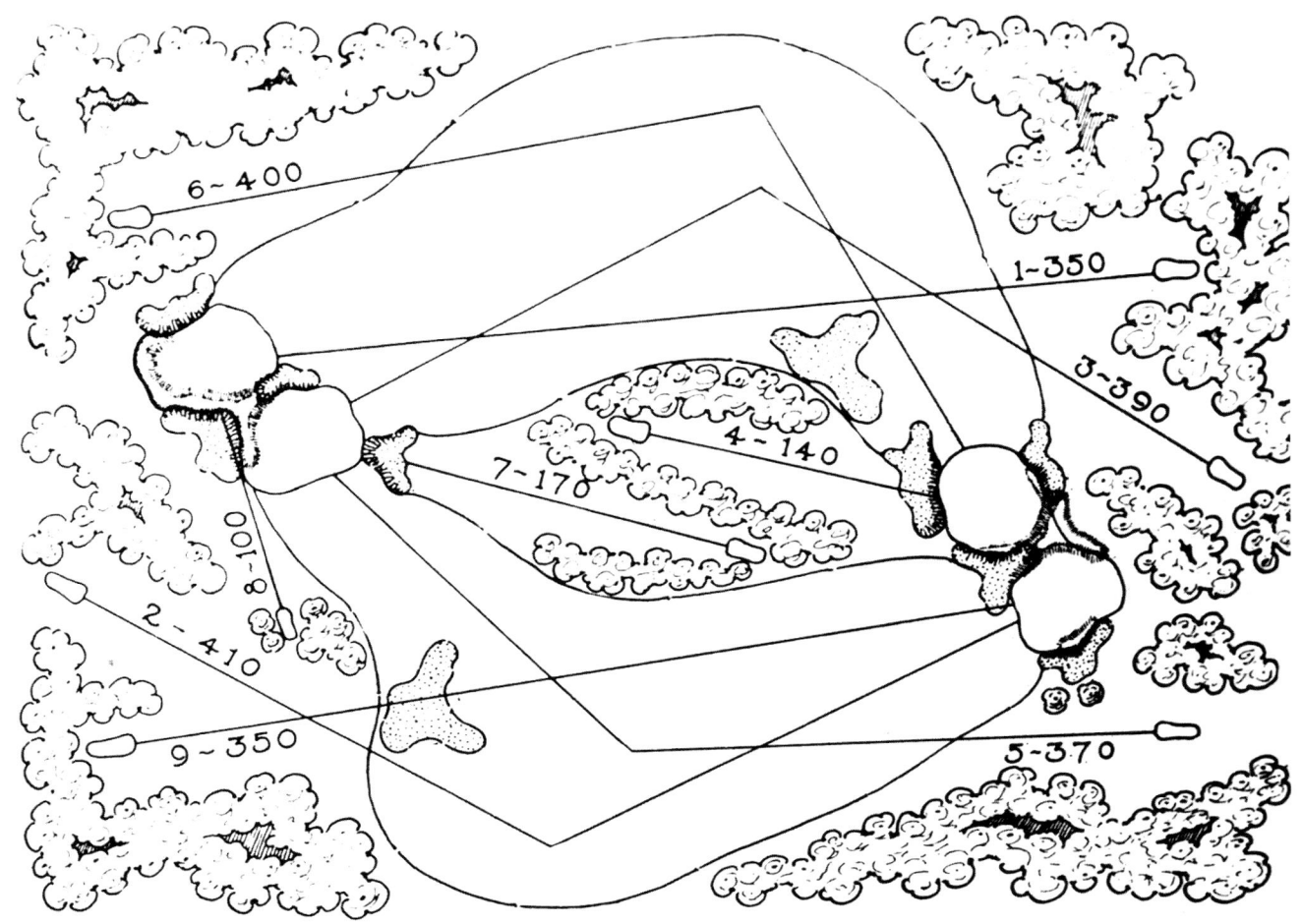

HERE IS A SPECIALLY DESIGNED NINE-HOLE COURSE
All within 30 acres with fine distances, clever greens, and not an easy course for any player.

THE CHARM of golf, indeed its very life, may be attributed to its great diversity. Unlike other sports and pastimes, the playgrounds of this game vary widely. No two are alike nor is there any rule of thumb to dictate the plan of a course. To be sure there are certain fundamentals, but courses generally reflect their greatness from the ingenuity of the plan which combines artifice with a true appreciation of natural features. If the game universally was played over many courses, each exact counterpart of the others, there is every reason to assume that it would lose much of its popularity and grip, which, ever tightening and spreading, holds millions.

It is obvious that the creators and builders of golf courses must be constantly alert to grasp new ideas. The successful entertainer must change his act for the better from time to time, and the conjurer must add to his bag of tricks. While the analogy may be timely, I do not quite like the word "tricks" as in any way applying to the work of the golf architect, for he should not be tricky. Without a doubt his creations may be subtle along lines consistent with sound, sensible play, but they should never be tricky enough to be freakish. This brings me the suggestion that I present to the readers a new and original idea of course design.

It will be my aim to discuss these thoughts briefly

and without embellishments, that he who reads in haste may not be halted, but that the student may find meat for thought, depending mainly on the sketch to carry the thoughts. If these efforts may make for more interesting play, they will not be wasted.

The thought for this chapter will not carry the general interest of those to follow, but I think it will be of peculiar significance to those who might develop a private course over thirty acres or less, a course which easily will provide for the simultaneous play of three or four foursomes. A glance at the plan will reveal nine different holes to but two double greens. The greens must be contoured carefully, a suggestion of which the plan shows. The scheme makes necessary tree planting and landscaping, but in the event of the selection of a wooded tract there remains only the work of clearing.

To make possible this arrangement it is obvious that the lines of play cross others, but this is not objectionable in the consideration of a private course where the play is confined to a few. The cost of construction may be little or great, conforming entirely to the whim or the purse of the owner, but over normal terrain the course may be introduced at very moderate expenditure. The plan shows that on a thirty acre tract this layout will provide a playing length of 2,680 yards, while on twenty acres it will yield 1,675 yards. Over the longer course, this miniature shows six two-shot holes running up to 410 yards. Comment of lengths is unnecessary as the cards are shown. Variations to suit other acreages are not at all difficult to conceive, following the two double-green idea.

As already mentioned, such a plan would be suitable only for a private course where play was limited to a few. The crossing of lines of play can not be even remotely considered on any course other than a private one where matches may be confined to three or four at most. More certainly would be dangerous and confusing. Yet, I recall a course over which the Open championship of the United States was played and which offered two holes which made necessary the crossing of play, one coming up the side of a hill very blindly. Any such arrangement of a club course today could not be conceived.

The private course illustrated is in no sense a practice course but rather one for actual competition. In another contribution I offered a plan of practice area which is conceived to accommodate a number of players simultaneously and which already has proved most satisfactory at a number of clubs. The provision of suitable practice grounds is a highly essential detail of modern course building, and one which often is quite disregarded until the last moment when something quite nondescript is sandwiched in.

The ideal setting for the building of our course is the estate of the wealthy golfer where sufficient money will be available to realize every vision of contour and landscaping. Without any great stretch of imagination we may see a lake introduced, extending irregularly across Numbers 4 and 7. Such ideas simply illustrate the elasticity of the plan. But we may conceive of this same arrangement in a less ambitious scale on any farmland where a few congenial souls might gather to do battle. If natural conditions are favorable a course of this description might be made playable for a few thousand dollars and kept in condition at a comparatively small annual expense. For example, I have built courses in Rhode Island, where the native meadows made good fairway with a little encouragement. Then again the plan might involve fifty thousand if carried on the last word of charm and excellence.

The chief criticism of private courses throughout the country is that they are too pawky. I recall one very good private course in the Middle West and on it are nine greens and individual holes over which more than a dozen rarely play. At less cost certainly a more satisfying collection of holes with only two large double greens might have been constructed, providing better tests of play with considerable more charm and at a lower annual cost of maintenance.

Isolating play is the object in planning club courses. Here it is desirable to get matches away and keep them going without seeing too much of the others. But this is not essential in the consideration of the private course. The conditions are very different. When a dozen men get together for a day's golf over a private course, invariably they are particularly well acquainted and the closer intimacy of play is not at all to be avoided provided the plan does not lay them open to an intimate visitation from the wayward ball from a friendly club. I believe the plan eliminates danger provided ordinary precautions are taken, and after all offers congenial play, which is the real objective of the private course.

20 Making The Most Of The Tee

THE PLACEMENT of the driving markers on teeing grounds is of far greater importance than most players realize, and the task should not be undertaken haphazardly nor by anyone not keenly alive to true golf strokes played under varying conditions. Assuming that the flags on the greens are sensibly located in spots, obviously fair and untreacherous to honest approach or putt, the selection of the exact area for driving is of even greater significance than the spotting of the cups. In brief, intelligent attention to this vital detail will make the hole a true test, but ignorance or nonobservance of the day's conditions may, and probably will, make it a very bad one.

The direction and velocity of the wind are the chief factors to dictate the exact limits of the teeing ground to be used. It is to be assumed that the size of the driving area is sufficiently large to allow considerable latitude, or that there be several teeing grounds for choice. Undoubtedly a great area, carefully graded to make one tremendous teeing ground, is the best design, for it presents many variations of play, as the markers are moved each day to permit the turf to mend. The wounding of the turf is particularly severe at one-shot holes, where irons are used, and, as we are considering particularly holes of the par 3 type in this article, we are dealing with the greatest of teeing grounds. So let us for a moment regard the sketch I have prepared.

This sketch shows, foreshortened for illustrating, a bird's-eye view of a hole measuring, let us say, about one hundred and eighty yards from the center of the dark colored parallelogram, which nearly represents the mathematically precise, solitary tee of other days, and which precluded any choice at all. In recent years, the driving areas have been increased in size and sometimes number, but I contend that the size still is not great enough. The sketch shows one extending the entire width of the hole with an extension of a hundred feet along the line of play. Why not? A properly graded area of this size is quite as easy to cut with a tractor mower as are the very small ones with hand

A CLOSELY GUARDED GREEN FOR A ONE-SHOT HOLE
With a teeing ground of ample proportions, the location of the markers may measurably change the character of play in the light of prevailing conditions at different times.

machines.

The green is guarded by side traps and a half-frontal pit cut into a pronounced hummock. The entire green setting indicates that any ball from the tee must carry to the green to insure the normal par figure. Assuming the day to be calm, probably A or D would be selected, depending upon the placement of the flag on the green, for in the case of one-shotters, there is a distinct relationship between the starting and finishing points. If the day be windy, fore or aft, it is likely that C would be selected, if the wind was coming from dead ahead, and B, if it was following.

Naturally a hole of this description would be more difficult to estimate and play, if a stiff breeze was coming across from either side. Under this condition rare judgment is necessary before locating the cup on the green and determining the driving angle (and distance). A study of the sketch will reveal many interesting conjectures concerning the exact direction of the tee shot other than the four indicated, with various locations of the cup and with the wind from different quarters. It will be noted that the shot along A has much more green length than that coming in from the right along D. The player may elect to play a firm iron with a slight hook or a high drifting ball coming in slightly with a fade to the right.

A TEE DESIGNED FOR ALL CONDITIONS OF WIND AND WEATHER
The tee preserves the character of the short eleventh at Essex County, no matter how the wind blows.

The green, such as this, should not have too many assisting flares for the true iron to the flag should have something on it.

It is likely that the sketch itself will take the place of a mass of wordy explanation. If it succeeds in illustrating my contention that to a great measure the value of any hole depends on a thoughtful placement of driving markers, it will have served its purpose. But let this thought be added. The attention to this detail should be a part of everyday procedure and not alone for the rare occasions of championships and meetings of the great ones of golf. It is true enough that, when champions meet, there must be some consideration given to their greater length. Any great course will provide a fine test for anyone at any time without a lot of grooming.

The reason why huge teeing grounds are advocated is to provide normal qualities to any hole even under abnormal conditions. The length of a hole is not yardage but how it plays. Frequently when champions meet they find the holes cut in all sorts of queer spots and, irrespective of wind conditions, every hole extended to its utmost like some poor creature of the Inquisition stretched on the rack. But more of this and the longer holes in a subsequent chapter.

THE TARGET FROM THE ELEVENTH TEE AT ESSEX COUNTY

21 TEEING GROUNDS FOR TWO-SHOTTERS

IN A PREVIOUS contribution, the teeing ground for a one-shot hole was illustrated. Briefly the comment strongly endorsed very large areas which offer great opportunity to vary the play under all conditions, particularly strength and direction of wind. Precisely the same argument applies in this chapter concerning the short or moderate length two-shotter.

The sketch shows six lines of drive from various points on the large and irregularly shaped teeing ground. The solid lines A, B and C illustrate elective drives from the extreme left; the first taking the long carry and leaving an open shot to the green. B takes the medium carry but although the route to the green is directly straight, the second has to carry the long pit and along the pronounced break of the ground on the right. The player from C, confessing his lack of length by playing safely to the right, must take three to get home for obviously the route for any second from this sector directly

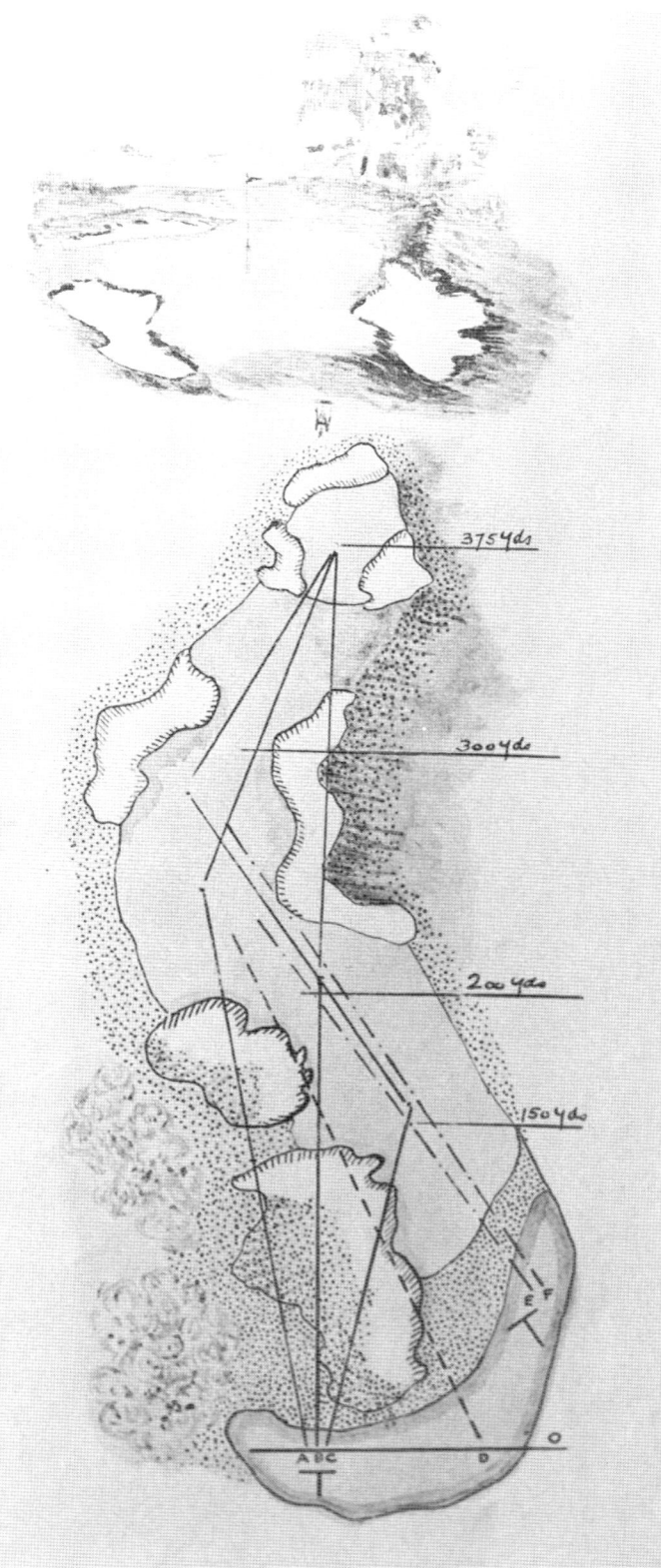

toward the green is quite beyond his ability.

The broken line D from the center of the tee shows a drive of exactly the same length as A with approximately the same carry, but from this point the hole is somewhat longer. Still another along the dot-and-dash line F, from the extreme right, is of the same length as A and D. In this instance there is no obligatory carry necessary to gain the coveted zone between the long hazards; although with about the same length of flight as is necessary for A and D to clear the first line of hazard from F, the corner of the long pit along the ridge may be carried to distinct advantage. It must be borne in mind that along the right side of the approach to this green, the ground breaks sharply to the right and the fairway, between the two long side hazards, is a swell rising gradually to the pits on either side.

This condition makes it possible to play boldly to this zone, provided it is close to down the middle. The arrangement of the entire bunkering scheme is intended to illustrate the fact that hazards should be something other than areas to be carried. This point is missed constantly in many plans. In reality, they add greatly to the merits of a course, if they are placed in such a manner as to bring reward to the judgment of distance and wind, and the accuracy of stroke that just misses them or "Cuts close" as the saying is. And, although the point has been debated often enough, the best players agree that it is not at all bad design that makes it necessary occasionally to judge length nicely enough to avoid playing a bit too strong into trouble. Glance at the sketch for a moment and it will be seen that B can reach trouble straight ahead in his elective route and so may F.

In placing the markers on a tee, such as we have provided for this hole, the direction of the wind must be noted. For example, it is fairly obvious that with the wind following or bearing in from the right, the left side of the teeing ground offers the fairest shots, while the right end is a good selection for the markers when the wind is against or from the left.

The semi bird's-eye-view of the green itself reveals a throw of the approach from left to right, and consequently it is evident that the shot must come falling to the green itself rather than running on. Of course such a condition would only be provided for the short or medium length two-shotter. The contouring of a much broader entrance would be quite different in the design of the green for the long shot home. The green of our illustration presents its most receptive length and holding contour to the high shot from the center or slight left of the fairway zone, which already I have mentioned as the desired spot. Mention was made in a prior contribution to the heinous offense of cutting the holes in the greens in tricky corners or too close to the guarding pits, an atrocious practice frequently encountered when courses have been prepared particularly for championships. If, for instance, the cup was cut, in our illustrated green, back in the rear left quarter, the value of the hole would be destroyed. The true qualities of any golf hole may be judged best by standing on the green and, noting its contours, seeing exactly from what sector of the fairway the proper shot should come. Then from that fairway zone study the line back to the teeing ground, observing the terrain, arrangement of hazards, and the driving area itself. If this makes placement of driving necessary to the successful conquest of par figures, the hole is well planned. And I place the configuration of terrain above driving pits in importance. Most of our courses are overbunkered.

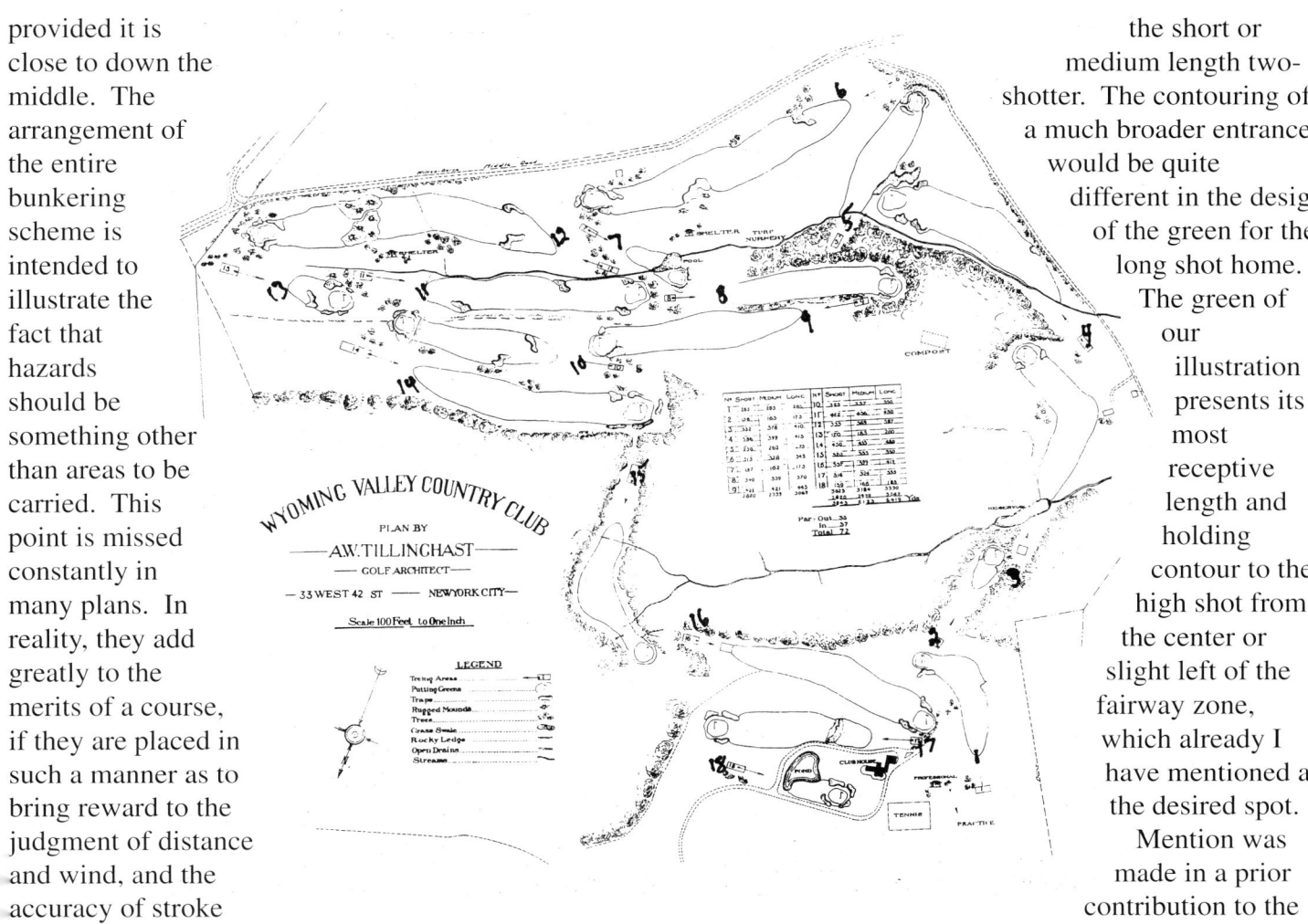

22   Sans Sand Pits

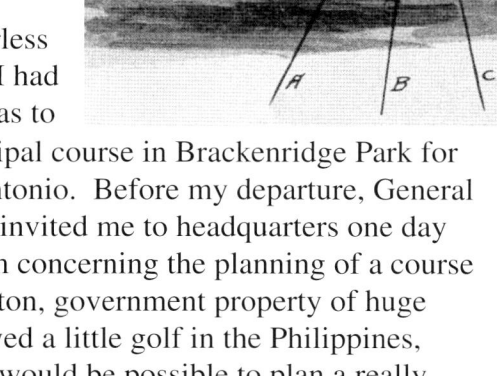

Golf courses are overbunkered. I frequently have made this assertion; now let me explain rather than merely repeat the conviction.

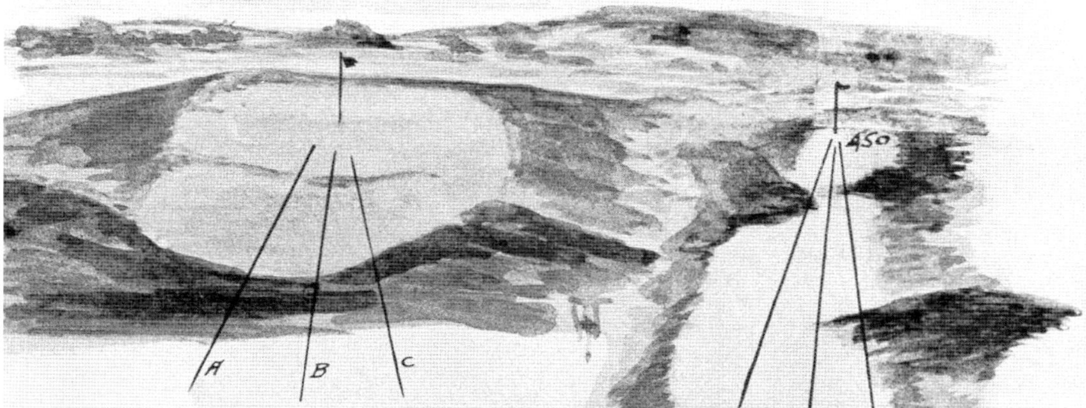

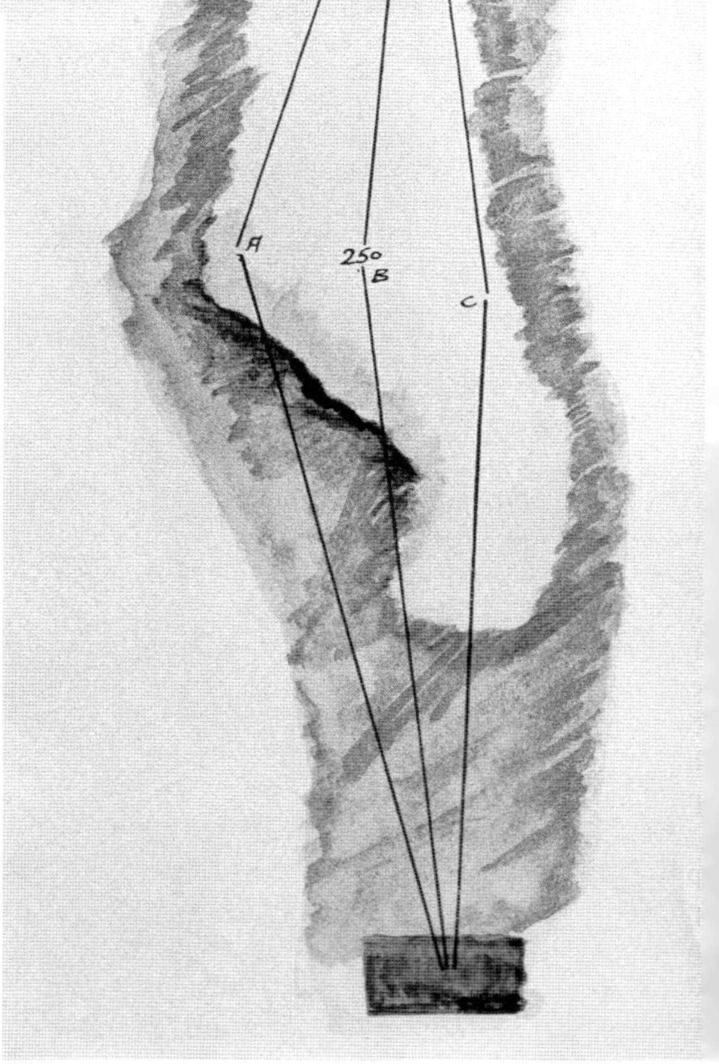

It was necessity of occasion which forced the idea of an absolutely bunkerless course. In 1915, I had gone out into Texas to lay out the municipal course in Brackenridge Park for the city of San Antonio. Before my departure, General Fredrick Funston invited me to headquarters one day to confer with him concerning the planning of a course at Fort Sam Houston, government property of huge area. He had played a little golf in the Philippines, and he asked if it would be possible to plan a really worthy course that could have no pitfalls on it, explaining that the proposed golf tract must be used frequently for cavalry and artillery maneuvers.

The drill grounds offered plenty of space, for it was prairie land stretching away in amazing distances. An inspection of the ground, rolling country dotted with bunches of mesquite and ouisache scrub growth, revealed the fact that judicious use of natural contours of terrain and encroachments of native growths could produce a truly interesting course. Here the calvary and artillery drills were practiced. Of course we could dig no pits, but a satisfactory method of using the prairie grass (which made a very useful rough) by swinging the fairway in elbows and doglegs was worked out. The course of eighteen holes was laid out and work started. Here we were aided by army prisoners under guard. But the officer's course was not completed. Just at this time the Mexican, Poncho Villa, was on the rampage, and I happened to be with the "little general" at the post when word came of the killing of the first American soldier along the Rio Grande. Funston was very short of stature, but in anger he was a giant. Had he free foot that night he would have started after Villa, "pronto." However, he declared that the Mexican bandit was a smart soldier and not to be underestimated. When the body of Corporal Schaeffer was brought back to Fort Sam Houston that was the end to any thought of golf play, for fight was in the air. The War Department saw fit to send General Pershing after him rather than Funston, and during the ensuing months the golf course project was rather lost in the shuffle. Afterwards I chanced to see a motion picture of army maneuvers on the same drill grounds and there, still standing, were several of our old directional targets.

However an idea had been born. For a number of years, I had been reconstructing many courses of the earliest American periods and of course ancient pits were being filled and obliterated. The antiquated cross bunker, hideous to view and quite worthless as a hazard, was the first to go. Then the builders of courses began to appreciate the fact that any man who could slice a ball only about one hundred and forty yards was experiencing enough tribulation without burying him to his neck in a sand pit.

And so it was that while pits in certain zones were being erased from the picture, others were showing in equal and even greater numbers in other zones but placed to trap the not-quite-good-enough efforts of the best players rather than the miscues of the duffers, as formerly.

After the dawn of the idea at the army post, I gradually found myself cutting down the numbers of fairway pits and trusting more and more to the contours of terrain for demands on placed tee shots and those to the greens generally. Contoured approaches to the greens and the shaping and contouring of the greens began to assume greater significance, as pits through the fairway were encountered with less frequency.

I have prepared a sketch of a hole of full two-shot length, which is wholly without pits. A break diagonally into the fairway from the left provides a higher level beyond. The ground slopes sharply away from the left of the green. The second shot along route A is a trifle harder than that of straight-down-the-center B, while C, having good length but declining the carry, must exercise extreme care to avoid the right front of the green or the slope on the left.

Obviously the badly pulled drive or one that is sliced have practically no chance of getting home in two, even though they are not bunkered. Here contours, either natural or artificial, created along natural lines, take the place of the conventional pits. It will be readily seen that such a scheme will admit of many variations. The sketch simply shows what might be done. Probably I would not go to the extreme of building a hole without any sand pit showing for there lurks the suspicion that there would be one or two about the green somewhere.

But there can be no doubt that close study of terrain and building holes to natural breaks will become more and more prevalent, and, as a consequence, driving pits in particular will decrease in numbers. All of which brings me back to the observation that most of our courses are decidedly overbunkered.

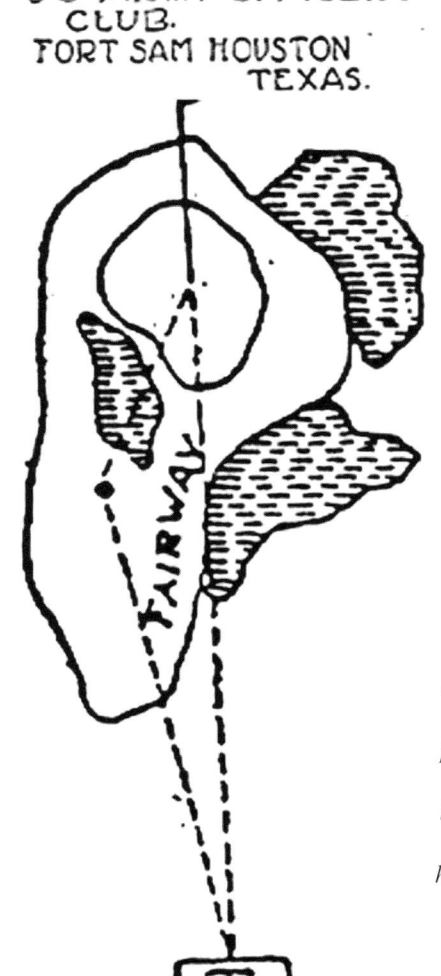

This sketch shows one of the short holes, with the teeing-ground facing the gently slope of the hill. The twisted fairway and rough grass hollows are illustrated. Ordinarily it would be out of the question to conceive of a course which was not provided with substantial sand pits, but in this instance Nature had been bountiful, and she must have had golf in her mind when she created this section of the Fort Sam Houston drill ground.

23 A Double Green

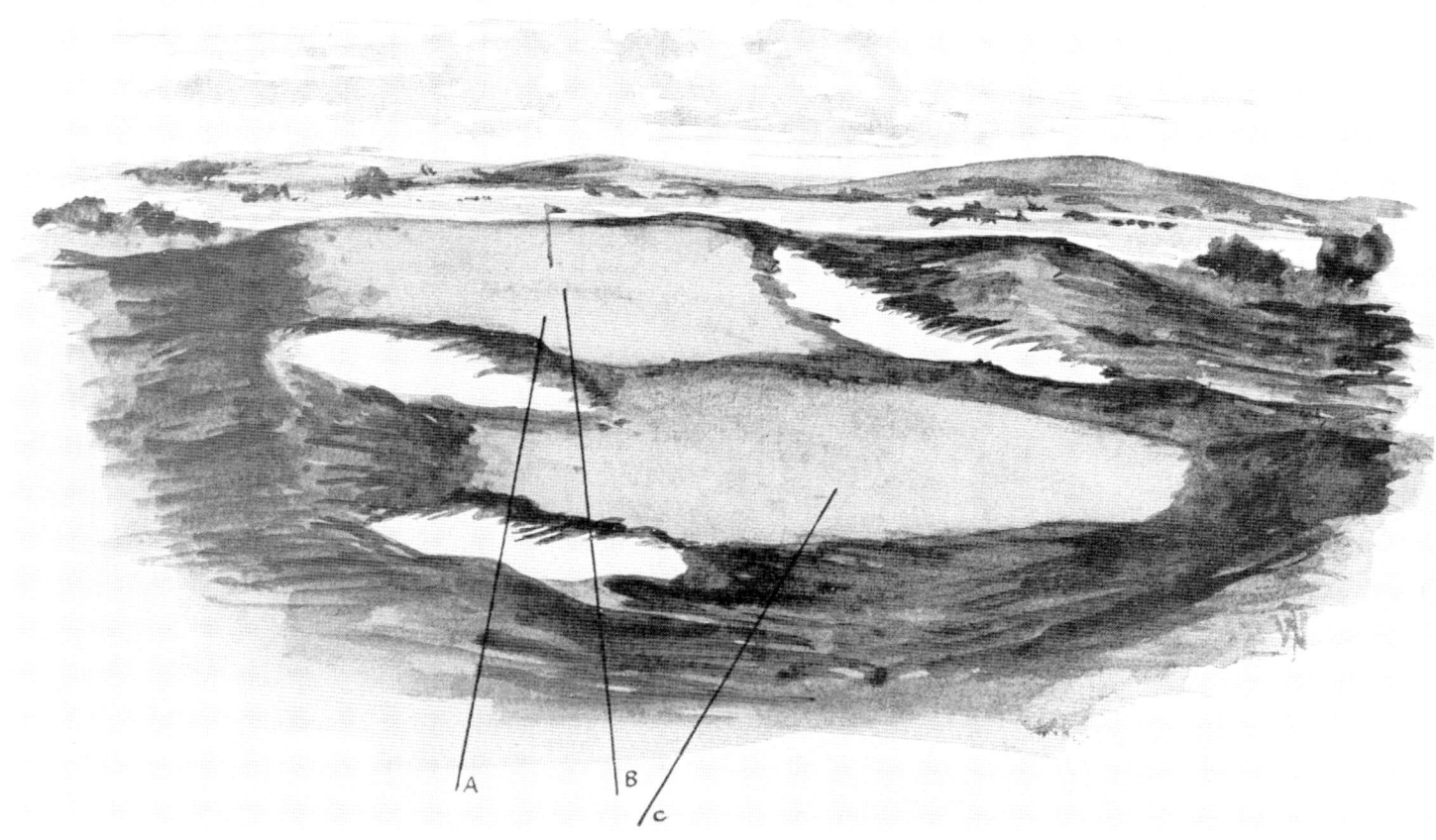

FOR A NUMBER of years the inclination of golf course architecture in America has been toward tightly bunkered greens, contoured definitely to receive certain shots and rather less in area than those found on British courses. In some instances, however, there are greens of even greater proportions than usual. No doubt each school of design has its defenders, and, while it is a well known fact that I stoutly advocate that the first mentioned produce the best golf, it is not the purpose of this chapter to debate the subject. I am illustrating an exceedingly long green, although I would prefer to designate it as two greens blended into one. In any event we cannot be far wrong in calling it a double green.

This particular design is conceived to end a hole of approximately four hundred yards or possibly a trifle more. Under normal conditions the class player probably would use his No. 4 iron for his second shot, while others, less expert, would grade all the way up to a spoon. The play from the tee is distinctly from the left with the fairway doglegging to the green. Three second shots are indicated—A, from the end of a drive of two hundred and twenty-five yards; B, from one of two hundred and fifty, and C, from the last inch that the one-hundred-and-eighty-five-yard hitter could get out of his wood.

The contour of the green makes it extremely improbable that the latter player can reach any part of it with his second. Even had he succeeded in getting two hundred yards with his tee shot, he probably would be pleased if he could reach the front half of the green with a brassie. Consequently, if light-hitting C is playing on a day when the pin had been placed on the rear half of the green, two of his best will get him home but a long way from the cup and with a trying approach putt.

The play of the second shots of both A and B is quite obvious, each is banging away for the flag, with the longer driver enjoying a trifle less dangerous journey with a bit more of the "carpet" to help to a fortunate finish. Naturally enough the rear half of the green would be selected for cup placement on days when the field was composed of the better players or to suit wind conditions. If each of these greens measured 80 x 80, making the entire length one hundred and sixty feet, it would be sufficient in my opinion. But the break between the two is very essential.

These double greens are highly satisfactory at the finish of holes where the shot to get home is a tough one, or where the opening up of the green depends upon the length of drive to an unusual degree, as it does in the hole in our illustration. Even though the light hitter cannot drive far enough out to see into the green entirely, he is satisfied if he can sight a corner of it to play for, as he prays for inspired length for his second, which may give him a chance for par figures after all.

The front half of the green, designed for a pitch shot, is a small one, but here again I recognize the opportunity for a double green (or as I insist, two greens blended into one) provided the dividing undulation extends with the line of play rather than across it. This green, much wider than long, makes it possible to change considerably the character of the shot in varying winds. It should be obvious that any distinct break in the contour, directly across the line of play, would introduce the element of luck when shots pitch directly on this area.

HERE IS THE FOURTH GREEN, WEST COURSE, RIDGEWOOD C.C.
The hole is a 545 yarder.

24 Miniature Golf Courses

"WHAT'S THE BREED of that pup of yours?" the wayfarer casually remarked. "Whisper, Stranger," replied the farmer as he drew the questioner aside, "He thinks he's an Airedale." It is not the intent of this article on Golf Architecture to comment closely on the form or structure of the thousands of so-called "Miniature Golf Courses" which have had such a bewildering vogue throughout this country, particularly during the year 1929, when they actually sprung up through the night like mushrooms. For the most part they have been tossed together in monotonous and garish array for proprietors, who know nothing about golf and care less so long as they prove profitable investments. However, they have given an incalculable amount of innocent pleasure to thousands and, consequently, they must be forgiven for the brazen adoption of a name, like the farmer's dog.

To be sure there have been some really excellent putting courses constructed here and there, miniature affairs which present true golf values, and, of course, these and many similar new ones will survive long after the Fuzzy Wuzzies gradually find the junk pile. Few real golfers ever took the latter seriously, and it has been only lately that golf architects have called into the new field of Miniatures, which after all is not new. From around 1910 to 1930 there have been designed and built many miniature courses throughout the country, generally on private estates and country club surroundings. In 1916 there was registered at the United States Patent Office a trade mark, "Lilliput Links" for miniature golf courses. Before the dawn of the twentieth century there had long existed at St. Andrews in Scotland a most excellent putting course over undulating turf. These are not to be confounded with Practice Putting

LADIES AT PLAY ON THE HIMALAYAS—ST. ANDREWS, SEPTEMBER 1894
Old Tom Morris looks on. The Grand Hotel is under construction.

PRACTICE COURSE AT HARRINGTON PARK IN BERGEN COUNTY, NEW JERSEY
Comprising thirty acres of ground in most pleasing surroundings and giving every facility to play all the true golf shots and providing first-class instruction besides. There are no freakish features. The place is lighted up for practice at night.

Greens, for in some instance the miniatures were close reproductions of the actual courses with their hazards in modified form. But now to this situation, which is quite unique and pregnant with possibility.

The recent vogue has placed golf clubs (of a kind) to knock a golf ball (or a sphere somewhat like a golf ball in composition) in the hands of several million folks who, a year or two back, would have scoffed at the idea of golfing in any form, but many of whom, now, are laboring under the urge to take a healthy swipe at a real golf ball with a real club somewhere, anywhere, they may do so without feeling like a squirrel in a cage. They crave plenty of room for their endeavors after a spell of getting dizzy trying to persuade a ball through a "what have you." This has resulted, first of all, in the demand for larger putting and approaching courses upon which only true golf conditions are encountered and second, in the building of great practice ranges where all of the long shots may be played as well as the short pitches, and expert instruction given. The better of these ranges are provided with both open and closed booths for all weather and the field flooded with light for night play. The third result of the popular wave is the pleas for many public courses of regulation requirements. More of this later.

As an illustration of the up-to-date miniature course and practice field, let us regard as a model the recently completed institution at Harrington Park, in Bergen County, New Jersey. Here thirty acres have been taken for the building of what may be called very properly a golf academy. The miniature course extends through a beautiful grove for nearly seven hundred yards, which is particularly attractive under the illumination at night. The fairways undulate in great diversity, but freakish features are not to be found. It is true golf all the way. These woodland courses are finding great favor for they afford privacy and are distinctly charming. A course of this type near Philadelphia took the play away completely from nearby corner enterprises of the conventional type. Naturally the winter will practically close all putting courses when it brings real chill in this region, but it is not all difficult to foresee what types will survive to carry on again in the spring.

But it is to the large range at Harrington Park that we may turn for a moment to visualize the sort of practice ground to which the public throughout the entire country will turn next to satisfy its desire to play real golf shots. Already it has been studied closely by representatives of other sections of America. The covered booths are sufficiently large to accommodate four players in each, hitting alternately, of course. They are oriented from the sun in the eyes of the players and protected from the prevailing cold winds of winter. Several are enclosed entirely and heated for indoor instruction, and one of the open stalls provides a sand hazard for coaching in the play of this most necessary but generally neglected stroke. However, the really great feature is the collection of greens which furnish a true objective for every shot from varying angles and distances. These are measured accurately and the ranges are indicated from every booth. Sand targets have been built into the faces of great mounds for pitch shots from various ranges. In brief, this will tend to indicate the thoroughness of the design of public golf playgrounds of the moment.

As an illustration of some of the hoaxes which naturally attended the scramble to meet the demand for public play, there came under observation one of the typical roadside balls-by-the-bucket variety. The measured distance from the teeing ground to the back fence was a trifle under 190 yards, yet on that same fence was blazoned a sign marked 300; fifteen feet in front was 275 and another fifteen feet found 250. It got quite a play for a time until the cash customers became painfully aware that the terrific drives they had been getting were not all they were cracked up to be. A certain professional who tried a bucketful at this same range actually knocked the cover off the first ball he hit, a composition affair which is sold at ridiculously low prices in the competition to secure the patronage of the golf-ignorant proprietors whose estimates of the proper requirements of the game have been quite on a par with their knowledge of the language of their newly adopted country.

It may be difficult to believe, but actually there was a miniature course of the Christmas Garden variety and as a stimulus to lagging patronage the proprietor introduced such added attractions as slackwire performers and snake charming. After a critical survey of the course itself, there persists the belief that had the reptile escaped and coiled, open mouthed on any hole, no one would have noticed anything unusual but would have exerted every effort to sink the putt into the innards of that snake, or was it an alligator? To such absurd depths did the honored name of Golf descend, but glory be, it emerges absolutely none the worse for its spree and bringing with it many thousands who want to know more about it all. Despite the fact that they happened to meet up with old man Golf when he was more or less down they soon appreciated that he was a gentleman and well worth knowing better. This chatty comment may be a bit trivial but, seriously, it does describe the situation.

While miniature course play has demonstrated that very cheap balls and clubs may be turned out, it by no means follows that these same implements would be of any use in playing real golf. The best quality accessories of the game will always be in demand as now, but the time is coming when the new throngs who will take up the game seriously will want serviceable weapons and durable balls, and it might be well for the manufacturers to see the handwriting on the wall and produce medium priced goods for the masses. But this is far from the field of golf architecture and the calls upon the profession to meet a situation which is a distinct break from the routine of years. To meet the demand for miniature courses the architects are planning and introducing interesting features and new ideas. Certain it is that the next year will see less miniatures and, already, the very ordinary ones are folding their tents like the Arabs. The supply far exceeded the demand. Many of the existing playgrounds of the next better grade will be patronized during the next year. But only the very good ones will survive permanently in my opinion, and these must present true golf and less of the freaks. The architects are studying the requirements of the large and costly driving ranges and practice fields. The better fields are being constructed and developed with the same care devoted to actual courses. Undoubtedly these will be permanent.

However, it is the public course of the pay-as-you-play manner of operation which must be built in great numbers in all parts of the country to supply the demand of the graduates from the small courses. Those which have been opened to the public have been highly

---

LILLIPUT LINKS REG U S PAT OFF

REAL LINKS IN MINIATURE
for Private Estates
Country Clubs and
Hotel Grounds

THE plans for this less strenuous form of golf are prepared by A. W. TILLINGHAST, who has laid out many courses of distinction. An accurate working-model in plasticine, showing every undulation and hazard, is created after either a personal inspection of the ground or a study of sketches or charts. LILLIPUTS are planned to occupy any space

For information in detail, write to
PETERSON, SINCLAIRE & MILLER, Inc.
"Rex Hunus"   25 West 45th Street, New York City

successful, and the idea that the public course may not rank with the best has been exploded. It is quite possible to offer a course of the greatest excellence, and conduct it profitably as it supplies every demand of the public. The assertion that the course of this sort eventually will outnumber the private club course may seem audacious to some, but I make it without hesitation. As the average high-class club is entirely beyond the means of most people, the large number of those who are coming to play the game provide the means of building semipublic and pay-as-you-go courses.

ALTHOUGH having been cognizant of the necessity of a suitable field for practicing, its real significance never impressed me quite so forcibly as throughout my tours of America as course consultant of the P.G.A. The practice grounds, which I find at golf clubs generally, are lamentably few and far between.

Time after time the pro says to me, "Will you impress my green committee with the necessity of providing a suitable place for practice and where I may be able to give lessons properly?"

Indeed it is of the utmost importance that such fields be provided, and it is important, too, that they should be rather close to the clubhouse and not away in some remote corner, which is inconvenient to reach. Only too often I find that the professional is compelled to give instructions and coaching from one of the regular fairways where interruptions are frequent and the element of danger is always present. And aside from the proper claims of the pro for a suitable place to follow that tremendously important department of his profession, the giving of instruction (and which daily is becoming of greater magnitude), there should be regarded the desires of the club members, who often enough have the urge to run out to the course for just a while for a bit of loosening-up or practice.

These will surely visit the club more frequently if convenient facilities are provided for a little golf, considerably short of a round. Maybe the player would like to doff his coat only and swing on a few. More than likely, with a match ahead, the golfers would like to limber up and get the kinks out before starting their rounds. A convenient practice field is not only something which will be genuinely appreciated, but the demand for it is so emphatic today that it must be regarded as something more than a passing fancy.

Of course the "fly in the ointment," found by the golf course architect, is the crowding of features in the immediate vicinity of the clubhouse. There is a commodious parking space to be included. There is the insistence that at least two swings of nine holes start and finish near the clubhouse. Sometimes there are tennis courts to be included in the plan. I know whereof I speak and fully recognize the difficulty. But today I appreciate better than ever before the absolute necessity for a conveniently located practice ground. While I admit that the plan presenting the first and tenth teeing-grounds and the ninth and eighteenth greens at the clubhouse is desired, I believe that the two swings are not of sufficient importance to crowd out the practice ground.

To some, a practice ground is something which is only used by players just before tournaments, and consequently not of great importance day after day. I do not concede any part of this argument but insist that it is of great daily value. But aside from its unquestioned desirability as a feature that must appeal to the club membership at large there should be another angle of contemplation and that is the obligation of the club to the professional. Teaching is of far far greater significance than ever before. Almost without any exceptions "the boys" all over America tell me that the past year has been the best of any within recollection, so far as instruction is concerned.

On every course we witness a lot of swings which are crudely grotesque—the familiar roundhouse wallop, etc., etc. It is evident that the swingers have had little or no training. They are self-taught and because they are they are losing a great deal of the joy of golf. Probably these crude swingers would admit that the reason why they had never followed a course of elementary instruction was because it was inconvenient. Certainly it would be inconvenient if a proper place had not been provided for it. It is human nature for the golfer to change to his playing clothes and walk out of the clubhouse and go right to it. If it is necessary for him to walk a quarter of a mile to some remote corner, and an unattractive corner at that, over by the railroad tracks, he just won't do it—that's all. If this brief plea for the practice ground may prove food for thought, it will not have been in vain.

CERTAINLY there are hundreds of young fellows who are causing their admirers to nod their heads in satisfaction and predict, "A future champion, sure!" But that last analysis, the National Amateur Championship, usually reveals that the young aspirants play well enough, yet fall short of greatness. A powerful, well rounded game is rare.

Without a doubt, few golfers practice intelligently. There is so much pleasure in going out to the club, every afternoon perhaps, and getting into active competition. To go by one's self and devote an hour or two in self-analysis and practice of definite strokes is not so alluring, but in this fashion, real champions are made.

To be sure there are some who indulge in this solitary, thoughtful practice, but as a rule they are those who do not possess the makings. Poor fellows! They follow the lodestar of golf fame, and, although their ambitions are never to be realized, the practice will make better golfers of them after all.

But there is a difference in the practice of embryo champions. One is likely to give some time to driving ball after ball away, while an energetic but tiring caddie retrieves them, first here, then there. Another may not hit nearly so many shots, but with every one there goes a thought. There is a definite aim, a careful observation of each effort, and a critical review. This is the sort of practice which brings great success after days of it, weeks of it, months of it, years of it.

Someone said once that golf could not be mastered inside of five years. Some of the greatest players will tell you that after twenty years they began to realize their ignorance. In a nutshell, they have told you the reason of their greatness. The really great golfer never knows perfection. No matter how thoroughly pleasing his strokes may appear to others, in his own eyes they are but unsatisfactory attempts to produce an ideal. It is a curious thing about this ideal, too. You can not catch up with it to save your life. Every time you put on a little extra speed and reach forth your hand to grasp it, Mr. Ideal throws a mocking laugh back over his shoulder and speeds it up a bit himself.

It seems to me that one must have a very good imagination to be a really good golfer, for the ideals of his thoughts represent the speed with which he will run. So dream on, golfers all. Let the mind create a good, sturdy pacemaker for each. Of course, it isn't going to do any good to wish for the moon, so don't conjure up some sort of will-o'-th'-wisp that you never can approach. Just chase something which always will travel a least bit faster than you can—and then chase it hard—not with the mad spurt of the sprinter, but with the enduring, methodical stride of the marathon.

All of these metaphors brings us back to the golf idealist and his patient practice with a fixed purpose.

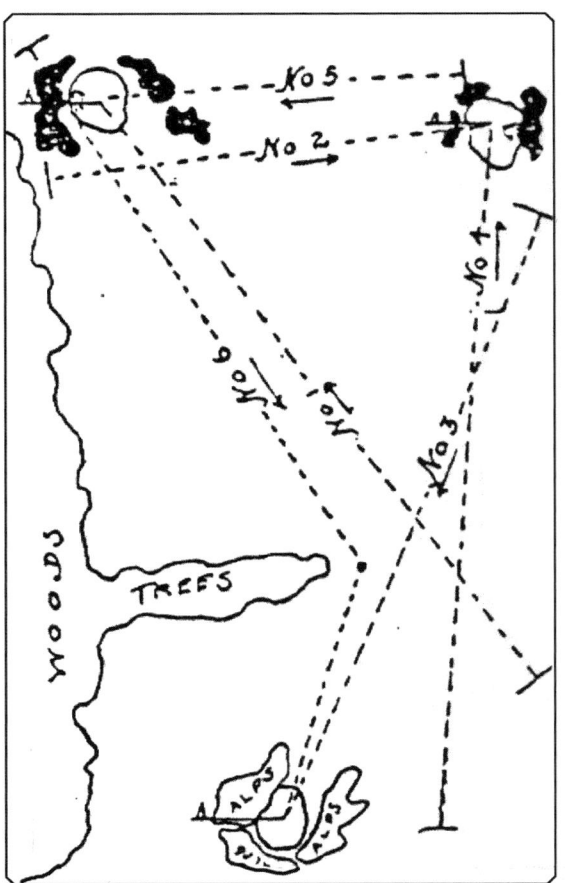

In the study of this sketch it must be born in mind that Mr. Rainey desired a course only for the exclusive use of himself and a small coterie of friends. Consequently, there was no objection to crossing the lines of play, which would be unheard of in planning regularly. The two greens at one end of the tract were half created by nature, but the lone green in the middle of meadow land is entirely artificial, yet built on such bold and rugged lines as to appear quite natural. In these six acres every club in the bag is called into play. The problem of making three greens serve for six holes was solved, although in each instance strokes of varying types find a green from different angles.

25   Popular Types Of Golf Holes

IN THE PLANNING of golf courses over a period of many years, it has been a natural thing to observe all classes of players negotiating the many various types of holes and to keep an ear open to their comments and opinions. Any course to be successful must be popular, and the architect who might persist in sticking stubbornly to features of his own personal fancy, even though they had proved not popular by test, would be foolish indeed. It is not to be assumed that all newly created holes will be generally favored immediately, for often enough they may require a bit of playing before being regarded as a "right un." However, it is not the intent of this article to select and compare the truly greatest testing holes of the world of golf today, but rather to cast a few observations about those which seem to give the most people the greatest pleasure to play. But, it must be conceded that there are some truly great holes, magnificent tests for the champions, which are not particularly popular with the rank and file, who, while respecting them, at the same time fear them, and this terror considerably interferes with their afternoon's fun. So, as this introduction already has stated, we are to regard briefly the types which apparently provide the keenest satisfaction to most golfers.

Without a doubt the one-shotter exerts the greatest appeal generally. Now the shot which seems to yield the greatest interest is one played from an elevation

THE SHAWNEE COUNTRY CLUB
At Delaware Water Gap, Pennsylvania. The eighth green is in the foreground and the ninth back on the left. Shawnee, which is laid out between two branches of the Delaware and surrounded by mountains, is famous for its fine golf and its fine tournaments.

considerably higher than the green or fairway below. It is spectacular to player and gallery alike, for the ball appears to travel prodigiously, much farther than it does in reality, although, of course, greater distance is achieved than on the level, and even the duffer gets great kick as his shot goes zooming forth in an amazingly cheering way. By like token the shot uphill meets with least favor and the backbreaking slog directly upgrade is made with no enthusiasm, particularly as it is accompanied by the distressing thought of the climb which has to follow; so enough of that.

THE ISLAND HOLE, FIFTEENTH GREEN, GALEN HALL C.C.

   We have now arrived at the conclusion that a one-shot hole, played from a stirring height, which should greet the eye with the added inspiration of lovely scenic beauty or panoramic grandeur, and to a green a trifle short of two-hundred yards away, is very desirable. This length is selected under the conditions for it gives the light hitters every opportunity to get home with the wood (for the elevation adds yards to the tee shot) to a green not so closely guarded as would be necessary were the distance less. Yet even this is not wholly satisfactory, for it is obvious that a hazard of major importance must be included to guard against the too fortunate endings of half-toppers from this easiest of all tee-shots. The player should look down on a hazard sufficiently imposing as to make it necessary to regard the shot from the tee with some respect. It might well extend two-thirds across the line of play, presenting unquestioned advantage to the courageous carry of the greatest length, an elective carry in brief. There are many ways of introducing this hazard and we are not so much interested in these in commenting on our particular topic at this time, for the character of the encroachment into the fairway is the point. To be most popular, it should be a lake—a picturesque and clean water hazard. Just why a hazard of water should be so much preferred over an exactly similar area of clean white sand or a combination of sand and rugged tuft grass is difficult for some to understand. Certainly the greenkeeper knows that it is easier to care for, but the players, including those of small skill and great timidity, favor the water, even though it may prove costly to them as its maw closes on erring balls. Beyond question, the water hazard is tremendously popular, so let us add this to our hole, and we have one that certainly contains all the elements of popular appeal.

   By the process of elimination we may find the more popular types, after leaving the better holes of one shot appeal—I think the par threes are more generally esteemed—let us take the long holes of par five description and the very short two-shotters. The latter have to be very closely guarded about their comparatively small greens to have any great value as a test.

   With the three-shotter, so frequently monotonous, and the very short two-shotter eliminated, we are left only with the longer two shot hole and for popular appeal we must eliminate the very long ones, those around four hundred yards, which demand some thought in electing the placement of the drive to open up the best route to the green—a green which may be gained either with wood or iron usually are not assailed by immoderate criticism.

26 An Exception To Rule

CERTAINLY the green, which I illustrate, as compared with the conventional type of modern green is, as the French would put it, "Tout au contraire." But, while it is contrary to the principals of putting green modeling of today, it is possible that a brief analysis will prove my thought that it has virtues other than lending of variety.

A GREEN SLIGHTLY SLOPING AWAY WITH THE SHOT
Usually a fault, but defended here, under certain condition, which is an exception to rule.

proper. But may there not be an exception to the rule? Is it not possible that in the thorough and ruthless elimination of all greens that were slightly higher in front than in the back, there may have been some truly great holes quite possibly spoiled by the application of the new principal or rule? I believe that there were; not often, I

Almost invariably the greens of our day are more or less higher in back than in front. This is as it should be and there is no quarrel with the principle. The early courses in America presented many instances of exactly the opposite contour, but it was not long before it was realized that most of the proper shots to greens pitched right up to the carpet, and the fade-away type of green would not hold or yield any bite to the ball. Then came the period of reconstruction and not only were such greens raised in the rear or lowered in the front, but the type was generally taboo wherever new courses were built. Frequently, the building up of the backs was overdone until most anything that came into the greens was held there, a condition often aggravated by soaking the turf by too copious sprinklings until the shots to the pins became little more than a matter of true direction with plenty behind them. As it was improbable that shots would run beyond, there was lost that nice sense of distance which made it necessary to put something on the ball to stop it with skill. However, let us agree that the green that is raised moderately and sensibly is entirely

grant you, but in some instances. My sketch may justify me.

Such a green should only appear at the end of a long two-shotter, where under all conditions the best players would find it necessary to use wood twice to get home, the second brassie naturally enough striking a bit in front and rolling on. Is there any reason why the shorter player or one who half-hits one of his two shots with wood, should find a green reared invitingly to gather and hold a third shot, pitched up and often yielding a half in a par after a missed stroke? It must not be inferred that I am discounting the value of recovery. In most instances I hold that the weaker player should be given the same chance to record his par as is given the crack to snare his bird, but in this instance of extreme length of the par 4, the ability to get home in two should be rewarded by reducing the probability of the third shot from behind evening the score here. This type of green might well be quite undulating in contour, but with the general slope slightly to the rear. It would add to the value of the shot chipped from off the green, for this stroke would have to be played with the greatest nicety. It might yield a half after a chipped approach to the player who had fallen only slightly short with his second, but the player from the ruck would have his own troubles in getting par figures on such a green. I insist that it is thoroughly sound even though unorthodox possibly and contrary to rule.

But may we not be sufficiently courageous now and then to be not afraid of getting out of the worm grooves of orthodoxy? So long as we do not introduce on our courses features which produce bad golf shots, but rather those which will adequately compensate for good ones, we cannot be far wrong, even though the usual thumb rule is disregarded. I have no patience with freak conceptions, and this type of green, in its proper place, will stand up under critical analysis and may not be classified as freakish in the slightest respect. Unorthodox? Certainly; but sound enough, I think. Had we feared to be unorthodox our courses today would be quite like those of years back. In those days who ever heard of a double-dogleg hole? At the very mention of the thought the heretic would have been roundly abused and generally condemned. New thoughts, if consistent with the best traditions of the game, must make the play more varied and correspondingly interesting.

As a matter of fact, some great holes on justly celebrated courses, particularly in Great Britain, have greens that slope somewhat away with the shot, without even the excuse which is presented in this paper. Yet critics concede them to be fine holes and do not quarrel with the green contours, even though in a few instances they are violations of the code of

THE TENTH ON BALTUSROL LOWER
Requires a well placed drive and a long second.

present day acceptance. But no rule may be without an occasional exception.

Following the first appearance of our sketch in *Golf Illustrated*, we received three comments coupled with inquiries. Fortunately the commentators were in accord with our idea of the slightly sloping-away, undulating green for the finish of the two-shot hole of extreme length, and curiously enough each of the queries was along lines identical with the others. Each immediately had grasped the idea of forcing the player, who was short of the green, to play an accurately gauged running approach to the hole and asked me if a green of this type would not be equally effective at the end of the hole of the extra long drive variety.

Most certainly it would, and the reason why an application of the thought did not embrace the hole of this character was solely because we endeavor nowadays to exclude this length from our plans. It is what is known generally as the par "three-and-a-half," the length beyond the accepted standard of 240 yards, which normally regulates the length of drive for computing par. Take for example the 300-yard hole, a nondescript as measured by the standards of our day, well beyond the range of the average golfer but often enough reached by the long drivers. Sometimes they stretch out even farther under favoring conditions. Frankly it is a bad length.

The green illustrated would take care of such holes very well, we think. However, the necessity would only arise in remodeling and reconstruction, for certainly we would not consider the type in a modern, virgin layout.

27 BLIND HOLES

WHEN is a hole a blind one, and consequently undesirable? Only when play of normal perfection does not make it possible for the player to see the green as he shoots for it. In other words blindness cannot be criticized if feeble or erring play makes it so. Some capable holes are only freed from a blind shot to the green when the properly hit and placed preceding stroke opens the flag to view. This is the reward. By like token the penalty for mediocre performance, obviously, is the blind shot home.

It is superfluous to observe that no one-shot (or par 3) hole should be blind to the teeing-ground. And it is most appropriate that the entire green be visible. This increases in importance as the distance decreases. With a very lofted, short distance club, like the mashie-niblick for example, the player knows well the necessity of pitching well up to the pin (provided, of course, that the green is bunkered and contoured properly), and it is highly desirable that every action of the ball when it strikes the carpet be in plain view. Not only should the flag be seen but the very bottom of it for, particularly at short range, no golfer is satisfied simply to find the green. The cup itself is the objective and a clear sight of it has much to do with successful effort.

But to return to those holes which some erroneously describe as "blind holes," just because they often are blind to them. We have prepared a sketch to illustrate the point. Here we have a hole of 385 yards. The teeing ground should be sufficiently expansive to give the hole this playing length under any condition of weather or wind. The drive is slightly upgrade and the ball should come to rest on one or another plateau. A well hit shot carrying about 185 yards will find the second plateau, from which the green is in full view. However, if the drive can reach no farther than the first plateau, the green cannot be seen. This is not a blind hole. It is only blind to the under-hit tee shots, and the fortunate terrain, which removes blindness to the proper drive, makes the hole entirely worthy.

Many plans may be conceived to introduce this same feature, viz—opening the green to full sight. It is this which gives so much value to the dogleg. You get far enough to see and play around the corner, or you don't.

A WORTHY HOLE PENALIZES A WEAK DRIVE
If the second shot to this green is blind, it is only because you make it so.

Author's note: *To digress slightly, in conning over the many publications which are devoted to golf we find numerous illustrations and diagrams of the various strokes, instructions by leading players and hints innumerable. Many are sound, many are not, but I think that often they are misleading and ruinous for one to attempt to follow. After building one's game around a few correct principles, every man is a law unto himself. Some of the very best players defy laws and advance ideas which would be fatal for anyone else to absorb.*

THE DALLAS C.C. CLUBHOUSE AND BATHING POOL

THE DALLAS CLUB'S FAMED WATER HOLE
It's number 6, and requires a water carry of 115 yards.

28   Down To Old Mexico

THE CHILL of winter was in the air as I made my way to the New York docks of the Ward Line to board S.S. "Siboney" for the port of Vera Cruz, Mexico, in November 1933. I had never been in Old Mexico and my destination was rather vague. My mind perhaps was about like that of the average citizen of the United States, harboring suggestions of spasmodic revolutions, fleabitten Indians in adobe huts covered with alkali dust, vicious bandits under huge sombreros, but at the same time realizing that back of it all there was color. Janvier had written of the Aztecs and their fabulous treasures and in my early youth I had read Prescott's history of Cortez and his conquest. Certainly a country which had been highly civilized centuries before the Continent was discovered to the eyes of Europeans must be intensely interesting. But now? What?

Old Mexico is magnificently gorgeous, the most foreign of any foreign land I have ever visited. Indians? Hosts of them. Fleas? Never observed a scratch. Bandits? Why, I met old friends in Mexico City who had lived there for more than twenty years and they asserted that their families could travel anywhere in Mexico in greater security than along the streets of Gotham. Certainly the conception of Mexico in the minds of so many, who have not been there, is entirely an erroneous one. I found this country of marvelous climate and extraordinary natural beauty to be a land of politeness, amiability and graciousness of manner. But, I am getting ashore a bit too quickly. I am on the "Siboney," a fine, comfortable Ward Liner, steaming out from New York to sea, with overcoat collar turned up. We round Hatteras in choppy foam-flecked water, but the overcoat is stowed away now in the cabin.

Sliding down the Florida coast. Through binoculars, to catch the flying fish, the water looks like morocco leather as the "Siboney" glides along with even keel on a flat, indigo sea. Morning comes and all are on deck to catch first glimpse of the hazy mountains taking form above the knife-cut horizon. Then Havana appears like a delicately tinted pastel in the morning sun. Just beyond austere Morro Castle in the hill-girt harbor lies the "Maine," watchful and patiently vigilant. Finally the long range of saw-tooth mountains ends and the western end of Cuba is astern; a brief stop-off at Yucatan to land mail, and clear water ahead to Vera Cruz and Old Mexico, mysterious and strange.

The air is heavy with the scent of gardenia, the bright blooming jasmine and the sweet, seductive odors of the tropics, as the train ascends from the sea through the resposeful indescribably charming mountain-country—up, up, until the great central plateau is gained, a climb of more than seven thousand feet. We have passed precipices and deep, wide valleys glimpsed through clouds and mists, which, in parting from time to time, reveal splashes of sunshine and color far below. This is a land of colossal inspiration.

Surely I have journeyed far and high to see Mexican golf and golfers for the event the National Championship. The men's title was won for the fifth time by Percy Clifford, a really fine golfer from the Chapultepec Club, but only after a stubborn resistance in the final by Max Wright, a plucky and tenacious player. Mrs. "Peggy" Chandler, of the Brook Hollow Golf Club at Dallas, Texas, outclassed her field to take the women's event.

CHAMPIONSHIPS OF THE MEXICAN GOLF ASSOCIATION

Percy Clifford of Chapultepec, a very convincing player who has seldom been out of Mexico.

Mrs. "Peggy" Chandler of Brook Hollow, Dallas, Texas. She won the Silver Sombrero.

The course of the Mexico City Country Club, originally laid out by Willie Smith, was that over which the championships were decided. It was in capital condition and, immediately after the meeting, work started to add to its attractiveness and testing qualities. The course at Chapultepec was laid out by Alec Smith over a particularly fine terrain and there, too, the committee anticipates an extensive program of improvement to bring it up to the high standards of the present day. But it is a real joy to play these Mexican courses, scenically so tremendously inspiring. The course of the Mexico City Country Club is rather flat but offers a good test of the game. Not so long after golf was introduced into Mexico by W.H. Townsend in 1900, this course was built in the Cherubusco section. In after years, through the support and magnificent efforts of Harry Wright, which have continued unflaggingly, the club is the center of country club social life. Here, the ceremonial presentation of trophies, following the recent championship, was a distinct event and one which added great significance and dignity.

Here, as is usual in Mexico, Bermuda grass on fairway and greens had been found best suited to climatic conditions, and while the run of the ball, particularly in the wet summer season, is not great, unusual distance is covered in flight, for the air is exceedingly rare. The twin, snow-crowned peaks of the extinct volcanoes, Popocatepetl and Ixtaccihuatl, usually are in plain view of golfers—truly an inspiring sight. From the Chapultepec course the scenic impression is of greater magnificence, as the wonderful panorama of rolling country unfolds from the heights. Knock a ball off the fairway here and you may find it resting snugly close against one of the numerous Maguey cacti, from which it is removed by local rule. This big plant, known to us as the Century, is cultivated widely throughout Mexico, for it is the very life of the native, furnishing food, drink, clothing, and many other essentials.

Visitors to the north country of course are familiar with the golf at Agua Caliente. There are other courses, too, and I am informed that the most recent one of nine holes at Tampicao, along the coast of the Gulf, is particularly picturesque and interesting.

Today Mexico is golf-minded to a degree, which augers well for the future of the game there. General Calles is an enthusiastic player of comparatively recent enlistment. The Presidente of the Republic, General Rodriguez, is an ardent enthusiast. It was my good fortune to talk with the Presidente in his chambers of the National Palace. I told him I was impressed particularly by the avidity with which many young Mexicans had taken to the game and referred to the finals of the several classes in the recent Caddie Championships, which I had witnessed. In this competition the lads really gave a fine exhibition of shot making together with poise and temperament. Young Mexico is a good golfer in every respect. I suggested to the Presidente that it would be a splendid thing for the government to foster and encourage this inclination to indulge in such a wholesome game of skill and character building. Quien Sabe?

This reference to the extreme interest in golf by the heads of the present government in Mexico recalls my visit to Cuernavaca, where a nine hole course was built especially sponsored by these high officials. There I was met by Senor Gustavo Duron Gonzales, who directed the construction of the new course. He eagerly sought my advice on certain problems of plan and development, and by his great interest and understanding proved that his conception of the requirements of modern golf was considerable. The holes at Cuernavaca extend over a high plateau, which shunts away on several sides to deep barrancas and stupendous valleys. One could almost drive a ball to the old palace of the conqueror Cortez or the ancient cathedral. It was there, in this old town, with its colorful houses walled in by gorgeous bourganvilla of purple and red, that Dwight Morrow resided. His gift, a mural by the Mexican artist Diego Rivera, serves as a memorial to our former ambassador.

I think the massive silver championship trophy certainly must be one of the finest in the entire world. Thirty inches high, of solid silver, it required eight months of the labor of a skilled silversmith.

I was honored when selected by the Association to present the championship trophies, and I know that this massive and wonderfully ornate cup was weight to lift. The exquisite design has developed delightful anachronisms, unrestrained by archaeological classic traditions. Here Aztecs are armed not with traditional weapons of destruction but with peaceful golf clubs. Here is depicted Macuilxochitl, the deity that always presided over the sports of the ancient ones, handling a mashie as he contemplates the crater of Popocatepetl and decides that for all time he will hold the record for a hole in one. In brief, he intends to pop a long'un right into old "Popo." Various of the deities are at golf, and surmounting the trophy is a golf ball, upon which is standing Centeotl, the water goddess, holding an iron, symbolic of the hazards she has crossed triumphantly. Altogether fantastic in its conception, the charming vagaries have been worked out ingeniously.

*THE ANCIENT PYRAMID OF THE SUN
AT SAN JUAN TEOTIHUACAN
A tremendously impressive relic of antiquity
well worth a day's truancy from the links.*

With a bag of clubs beckoning from a corner of the locker room, and all Mexico calling from without, siren-like, luring to a feast of strange sight-seeing, one who goes down to golf in Old Mexico is torn between two charms. I confess that I deserted the game, of which I have seen so much, in favor of this gorgeous and absorbing land, of which I had seen so little. Standing beside the great pyramid of the sun at Teotihuacan, and in the recently excavated citadel, I know that I reacted to a greater thrill of gazing bewilderedly into the dim past than I had in the Roman Coliseum.

The haciendas proved of peculiar interest, not in themselves perhaps but because they offered a simple yet mighty effective setting for the picturesque. Here comes a peon mounted on a burro. It is fascinating to conjecture how he manages to stick on, for he is

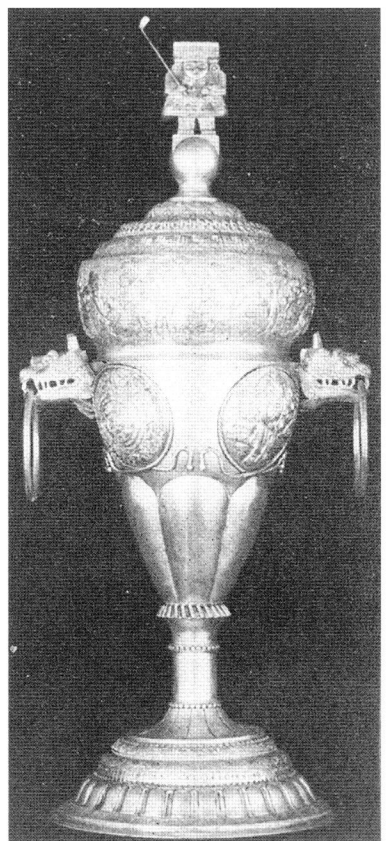

*MEXICO'S CHAMPIONSHIP CUP
It would be difficult to imagine a
more gorgeous trophy or one more
typical. This superb example of
the silversmith's craft took eight
months in the making and reveals
the ancient Aztec's playing at golf.*

In Old Mexico

seated so far back on the rump that one could well imagine that donkey's hind legs belonged to the man, were the illusion not destroyed by the man's swinging heels. Maybe if I rode a burro I would understand why every rider swings his feet in Mexico.

The Indians, and they are everywhere, are calmly peaceful folk, cheerful enough, for they will usually answer a smile with another, and they appear to be a contented lot in their adobe villages. But they are a big part of this big Mexico.

In addition to the organizations already mentioned, the golf clubs of Monterey, Alondra, Los Mochis, Cananea, Santiago, Tlahualilo, Fresmillo, Hermosillo, Pachuca, and Guadalajara comprise the Mexico Golf Association.

GENERAL CALLES

To all who travel for golf or who incidentally golf as they travel, the author recommends Old Mexico. I went down there because I, too, had been told that it would be a delight. It was all of that, and more. Casting aside superlatives let me simply say, "Wonderful!"

Editor's note: *The late Percy Clifford was a long time friend of Geoffrey Cornish and an A.S.G.C.A. member. His daughter Sandra is Mrs. Paul Fullmer, wife of the A.S.G.C.A. Secretary, Paul. She was winner of the Women's Amateur Championship of Mexico, Spain and Germany in one year and four times Chicago District Champion. Percy was present for all her European triumphs. Indeed, as a boy he attended school in England and later acquitted himself well in the Western Open and other U.S. tournaments. Obviously he spent a lot of time outside Mexico.*

THE PRESIDENT OF THE REPUBLIC
General Abelardo Rodriguez.

SENOR DURON GONZALEZ AT CUERNAVACA
With Harry Wright, President of the Mexico Golf Association.

29 Winter Greens

THE 1949 P.G.A. CHAMPIONSHIP STARTED ON THIS FIRST HOLE AT HERMITAGE COUNTRY CLUB, RICHMOND

On several former occasions we have given to green committees our opinion of the closing of play of the putting greens of our northern courses through the winter months. Only the other day we happened to overhear mutterings in a locker room. The committee had just announced the intention to close the regular greens for the winter, limiting putting to "temporaries" on the approaches. We harbor a feeling of sympathy for the grumbling players who can see no reason for it. Neither can we. At the same time we realize that the golfers taken by and large in every club are wholly selfish individuals, who offer objections to every effort of a conscientious committee to improve the condition of their course, and sometimes effect an obviously desirable change to one hole or another. If these mutinous kicks could be traced accurately to their sources, it would be found that they had been inspired entirely by the selfish reaction of the individual. "Does this suit me?" Probably a slight alteration about the green of a certain hole is anticipated. Immediately this assumes terrifically fearful proportions to the player, who finds that his own shortcomings fit rather well into the old scheme. He does not allow his thought to reach beyond self to a possible consideration of the fact that maybe the proposed might after all benefit the course and inspire the play of others. No, the whole affair is outrageous because it outrages the individual.

Yet sometimes the resenting forces may be right, although we cannot give them credit, for if the playing on the regular greens throughout the winter might injure the turf, they would be indifferent so long as they had what they wanted. But as a matter of fact the closing of the greens for the frozen months is unnecessary. When the turf is inactive no harm may be feared (more to the point if greens were closed to play in the early spring when the frost is coming out of the ground and life is stirring in the plants).

When greens are so softened at any time that sinking feet obviously must make a mess of things, the sensible greenkeeper keeps players off until the condition ends. This is more likely to happen in the early spring, so why deny the players their regular greens when they are firm with inches of frost?

30

SNAKE HOLES AND GOLF HOLES

THERE are thousands playing over verdant golf courses throughout our country today, who take things as they find them but without any conception of the virgin condition of those particular spots. Why should they? Yet often enough the transformation has taken a full toll of labor and fatigue, and sometimes it seems to me that a fleeting thought bestowed by the players on the pioneers might be not inappropriate. After so many years given over to the creation of golf courses, here, there and everywhere, it stands to reason that I am qualified in a measure to comment on the arduous work involved in turning snake holes into golf holes, and I must admit that snakes have always worried me more than any other of the pests that the course architect has to encounter and endure.

It is probable that this distinctly violent aversion may be traced back to the days of early childhood, when a quite harmless garden snake threw a scare into me, but whatever may have been the cause, I don't like snakes of any description, even when back of glass in the zoological gardens.

This aversion became sort of panic, which I have striven desperately to conceal, when some years ago in the South, a cook-woman was struck in the face by a big "rattler," and died in great agony shortly afterward. She was a part of the labor camp, organized on the acreage where I had laid out a course, which was then under construction. She had bent low over a woodpile, which accounted for the fangs taking her in the head. Of course, no tourniquet could stop her poisoned blood from getting back into her heart. Yet I have seen laborers walking unconcerned in bare feet through grass where there were rattlesnakes and swamps, where moccasins lurked. It used to give me the creeps!

IN THIS SORT OF COUNTRY, GOLF HOLES ARE BORN
Swamps, thickets, and jungle-tangles are replaced by contours of fine turf. Yet few who may golf there give a thought to the things which were.

When the municipal course at San Antonio was laid out in what is now Brackenridge Park, the presence of rattlesnakes here was rather disturbing at first, but after seeing the little children, from a nearby dobe house, toddling and playing fearlessly around a brush heap from which issued the sound of more than one set of vibrating rattles, the feeling wore off. Nothing happened other than the nervous chills which ran the gamut of my spine. That was years ago, and in March of 1935, I stopped to look over this course. The thickets are gone and no doubt there isn't a snake about the place, yet I fear I trod cautiously over the fairways where many golfers played. But I could still hear rattles.

It may be said that in laying out many courses in rattlesnake country, I have seen but one rattler, a seven-foot diamondback, which I shot with a revolver as he sunned himself by a gopher-hole on the West Coast of Florida. But moccasins and copperheads are different. They are not gentlemen who give warning.

THE SECOND SHOT TO THE NINTH GREEN
Representing the most daring features at Aronimink.

billy-goat methods, butted me in the back. My hand had been resting not many inches from a coiled and sleeping "cottonmouth," and the quick thinking of my companion moved me out of danger without any delay whatever.

Cameron Buxton, who accompanied me on our first explorations of the Trinity River Country, where we built the Brook Hollow course near Dallas, Texas, discovered a half dozen moccasins one day and hastened to show this delegation to me. He thought he was doing me a favor and was perplexed at my entire lack of appreciation. And so I might recall a score or more of courses in the South and Southwest, where velvety greens now cover spots which were once snake holes.

I recall vividly one day on the West Coast of Florida (it was 1915) when the rainy season was just over, leaving many mucky holes across the trail through the palmettos. Suddenly, the laborer who walked just in front of me, struck viciously with his "brush-hook" and neatly decapitated a big moccasin and left the remains lying there. Just at sundown I returned along that same trail, thinking of snakes, of course, when suddenly I trod squarely on one and felt it twist in the ooze under foot. I still am convinced that the world's record for the standing jump was broken then and there, but needlessly, for investigation showed that I had run afoul of a thoroughly defunct and headless snake, the villain of our morning's adventure.

The very next day brought forth another moccasin scare. The day was blistering hot and thirst soon demanded assuaging. One of the laborers guided me to the nearest spring, which was considerably more than a mile distant, and which incidentally turned out to be sulfur water of remarkable potency and of unpleasant odor. We had been removing thousands of palmetto roots, and piles of them were here and there. By one of these I stopped and rested. Suddenly I was hurled violently to the ground, as my guide, adopted

An amusing incident is called to mind, and it concerns reptiles, although not of the poisonous variety. When we were building the course at St. Albans on Long Island, many blacksnakes were in evidence in a swampy corner. The chairman of the committee shared my abhorrence of creeping things, and he very properly concluded that their presence would fill prospective members with no enthusiasm. Consequently, he offered a bounty of "two bits" each for dead snakes, and a tribe of gypsies reacted to the proposal with alacrity and thoroughness. Each night they collected, and the snakes were buried. Finally, Mr. Meehan had a feeling that some of the day's bag were none too fresh. As a matter of fact, their odor was rather fancy. Those gypsies had been selling and burying snakes at sundown, digging them up by moonlight, and repeating—well, even a snake won't remain pure forever.

THE LOVELY FIFTH AT ELM RIDGE C.C. IN MONTREAL, CANADA

GRAND OLD TREES—THE GLORY OF A GREAT GOLF COURSE
Tee and green of the third hole (now the fourth) of the Scarboro G.&C.C., near Toronto, Canada. "Chick" Evans said it was one of the finest one-shot holes in North America. Its rich setting makes it one of the most beautiful.

31 THE FIVE FARMS COURSE

MR. FRANCIS OUIMET HAS LONG BEEN RATED ONE OF THE BEST PUTTERS AMONG AMATEURS
His stance is slightly open; he addresses rather off the toe of the club and takes it back on an arc inside the line to the hole.
He hits through the ball, and the club-face remains open at the end of the stroke.

IN 1928 the Professional Golfer's Association chose the Five Farms course of the Baltimore Country Club for their annual championship. At that time the turf had not fully found itself, and there was a certain newness about the entire layout. Yet the conclusion of the championship, the consensus of opinion among the crack professional players of the country who took part in that championship, was that Five Farms was a thoroughly testing collection of golf holes, and eminently fair.

It would seem, therefore, that the action of the United States Golf Association in choosing the course for its amateur championship of 1932 was deserved recognition of this course. I may explain that the name under which the course goes traces back to the fact that the property was formerly a tract of land belonging to Mr. Stuart Oliver, and that it had long been known as Five Farms, so when it was converted into a golf club, it continued to be known as Five Farms, or the Five Farms course of the Baltimore Country Club.

I was called in by the Baltimore Country Club in around 1922 to plan thirty-six holes, with work on the first eighteen to begin immediately. As soon as the plans were ready this work was begun, and the course completed in due time. And in this connection, I want to say that the club has the benefit of the services of one of the best greenkeepers to be found anywhere in Bob Scott. He has been in charge constantly, and to his care and attention much of the condition of the course can be attributed.

These eighteen holes are the first half of those which I planned for the club, and I should judge that the new course is some four or five miles from the old club in Roland Park, one of the most distinguished organizations since its foundation in the late nineties. The course has remained unchanged since the Championship, with the exception of several bunkers and the lengthening of No. 16 to the extent of twenty yards by the introduction of a new teeing ground. The official distances for the National Amateur Championship are as follows:

Out	Par	In	Par
1.....424 yards	4	10.....378 yards	4
2.....438 yards	4	11.....424 yards	4
3.....376 yards	4	12.....388 yards	4
4.....163 yards	3	12.....141 yards	3
5.....443 yards	4	14.....585 yards	5
6.....590 yards	5	15.....425 yards	4
7.....344 yards	4	16.....402 yards	4
8.....355 yards	4	17.....155 yards	3
9.....<u>179</u> yards	<u>3</u>	18.....<u>385</u> yards	<u>4</u>
3,312	35	3,283	35

Total 6,595 yards—Par 70.

The par of 70 is a trifle misleading in estimating the testing qualities of Five Farms, for the course certainly is somewhat more difficult than these figures might suggest, but it is eminently fair and quite without freakish features. As is usual with courses of my design, there are no mighty carries necessary from the tee and the fairways are comparatively open, but the contours of the greens make careful placements necessary to getting home. It may be remarked here that the greens generally call for lofted approaches.

A part of the course was cut out of wooded land, and certain of the holes are very attractive in a scenic way. The tee for the tenth, for example, shows a view down a lane, flanked on either side by trees, beyond which the fairway broadens out with a bit of a slope from right to left. A ditch extending along the left side will prove troublesome to a hooked shot, especially because of the right-to-left slope. The green is located on a small island; an accurate pitch will be needed to hold it.

There are four one-shot holes, no one of which exceeds one hundred eighty yards in length. The first is Number 4, just over 160 yards; the green is an elevated plateau with the grounds breaking away at the front and from both sides, with traps cut into the slope. A well-controlled tee shot is needed to hold here. The ninth, one hundred seventy-nine yards, has the green on a level higher than the tee and calls for a good iron. The thirteenth, only one hundred forty-one yards, has the look of innocence, but may prove quite annoying, for the ball must be hit to hold on striking, since the shaping of the green affords no help. Unless the ball has a "bite," it is likely to pull up off the putting surface. The seventeenth is on an elevation quite well above the level of the tee, with quite a steep slope leading up to the green. There is trouble short of the slope, and traps both right and left.

There are only two three-shotters on the course, but

THE NINTH GREEN
Here is a view of the ninth green of the Five Farms course, taken from the back, and looking toward the tee in the low ground in the distance. The hole plays around one hundred and eighty yards, and the call is for a well-played iron.

both of them are all that the term implies. The first of these is the sixth, measuring five hundred ninety-six yards. There is a bend to the left, and in the corner providing this bend is a large barn, which makes it exceedingly difficult to attempt a short cut. Extraordinarily long hitters may negotiate the short route, but it is a dangerous gamble, and there will in all probability be few to try it. A well placed drive leaves the player with a brassie second needed to carry an array of traps on his way. If he negotiates these

THE TENTH GREEN—FIVE FARMS COURSE
Baltimore Country Club is one of the most famous in America. The United States Open, won by Willie Smith, was held at the old course situated at Roland Park in 1899.

successfully, he has a fairly simple pitch, but the green which is the target is not very large, and there is trouble aplenty, if he fails to hit on and hold it.

The fourteenth, measuring five hundred eighty-five yards, is the other long one. Two soundly-hit shots are needed to get within range of the green here, and furthermore the second shot must be rather accurately placed in order to avoid trouble from bunkers on the right. The green demands a pitched approach to avoid a bunker just short of it.

The course is a particularly interesting one for match play by reason of the sequence of finishing holes. Fourteen, a long three-shooter, does not play quite as long as the carded distance would indicate for it is partially down grade, but, like the others which follow, it must be played with courageous accuracy. While the short seventeenth is a particularly beautiful hole, in my opinion it is not so difficult as any of the other par threes and while it calls for careful play, its scenic charm is its greatest merit. Five Farms must be regarded as a good gallery course and in the event of extra hole matches the second returns to the clubhouse vicinity. Prophecies are dangerous in this day of mighty players, but rounds of 72 ought to win the medal and most matches.

THE 1932 AMATEUR BATTLE FIELD

Editor's note: *Mr. Tillinghast's prophecy was close—within two shots. The medal was won by John W. Fischer with a 36-hole score of 142.*

107

BOBBY JONES IN PANAMA HAT
Follows the matches at the 1932 U.S. Amateur Championship.

A HATLESS CHARLES SEAVER
Shaking hands with Bobby Jones, accompanied by Grantland Rice at the 1932 U.S. Amateur Championship.

THE WINNING PUTT
At the seventeenth in the second round, Mr. Goodman, who was two down, was just short of the green and chipped dead. Mr. Somerville, forty feet away after his tee shot, putted to within six inches of the hole and the U.S. Amateur Championship was won.

AS THE CHAMPIONSHIP WAS WON
Mr. C. Ross Somerville to right of flag, shaking hands with Mr. John Goodman, the runner-up, with onlookers starting forward to offer congratulations. At these big championships provision is always made to protect the finalists from too enthusiastic a crowd.

PLAYING FROM THE SAND
Mr. C. Ross Somerville plays this shot very well. His hand is open with feet closed and kept firmly on the ground while making the stroke—it is a right handed shot.

MR. C. ROSS SOMERVILLE
On the right Mr. H.H. Ramsay, President of the USGA, who just presented the Championship Havemeyer Cup.

32   Out Of The Adirondacks

IN THE YEAR 1901 it happened that I was at Lake Placid in the Adirondack Mountains of northern New York, playing considerable golf with George Stevens, father of those husky lads who broke records on bobsleds. In that same year, just after the twentieth century was getting well under way, in this same Adirondack town, there was born a boy baby and the household of the woods rejoiced. Little Craig came along through childhood like all the mountain youngsters do, growing sturdy and strong as they take into their lungs that bracing, balsam-tanged air, which goes to make big, virile fellows. My friend, George Stevens, was a wonderful example—one of the most powerful men I ever knew. In his hands a golf club seemed small indeed and how he could lash them out, mostly by main strength, for he was a hitter if ever there was one. There were, and are of course, countless rocks of all sizes in that country, and golf courses in those days were not developed with quite the same care as is the method of the present. I have seen George Stevens unearth them as big as your fist as he went deep with his niblick but he always managed to get hold of the ball, too, and it went off plenty far. An Adirondack golfer was about as rugged as Old White Face mountain that looked down upon him.

CRAIG WOOD
Adirondack Mountain Man.

Young Craig (I almost lapsed by saying little Craig but he never was that) did not get to know golf until he was seven years of age. He was too busy growing big. But when he was seven he did as most of the village boys did and wandered over to the nearby golf courses to caddie. Although he was but seven they could load some pretty big bags on him, yet he never murmured as he lugged them over those Lake Placid hills. Naturally enough he took to swinging clubs early and from the beginning he showed great aptitude. At first he hit them in typical Adirondack mauling fashion, but as he watched the better players he copied their trained swingings and his supple young muscles quickly attuned themselves to proper functioning in stroking a golf ball. In brief, the young Craig acquired good form at a very early age, and this, coupled with a real liking for the game and bodily strength, gained for him such skill that he was beating the older boys when chance gave them the opportunity to play, and at the age of thirteen he won his first tournament.

But it was not until he was twenty that he played much serious golf. In the meantime he had gone through prep school, Dean Academy at Franklin, Massachusetts, and afterwards entered Clarkson Tech at Potsdam, New York, to take a course in engineering. Now it came to pass that as Craig Wood found more opportunities to golf he got to like it more and engineering preparedness the less, and when he had a chance to chuck college and go to Winchester, Kentucky, as professional at a nine hole course, he needed no great urging but hopped to it with alacrity. He was twenty-two then and had been at Winchester only a year when he succeeded in finishing as runner-up in the Kentucky State Open at Louisville. Here at the Louisville Country Club he made many friends during the playing of the tournament and he was offered the berth of pro at this club. He remained there for three years before going to Norwood, New Jersey, as assistant and soon on to Forest Hills in the same state. After three years he went to Hollywood, on the Jersey coast.

To an already powerful game, Craig Wood gradually added finesse until he was rated among those of America's top flight. He won many open tournaments and already has been twice on the Ryder Cup team and, undoubtedly, will again be selected to represent his country in this classic at Ridgewood in September of 1935.

Those who have watched Craig Wood's play critically are keenly alive to the fact that he is one of the country's longest drivers. As he plays any course he will be using little irons with the big numbers on their backs in most instances as he approaches to the green. He should be a decidedly indifferent performer with the long irons for he uses them so comparatively infrequently. His low raking drives carry him so far down the course that we find him continually pitching with a mashie-niblick to the cup when others, and not short drivers either, are taking out their 4 irons to gain the green. He is particularly effective in the face of a strong wind, a fact which strongly impressed on the British gallery, which saw him finish at St. Andrews to tie Shute for the Open title in 1933. When the winds off the sea sweep this course there can be no doubt that "She blows" but his shots were raking long and splitting the fairway. I think that it takes an occasion such as this to show Wood at his best.

I did say that because he does not find occasion to use the long irons to any great extent, Craig should be rather green with them but, as a matter of fact, he plays with great power and accuracy when he does take them out.

However it must be apparent to those who have watched him closely that one of the greatest clubs in his bag is his putter. His stroking of putts is wonderfully delicate. It seems that such a strong fellow should be more bear-like around the cup. But no, our golfer from the Adirondacks is smooth as silk with his putters, so let us simply say that Craig Wood is a great, well balanced golfer; and have done with it.

Editor's note: Craig Wood earned a reputation of finishing second in major championships until the year 1941 when he won the Masters and the U.S. Open.

THIS SCENIC VIEW SHOWS THE THIRTEENTH HOLE ON THE SLEEPY HOLLOW COUNTRY CLUB COURSE
With one match on the tee, another seated on the bench and still a third arriving.

33   WAY DOWN AND WAY OUT

MILES ON MILES OVER ARID DESERT STRETCHES
The only departure from the primeval is the excellent motor road, which frequently winds through passes of stark, stony mountains.

IT IS FEBRUARY of 1935, and I am so far out in the West that should a California trembler (earthquake to you) roll me out through the patio and on down the hill, I would be in sudden contact with the Pacific Ocean. Down, just a few miles to the south, the United States decides to call it quits at a boundary fence, beyond which is the Mexican town of Tia Juana, hard by a river running underground, as most of the rivers in these parts do. A goodly portion of the U.S. Navy in the harbor of San Diego guarded me on the left, so I felt tolerably secure even though I was a long way from home, a trifle more than three thousand miles to be exact. Urged by the desire to extend my golf horizon, every one of these miles was covered by motor car, more or less on all four wheels, the exception being a short period in Tennessee when my car was overturned in a ditch. This was by no means in harmony with the inclinations of an old gentleman of my years nor did it help any when they put me under covers for repairs at Knoxville for two long days. Needless to add that the car needed them, too, and after recovering enough wind to inform all and sundry of my low opinion of the viciously crowned road of Route 11, the journey on out was resumed.

The southern route to California may well be recommended to the winter golfing traveler. Good roads are the general rule, leading through Memphis, Dallas, Texas, to El Paso, and over a corner of New Mexico to Phoenix and Yuma, Arizona, into California. All is wonderfully interesting, even the long stretches through the deserts and bad lands. One morning, along the desert road, I made a stop for a glass of milk. The skies were overcast and it did seem to me that rain was in the air. The hostess of this isolated shack was a tall, angular female of sad countenance. She was standing by a window looking hopefully at the dark clouds.

"Do you reckon it might rain?" she queried but without much spirit.

"It does look like it," I answered. "Do you need it hereabouts?"

"Mister," she said and there was bitterness in her tone, "We ain't had one good rain in nigh on three years; just a spit once in a while, and I reckon that we

LOOKING OVER THE FIRST HOLE
Through a pepper tree. This course of the San Diego Country Club offers the best golf to be found in the far southwestern corner of California.

won't git nothin' more now."

But it didn't even spit.

The desert country is not altogether continuous. After fifty miles perhaps, a town will come forth from the nowhere. Near one of these bad lands towns I actually encountered a golf course, or at least the sign bravely announced that it was a country club. Of course there were no greens nor could grass of any description be discovered. The putting surfaces were brown patches of adobe, but maybe those desert

SECOND GREEN OF THE OLD COURSE AT CORONADO
Beyond is the haven of battleships, the harbor of San Diego.

golfers get quite as much kick out of their play as any in our land. More power to them!

But mountain passes, many of them, must be traversed. Usually the desert vegetation climbs with you well up into the laps of the hills, giant cactus and the Joshua tree growing on all sides. The landscapes are sepia-toned rather than green at this time of year, particularly in Texas, and as we reach farther into the West we encounter the bristling mountain ranges. But mountain roads are safe enough if taken with careful respect. The air is glorious to take into the lungs. It is very noticeably different and the atmosphere is so clear that landmarks, twenty-five and even fifty miles away, seem quite close at hand. I think that nowhere are skies more strikingly beautiful than in New Mexico and Arizona, where mesas and buttes are silhouetted against delicate pastel tones of turquoise, pinks and ambers. The clouds are fleecy puffs, small indeed as compared with my usual Eastern banks, but the brilliant skies are filled with hosts of them.

California was gained after ten days of easy driving. Some boast of doing it in seven days, but this calls for driving relief, very early starts and late stops and a heavy foot on the gas.

On looking about I found everything pretty much as I left it a few years back, which gave me great satisfaction. Everything, did I say? Well, everything but the weather, for Southern California was having an unusually rainy time of it and for the greater part of two weeks the oldest inhabitants snarled at the downpours, drained their galoshes and explained to visitors that they had never seen the like. Just to square matters I must recall my first visit to the West Coast of Florida, in 1915, when that esteemed section was getting a similar dose. Then the old-timers were driven from their sunny perches on the benches along St. Petersburg's main street, took it on the run for shelter and as they wrung the moisture from their beards, swore that nothing of the sort had happened before in thirty years. Anyhow, it has been wet but the skies are smiling again now in strict accordance with the usual program.

Between drops but generally over sodden golf courses, tournaments have followed in uninterrupted procession. When I set foot on the Lakewood course at Long Beach, to look over the California Open, it seemed that I must be in the East again for there were

Johnny Kinder, Henry Picard, Jimmy Hines, Victor Ghezzi, Clarence Clark, "Wiffy" Cox, Maurie O'Connor, Charley Lacey and others added to western pros headed by Walter Hagen, Horton Smith, Dick Metz, Eddie Loos, Abe Espinosa, Harold McSpaden and the usual coterie of California's best. Here was the nucleus for a great field, but let us add MacDonald Smith, Willie Hunter, Lex Robson, John Rogers, Ralph Guldahl, Willie Goggin, George Von Elm, Charley Guest, John Revolta, Fred Morrison, Ray Mangrum and other good local talent, and you have assembled a very fine field indeed. Then to climax this ensemble the Australian boat dumped off at San Francisco no less than Paul Runyan, Craig Wood, Ky Laffoon, Harry Cooper, Denny Shute, Leo Diegel, Gene Sarazen, and Jimmy Thomson, while champion Olin Dutra arrived on the scene, too. All this has given Southern California a great break and the field contesting for the Los Angeles purses was the greatest in the history of the event.

Paul Runyan departed for Florida and the Miami

AGUA CALIENTE G.&C.C., MEXICO
Where Paul Runyan won the Agua Caliente Open from a splendid field.

tendency in a *Golf Illustrated* editorial and the United States Golf Association has warned against it. Undoubtedly the national officials of the P.G.A. stoutly opposed it and I should not be at all surprised if they took specific action to check it. Out here the level heads of golf expressed regret that the idea received any encouragement, for certainly it was not in keeping with the traditions of the game and should be regarded as a menace.

Such courses as I have studied in Southern California are not so testing as those, which we regard as real championship layouts in the East. The great frequency with which scores in the 60s are recorded in the open tournaments, I think justifies this opinion.

There exists a rather monotonous plan, more or less adhered to in contouring greens, and only too often values for the placement of shots are unrecognized and neglected. This must not be regarded in any way as a

A CANYON HOLE AT AGUA CALIENTE
Putting on the green is Ellsworth Vines, of tennis fame, who, by the way, takes his golf quite seriously. A fine field entered the February Open Tournament of 1935 over this course, which is less than three miles from the United States border.

Biltmore, but with this exception the same field competed at Agua Caliente, for so I was informed by Bill Hickey, president of the Southern California P.G.A. At this event it was intended to introduce public gambling by means of the pari-mutuel machine system. Already I have deplored this

THE EIGHTEENTH AT AGUA CALIENTE
Bobby Jones putting.

criticism of California courses in general for certainly there are some excellent courses, which as yet I have to lay eyes on. It embraces only the comparatively few I have observed at this writing.

In the San Diego section the country club of that name has an interesting if not a particularly testing course. Certainly its condition is better than any other in this far southwest corner. Many years ago the course at Coronado Beach was popular. I recall it was a favorite of Walter Fairbanks, or Foxy Grandpa as his intimates used to call him. But that was around 1910 and the old course has changed but trivially during the years. But it is a favorite rendezvous for the golf-minded officers of our navy when their ships are anchored in the adjacent harbor, and there are always a number of them there.

The only course here that I have yet to visit is the Rancho Santa Fe course. I am told that this course was designed by Max Behr, and I would like to walk over it, which I must do. To the north I have wandered as far as Los Angeles, but thus far I have seen only the country club course (during the Open) and some of the holes I liked very much; the course

AT LAKE MERCED GOLF AND COUNTRY CLUB
One of the trying par 3 holes.

at Annandale, Pasadena; the new Lakewood course at Long Beach; and the Victoria Club at Riverside, one of the oldest on the Coast. Lakeside I have yet to see although I hear good reports of it.

And now that the sun beams warm during the day, I may be forgiven I hope, if just a few words of appreciation are given to this wonderful climate. If any mention was made of a rainy spell let it be forgotten for I am sure that it was all a mistake. Why here in the far down and the far-out country and far to the north, too, they golf uninterruptedly almost throughout the entire year. Is it any wonder that fine golfers grow big out here?

SEVENTH AT MONTEREY PENINSULA

34 What The P.G.A. Course Service Really Means

LET US BRIEFLY regard the newly instituted service of the Professional Golfers' Association, extended without fees to golf courses throughout the United States wherever a P.G.A. member is affiliated.

It is a sincere gesture from the professionals to do something more for the game from which they derive a livelihood—something which will gradually improve courses generally by making them more pleasurable for more people. Obviously this is a farsighted policy for as more players are attracted to the game, naturally the field of the professional is broadened.

Expert advice, which emphasizes a concentration on vitally important details and the elimination of obsolete and unnecessary features, must direct budgets to doing the most good.

When I was selected and retained by the P.G.A. to visit courses throughout the country, solely to advise them and help them with their various course problems, I was little prepared for the spontaneous reaction to the plan. It is amazing. In the middle of August of 1935 I started through New York State, apart from the Metropolitan district, in response to requests from P.G.A. members, and within fifteen days I had been called on to visit no less than twenty-six courses to help solve their problems. These examinations extended from Schenectady as far west as Buffalo. In every instance I was accompanied in the examinations by the club's pro and greenkeeper, and in most cases by green committeemen and officials. On two occasions I was contacted by local golf architects and course builders, who expressed their pleasure and satisfaction.

A GENERAL VIEW OF THE COURSE OF IREM TEMPLE

Let it be thoroughly understood that the P.G.A. does *not* propose to make plans and construct courses. Where any considerable work in this direction may be involved our policy will be to recommend reliable local experts and in everyway help them with advice and suggestions, a fact that stimulates their activities and which evidently is being appreciated. In three districts of the P.G.A. I addresssed meetings of member professionals with greenkeepers and green committeemen from their clubs and 0afterwards, animated and informally, general discussions of many interesting points, which were mingled with various questions and my opinions.

The following incident may be indicative of the early success of the service. The secretary of a P.G.A. district advised me of the requests for my presence (and may it be borne in mind that the service is rendered only on request) and stated that a certain pro had remarked that it would scarcely be worth while for

THERE ARE PLENTY OF TRAPS AND CHOCOLATE DROPS ON THE LINKS AT DELAND

me to travel forty miles to his course—"for my club has no money."

His course is not included in the twenty-six already noted but I did travel the forty miles just to explain to him that our intention was not to devise plans for the spending of money but rather to save it. Finally he asked me to visit three of his greens that needed recontouring. I was able to show him how one of them could be changed at little cost, how another needed only the introduction of one guarding pit, and in the other instance an entirely new green in a perfectly natural location would improve the hole and cost no more than the fixing up of the old green, which was wrongly placed.

"Why I can do all that this fall!" he exclaimed. "And not have to ask the committee for any money at all." That detour seemed very worth while to me.

Certainly one of the greatest benefits to the average golfer to be accomplished under the new service is the elimination of what I term "Duffers' Headaches," the many traps placed only to catch the poor shots of poor players. These add aggravation and are of no value, for modern planning seeks only to make the par shooters mind their Ps and Qs. Yet these ancient relics (and unfortunately some of later vintage) are scattered about many courses serving to add to the upkeep to a marked degree, for usually they demand an unholy amount of handwork. At one place these "Chocolate drops" and sand pits ran about in a perfect riot and utterly destroyed the natural beauty of an otherwise beautiful course. But above all else they brought dismay to poor golfers and were very expensive to maintain. After only a rather brief discussion with the chairman of the green committee, who accompanied the professional and the greenkeeper, his notations sealed the doom of no less than twenty-five of these monstrosities and I believe that more will follow as a natural consequence. The course was built in 1915, which of course was nearer the period when hazards said to the humble golfer, "You must" rather than "You may." One must surely understand by this what the P.G.A. service really means when it is declared that it will make golf more pleasurable for more players.

The service was extended to all parts of the United States and as rapidly as possible routes were established. To reach as many clubs as request the service, applications were made by P.G.A. members, either through the sectional association or to the national headquarters.

35 THE MASTERPIECE OF DONALD ROSS

A BIRD'S-EYE VIEW OF PINEHURST

EARLY IN DECEMBER 1935, two old golf course architects put in a morning together at Pinehurst, N.C. One, Donald Ross, may be said to be Pinehurst itself. His companion, myself, was on tour as the golf course consultant of the P.G.A. Needless to say it was not in this capacity that I turned a bit aside from my scheduled route, that my path might cross again with that of my greatly esteemed contemporary. This was a meeting again after many years. As I alighted at the door of his charming house, Donald gave me a warm greeting and after just a bit of chat about this and that, he had me out his back door and we were on the No. 2 course.

And what a course it is! Without any doubt Ross regards this as his greatest achievement, which is saying a great deal. Every touch is Donald's own and I doubt if a single contour was fashioned unless he stood hard by with critical eye. As we stood on hole after hole, the great architect proudly called my attention to each subtle feature, certain that my appreciation of his artistry must be greater than that taken in by a less practiced eye. Nothing was lost on me, and after our round together I told him with all honesty that his course was magnificent, without a single weakness, and one which must rank with the truly great courses in the world today.

To those who have been accustomed to Pinehurst's sanded greens, the fact that No. 2 presents finely

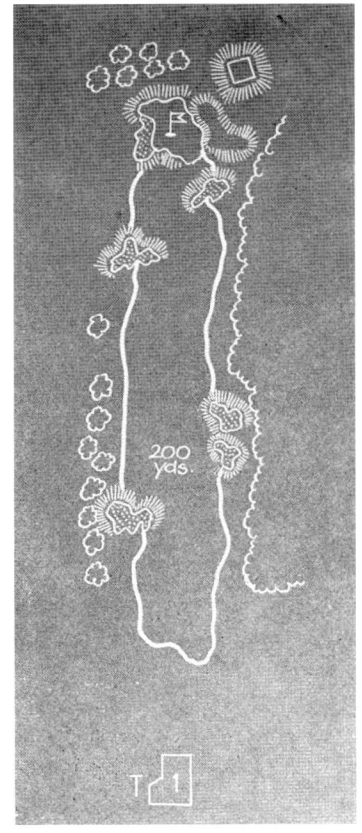 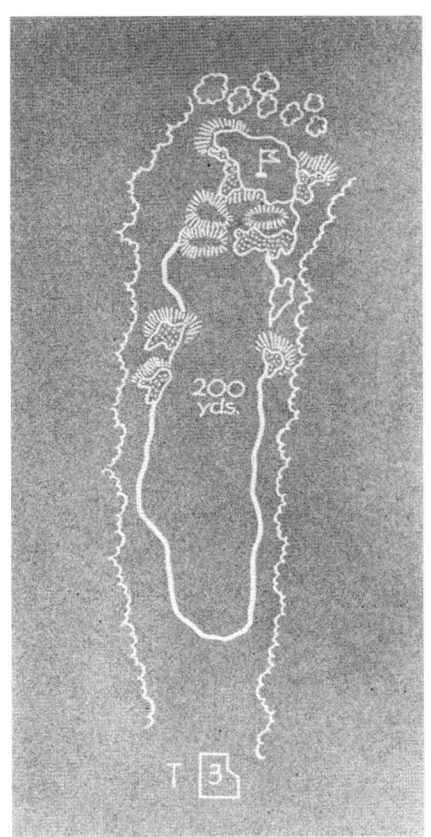 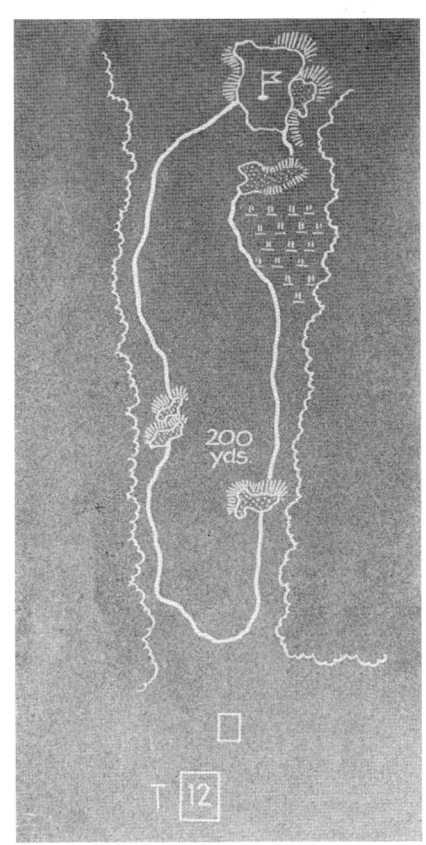

FIRST HOLE, 419 YARDS *THIRD HOLE, 334 YARDS* *TWELFTH HOLE, 409 YARDS*

turfed putting surfaces must come as a revelation. I had never seen Pinehurst before and I often had wondered why turfed greens had never been developed there. Really I am still wondering for these new greens are quite as fine as anyone could wish to play to or putt over. Of course, as is necessary in that section, they are of Bermuda base with Italian Rye, but they are undeniably fine, of lovely uniform color and true as steel.

Measured at its longest, the course covers 6,879 yards, but compared with northern fairways Pinehurst's two-shotters will probably play fifteen yards longer. So it will be apparent that it must favor the long hitters when extended to tournament lengths. But hard hitting in itself will not be enough, for every hole demands placement as well. Starting with the very first hole, 419 yards, the drive must be directed with extreme accuracy, which is as it should be of course, but Ross never permits one to forget this for an instant. The long tenth, 598 yards, a very fine hole indeed, must prove a thorn in the flesh to the shorter shot-makers.

I have always contended that no course is any greater than its one-shotters. Each par 3 here is a gem. They come at the sixth, 209 yards; the ninth, 143; the fifteenth, 204; and the seventeenth, 186. To stand on the teeing ground of any of these and look out to the green is inspirational. None has an apology to make. It seems to say: "I am a grand golf hole and I know it as you will, too, in just another moment."

Donald Ross at his best was never greater. The length of the holes from the back tees on the No. 2 Course are as follows:

Out	Par	In	Par
No. 1 - 419	4	No.10 - 598	5
No 2 - 434	4	No.11 - 433	4
No. 3 - 334	4	No.12 - 409	4
No. 4 - 476	5	No.13 - 377	4
No. 5 - 467	5	No.14 - 442	4
No. 6 - 209	3	No.15 - 204	4
No. 7 - 386	4	No.16 - 473	5
No. 8 - 466	4	No.17 - 186	3
No. 9 - <u>143</u>	<u>3</u>	No.18 - <u>423</u>	<u>4</u>
3,334	36	3,545	36

Total 6,879   Yards—Par 72

36 GLEANINGS FROM THE WAYSIDE

IT HAS been suggested that as golf course consultant of the P.G.A. I give our members throughout the country some idea of the problems encountered along the routes of the tour.

Probably it is known generally that this service is extended gratuitously to clubs where P.G.A. members are retained, and who request our assistance in helping them with their problems, suggesting methods for reducing maintenance costs, and improving courses without great expense simply by adhering definitely to a sensible program. In brief, we are only trying to be helpful.

Thus far my travels have taken me to courses in our various sections of Connecticut, Illinois, Wisconsin, Philadelphia, Pittsburgh, Washington, Virginia, Georgia, Florida, New Orleans, Albuquerque (New Mexico), Tucson (Arizona), Southern and Northern California, Portland (Oregon), the State of Washington and the newly organized Rocky Mountain Section (from whence I am now writing on my way to Denver, Colorado, after visiting our members at Ogden and Salt Lake City, Utah). And everywhere our efforts have been most warmly welcomed.

Now the conclusions I have formed are many and various. Conditions differ so widely in the wide sections of our country that no fixed rule may always be applied. These I will refer to in later articles, discussing definitely these sections as they are investigated. But there are situations which are quite general and common. It is my belief that too many American courses are retarded in proper development and improvement by unintelligent although doubtless well-intended criticism and advice from the locker-rooms. Without a doubt, there exist more amateur course architects and turf authorities among the members of some of our clubs than there are following these crafts professionally.

Types of closely cropped and glaringly artificial mounds; now generally referred to as "Chocolate Drops" in ridicule.

Of course, it is wise for green committees and club officials to lend an open ear to the comments of the rank and file of players, but it is not a wise thing to take them all too seriously nor attempt experimentally to please too many. For example I conferred with the professional and the president of his club as we faced a certain green, which presented a truly grotesque contour of surface. A gigantic, wart-like mound occupied not only the center of the green but flared so violently on all sides, that only about a third of the green's floor could possibly be used for cup-cutting. In addition it played havoc with many well pitched irons, and any shot to the hole was a pure gamble.

Now it is entirely contrary to the policy of the P.G.A.'s consultant to criticize harshly. Rather am I inclined to slip in a suggestion as inoffensively as possible. This I did at this stage and immediately the club's chief executive observed, "So you do not like that feature of our green?"

Then I told him that I did not like it at all and gave him my reasons. I was staggered by the reply, "Well, I see clearly the sense of your objections,

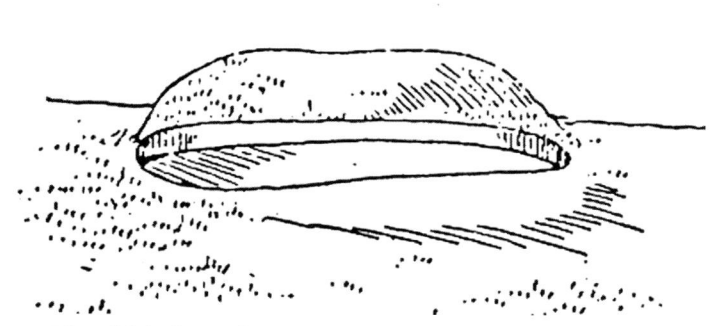
The old-fashioned type of the mathematically precise and obviously artifical, symmetrical bunker.

but we cannot possibly alter this green. You see it was designed by one of our oldest members, and we must not hurt Mr. Blank's feelings."

And similar situations are not at all uncommon. I have encountered numerous instances where the committee is on a thoroughly uncomfortable spot just because "locker-room" experts have put them there.

In another state I saw one of the most atrocious greens which I ever have encountered. It was just awful and, incidentally, had cost the club some ten thousand dollars to build after scooping away quite a lot of hillside. It was elementally wrong in every detail. Sufficient to remark that the hole called for a short pitch and the entire floor of the green was blind as a bat. That green had been designed by a member of the club and a very indifferent player at that. But he was a convincing talker and sold the idea to the green committee and only within the past three years. "Ten Grand," as they put it, had been burned up, and it was entirely unnecessary for me to say much about it in condemnation. They all knew it by this time. The designer plays his golf at another club these days. The tragedy of it is the fact that this course really needs money spent on it right now to keep the turf from going to pot, and they can't afford it.

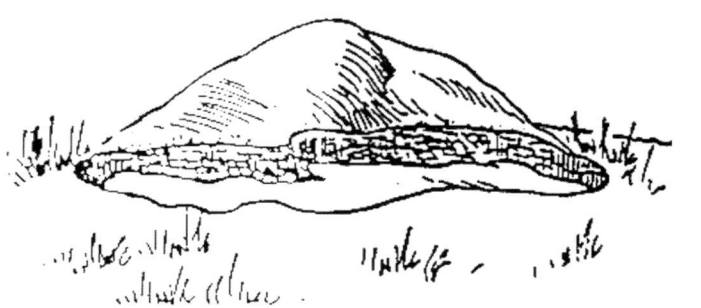

A modern idea of the building of a natural looking sand trap and mound. The lines are irregular, but care has been exercised in avoiding angles where a ball might find a well-nigh unplayable lie. Tufted but not rank grass adds to its simplicity.

Author's note: *In the year 1913 the discoverer and developer of Pine Valley, Mr. George A. Crump, accompanied by Mr. Howard W. Perrin, Mr. Richard Mott and Mr. A.W. Tillinghast, played golf there for the first time. To the founder was given the honor of driving the first ball and he selected a faithful old driver as the club in his bag most deserving of the historic first stroke. "Bolivar," as this particular club affectionately is named by Mr. Crump, is huge and powerful, and on this occasion it was at the business end of a long straight ball from Pine Valley's first teeing ground. Mr. Perrin, firm in his conviction that the new course will prove to be one of the most notable in America, asserted that in years to come these four pioneers would look back to the day with great satisfaction. As he expressed it, "We are making history and with this in mind we must fancy 'Bolivar' hanging in a prominent and honored place on the club-room walls." Mr. Tillinghast secured a first par – a 4 on the first hole played, and likewise the first "bird," – a 2 on the third. To the same player must be given the rather doubtful distinction of slapping first into the lake in front of the fifth teeing ground, which he did to his great disgust on this history-making day.*

37 From The Gulf To Puget Sound

A FINE SETTING FOR A FINE SHOT—1929 U.S. AMATEUR FINAL AT PEBBLE BEACH
Harrison R. Johnston playing his spectacular shot from the water's edge at the eighteenth in the final against O.F. Willing.

THE FIRST DAY of the year 1936 found me skirting the Gulf of Mexico. With the breaking of spring I was making my way to Bremerton from Seattle, Washington, on a Puget Sound ferry boat. Throughout the intervening three months the path of the P.G.A.'s course consultant had taken me from New Orleans, generally along the coast, to the far northwest of our country. I had investigated numerous courses, in response to requests from P.G.A. members, and it is likely that my reactions to them will be timely and, I hope, of sufficient value to assist the work of bettering our courses.

Let us regard the conditions as I observed them in the territory I have mentioned. Undoubtedly there has been a marked improvement in recent years. New holes reflect a better thought of design and construction work has been more pleasing, too. These efforts of local craftsmen are particularly pleasing to record and they augur well for the future.

Only a few years ago sanded greens were not uncommon in Texas and Oklahoma. Many natives contended that good turf greens could not be developed and maintained in those states. And let me pause to add that the cry of "It just can't be done here!" has hindered the proper development of courses to a lamentable extent in many sections. Indeed the "doubting Thomases" have been astonished when intelligent experiment has proved conclusively that it could be done despite tradition. The many excellent turfed greens in Texas and Oklahoma today are evidence of this. Some five years ago Seaside Bent was introduced in these parts and numerous successful results are in existence now. Francis Scheider at Oklahoma City has every reason to be proud of the greens of this strain at his course, and it is significant that he uses a very sharp and rather coarse sand in his top-dressings. This is available locally, which is most fortunate, and I regard it as a point well worth keeping in the minds of greenkeepers, particularly those who have to contend with a tight and heavy soil.

Bermuda grass is very satisfactory as fairway. In many instances I found it on the putting greens, alone during the summer months and as a base during the cold weather with additions, frequently with Italian Rye. This variety however is liable to put up quite a battle in the spring, reluctant to give way to the greening Bermuda. At Houston, Texas, I found that Willie Maguire had developed beautiful turf at the Country Club. But instead of using any Rye he depends on a combination of Red Top, Meadow Fescue and Blue Grass for his winter greens. He has found that these get along beautifully with the Bermuda and his greens prove the contention.

After calls in New Mexico and Arizona I made my way very thoroughly through California all the way from the most southern part, San Diego, to the last hopping-off town, Eureka in the north. This state has developed some fine courses, several truly great ones. But I believe that these would be even greater if greater premium followed a bit more accurate placement of tee-shots. However the courses generally are well kept and interesting, although somewhat hilly in spots. Putting turf is excellent as a rule, but the proper estimate of the line to the cup is extremely difficult to determine as time and time again the surrounding mountain-slopes play queer tricks with vision. Both seeded greens and those vegetatively developed from stolons are of good texture, for the most part, although inclined to be somewhat tight of soil. It must be remembered that throughout this entire section, with few exceptions, the courses have been constructed on Adobe, which naturally is heavy and close. Yet in only too many instances the greens were built without any real effort to remedy this condition.

Before true golf turf may be developed and maintained, it is absolutely necessary that the construction provides an open and friable topsoil structure, in which proper root growth may be encouraged without the handicap of shallow-rooted weed invasion. Greens must drain and roots must breathe. During the time of the inspections mentioned at the beginning of this paper, I am certain that the most common fault I encountered nearly everywhere battled this fundamental truth. Tight greens were seldom spiked and a good old-fashioned forking was a rarity.

"Do you use sand in your compost?" I frequently asked when a plug failed to reveal any.

"Oh, yes, we use a third part of sand."

But when I was shown what they used for sand, it turned out to be fine, silty stuff that only served to bind the soil closer and tighter than ever. There were exceptions of course, where sand with a "real kick in it" was used. But forking occasionally? That was too slow, and exacting—yet it would have spelled "Salvation."

While, as I have said, the courses generally are structurally and strategically improved over those of a few years back, yet there are enough of the Cheap-

HERE IS THE FAMOUS SHORT SEVENTH AT PEBBLE BEACH WITH THE WATERS OF THE BAY JUST BEHIND
A casual glance at the cluster of traps lurking around shows the woe that may be encountered by an errant shot.

John, amateurish sort, rather cluttered with sand pits that cost money to maintain for no other purpose than to discourage the very players at golf who need encouraging most. When speaking of these abominations in my reports to the P.G.A. for brevity's sake I simply call them D.H.'s (short for Duffers' Headaches). I am thoroughly delighted by the reactions of green committees everywhere to our doctrine of the elimination of these relics of golf's dark age. There will be more about them in subsequent papers.

I am thoroughly convinced that many of our country's courses are hurt tremendously by stretching holes out for no other purpose than to bolster up score-card distances and par figures. There seems to exist the feeling that the collection of par figures must determine the worth of a course. Let it be remembered that in golf we do not measure pleasure with a yardstick.

When I got into Oregon and Washington, where I had never been previously, I found about the "growingest" country my feet had ever trod. Up there grass really does grow. One course which I inspected has its fairway cut three times a week. I knew that Coos County, Oregon, was the native habitat of Agrostis maratima, the Seaside Bent, which has been found so satisfactory in many sections of America. To my utter amazement I found but little of it on the greens of Oregon or Washington courses. Greenkeepers of that section told me that after a year or two it turned very grainy and coarse and attributed this condition to the very moist atmosphere and long rains. Now I have formed no conclusion myself in this matter, for I realize so well that conditions vary so greatly in the various sections of this vast country of ours that no amount of theory and conjecture can ever stand up against intelligent observation and experiment in each particular locality. Fundamental principles will hold true anywhere but Nature has curious vagaries. No doubt those northwestern lads know what they are talking about. It is their country and their climate. And if they turn thumbs down on their own native Seaside Bent so far as permanent greens on their courses are concerned, I will trust to their judgment, but for most parts of the country I can only say that it has proved satisfactory, even in texture and color. It resists fungus attacks well and I like it.

When I was at Seattle, my old friend Chandler Egan died at a nearby town. I was greatly shocked, and the game in that section has suffered a great loss for Chandler had been

THE NINTH AT PEBBLE BEACH
Looking along the line of play.

THE SEVENTEENTH AT PEBBLE BEACH
On the edge of the Pacific Ocean.

instrumental in improving golf course conditions on the Pacific Coast to a marked degree. His reconstructed course at Pebble Beach, on the Monterey Peninsula, must be rated among the country's great ones. Leaving Washington, my path led to Utah and then through the Middle-West.

THE FINAL HOLE AT PEBBLE BEACH
Is nestled in a woodland nook.

THE BASTIONED EIGHTEENTH TEE
At Pebble Beach jutting out into the bay, with the green five hundred forty yards away and plenty of grief awaiting along the way.

THIS IS THE PROSPECT
Which faces the player on the eighteenth tee at Pebble Beach. The fairway swings around toward the left with the green in the far distance. Bargain for what you want in the tee shot.

There are many men who have in their hearts all the love of nature of Joyce Kilmer, but very few have expressed it quite so beautifully as he:

> I think that I shall never see
> A poem lovely as a tree.
> A tree whose hungry mouth is prest
> Against the earth's sweet flowing breast;
> A tree that looks at God all day,
> And lifts her leafy arms to pray;
> A tree that may in summer wear
> A nest of robins in her hair;
> Upon whose bosom snow has lain,
> Who intimately lives with rain.
> Poems are made by fools like me,
> But only God can make a tree.

A TREE LIKE THIS HAS AN APPEALING CHARM
To golfers who know it well from playing over a course day after day.

DR. JOHN MONTEITH, JR., TURF EXPERT
He and his assistant Kenneth Welton shoulder the technical research work for the USGA. His studies on the Arlington Turf Garden date back many years, encouraged by Drs. Piper and Oakley, who originally directed the work of the Green Section. The Green Section has made exhaustive study of turf problems so far as they apply to the golf courses of the United States. These experiments, researches and conclusions, carried through the years, have enabled the department to advise and instruct the nation's greenkeepers, to solve for them their individual problems and to bring the quality of the turf of our courses everywhere to a high degree of excellence. But to far greater purpose, the work has shown exactly how every detail of golf course development and maintenance may be achieved at the lowest possible cost.

THE ARLINGTON TURF GARDEN, WHERE THE GREEN SECTION OF THE USGA EXPERIMENTS SCIENTIFICALLY
Here also the greenhouses and laboratories, operated by the Golf Association in cooperation with the U.S. Department of Agriculture.

38   Things I Am Observing

AMONG the "wise saws and sayings" that have been handed down throughout the years is this one, "There is no disputing tastes, as the old lady remarked as she kissed the cow." Certainly this must be applied to golf and its courses. The merit of any course should be judged by the satisfaction it affords to those who play it. It may not measure up to the standards of the most discriminating players but, after all, it all is a matter of taste.

But is there any authority in the world, any mind so finely tuned to the true harmony of a set of golf holes and so profoundly analytical, that individual opinion must pass unchallenged? During forty years I have probably trod as many golf holes as any man in the world, many of my own creation and many, many more designed by others. I know a good hole when I see one and I think I know a bad one, too. Some of the latter type obviously are atrociously faulty, others just over the border of mediocrity, while some apparently weak ones may be open to debate. Any man has as much right to his own opinions as have I. So let it be understood that as I examine course after course throughout the United States in extending the service of the P.G.A. I do not assume the attitude on a pedestal that would suggest "When I ope' my mouth let no dog bark." There is no disputing tastes!

However, I do know what I like, and when I encounter something contrary to my ideas, but nevertheless liked by others, it seems a good idea to consider the pros and cons whenever possible. And it possibly will be interesting to refer to some of these discussed points from time to time.

THE SUNEAGLES CLUBHOUSE AND COURSE
The eighteenth green is across the lake.

The first concerns the fitting of guarding pits close up to the green itself. As is well known, and already indicated in past chapters on these pages, my personal preference is for this type. However I often find the sand pits fifteen or twenty feet off from the carpet of the green areas which are never cut by the greens mowers but allowed to grow shaggy and long. I have always regarded these frowsy patches with considerable abhorrence not only because of their unkempt, back-lot appearance but for the reason that considerable hand work with a sickle was necessary, when the matted grass became too long. I believe that in these days of modern equipment it is foolish to revert to the hand-labor, which was necessary twenty years and more gone by. Now for the argument defending them.

In most instances it is contended that when the pits are "Smack-up" against the greens, every explosion shot heaves not only a lot of course sand on to the turf of the green, but very often small stones, which interfere with putting and dull the knives of the mowers. Well, certainly here is an argument that has some sense back of it. Of course I may suggest that it would be well to place in the pits sand of the proper quality, free from the objectionable gravel stones.

THE GREEN ON THE SIXTH AT SUNEAGLES
This is a fine hole whereon the second must carry a brook which expands to a lake on the left. The shot must be well placed due to the slope of the ground.

THE FIFTEENTH GREEN AT SUNEAGLES
The greens in general are generous but quite undulating. The turf is uniformly excellent and, in general, the design is such that the good golfer must play well to score, while the less accomplished are not faced with the tee shots too severe.

That's a fine idea, too. But the retort rather disturbs my knowing smile of complacency, "That is the only sand procurable in these parts." So there we are, right back where we started.

However, I still think that the sand-pits should nestle close-up, with the sand showing up into the slopes, and if small stones are deposited on the greens (because it is impossible to secure sand which is free of them) frequent sweepings to remove them are warranted and preferable. But that is only my own idea. You have yours to be sure.

I still observe the tendency to preserve pulpit-like, raised teeing grounds. In some sections there prevails the idea that any teeing area, down to the grade of its surroundings, is not a proper teeing ground at all. New ones are still being built to conform with this thought. It must be admitted that at times a raised teeing ground is necessary to provide visibility, and terraced side slopes are unavoidable when "cut and fill" must be resorted to when building from a side-hill. But I see these small platforms, which limit the areas of wear and tear to spots, soon denuded of turf and offer absolutely no opportunity to shift the tee-markers to suit wind conditions. In the nineties, when our first American golf courses were built, it was the common procedure to construct a "Tee" by planting some two-by-fours at the sides of a small rectangle and filling in the center with clay. This provided just about enough room for the player and his ball. It took some years to enlarge the teeing grounds and gradually get them to turf. As time rolled on, the grounds assumed greater proportions and they were graded and blended

A SPLENDID HOLE IN LOVELY SUROUNDINGS
The short seventeenth at the Suneagles. The green is surrounded on every side by a stream, expanded into a pool in front. Fine trees form a background most pleasing to the eye and add a further hazard for the errant pitch.

naturally to meet their surroundings. These did not dry out as quickly as the platforms and besides they were more easily cut. Consequently the larger, natural-looking teeing areas are to be found on most of our first class courses today, but I still observe the "relics of the dark ages" on too many links.

Up here in the New England Section, which I am touring at present and extending the P.G.A. course service, I have been observing the development of a comparatively new strain of Velvet Bent. It was discovered by the Green Section at Washington, where the activities of the very capable Dr. Monteith are doing so much for our courses. It is known as Government Bent No. 14276. I like it tremendously, for it is uniform in color and texture and such greens as have come to complete maturity here are excellent. I recommend it to your attention and experiment. It is reported to me, too, that in this district it has manifested great hardiness and has resisted the diseases of turf admirably. Let me take opportunity here to remark that the New England greenkeepers have been most sympathetic with the work of the P.G.A. in this section and they have been exceedingly gracious and helpful to me. Indeed the entire reaction to our Association's work here has been splendid.

AT WORK ON THE SEVENTH AT SUNEAGLES
Seymour Dunn plays the pipes for the flock of green cutters.

AN OLD INDIAN SPRING
The spring is right outside the Suneagles Clubhouse, and has been preserved and enclosed in a grotto. The Indians ascribed healing powers to these waters to which from time immemorial a well-beaten path has always wended its way—the Colonists following the Aboriginals as users.

Author's note: *In every possible manner I have endeavored to impress green committees everywhere with the vital importance of the greenkeeper. Yet I have been shocked to learn of the scant remuneration they receive, in some instances but little more than men under them are paid for manual labor. Brains are surely worth more than this. Inside the skulls of the capable modern greenkeepers there must be more than good old-fashioned "Horse–sense," which is essential to be sure. But with the sources of information today, scientific research has crammed craniums with knowledge which has developed greenkeeping far above the old hit–or–miss methods of experiment to definite ways of certainty. I believe that the club officials are gradually recognizing this. The true greenkeeper is not an ordinary laboring man but a highly specialized thinker, — and brains have always been worth something. They always will be.*

39   Intimate Survey Of Oakland Hills

THE SEVENTEENTH HOLE ON THE OAKLAND HILLS COUNTRY CLUB COURSE
Inserts left to right: Mike Brady, MacDonald Smith, Jock Hutchison, Gene Sarazen, Walter Hagen,
Jim Barnes, Joe Kirkwood, and Bobby Jones in center.

ON MY TOUR as course consultant of the P.G.A. I was requested by P.G.A. member, Al Watrous, to visit the course of the Oakland Hills Country Club, at Birmingham, Michigan, for an exchange of ideas regarding the preparation of that course for the National Open Championship of 1937. With Al and myself were Chris Brinke and greenkeeper Bert Shave, who has been at this club for sixteen years. It is rather significant that this course, which was the scene of the National Open in 1924 should again be selected for the same event. Certainly it is a tribute to its worth—and make no mistake, here is a truly great course.

It may seem premature to review this course so far ahead of the event but it seems to me to be well to do it while the impressions are fresh in mind. It is likely that the review may be of interest to professionals and others generally but, to a far greater extent, to those who will likely compete in the classic. What in particular will be required of these? In brief, what is the course like? It is a long while to look back over twelve years since the last Open there, when, as I recall off-hand, Cyril Walker won the title by knocking his second shot across the lake, stiff against the sixteenth cup, or close by. (Remember I am trusting to memory.)

I will not attempt a detailed description of each hole, but getting right down to brass tacks let me say that aside from the shifting of five teeing grounds, extending the entire length to a trifle over seven thousand yards, there will be no changes in the course and no more sand traps than the usual collection will be added to the day the USGA officials will call for "Silence, please," as the first contender steps on the first teeing-ground.

While the length indicates that long and sturdy

hitting will be very necessary there is something more to it than this, which I will speak of shortly. It must be remembered that seven thousand yards of fairway not only calls for stout hitting, but KEEPING IT UP for three strenuous days of tournament pressure. That means Stamina. If I might visualize the next Open Champion of the United States I would picture a very sturdy player, in fine physical condition—but with the putting touch of rare delicacy and with a sure feel of the greens.

Now about those greens. They are rather on the large size but for the most part they are very undulating, and if I may venture to say so—likely to be somewhat tricky entirely because of the many and varied undulations. I am very sure that the excellent turf will not be open to criticism for both on fairway and putting green it is excellent and true. I rather incline to the opinion that there will be fewer "birds" registered at Oakland Hills than during any Open for a long time now. Take for example the 210-yard ninth —I would call it a "sucker shot" for any one to bang an iron up to the cup on this green. From beyond the flag the putt is very trying. It is likely that most of the play here will be "percentage shots" for the front of the green, with visions of a sure 3.

To those who are at all familiar with the course, it will be interesting probably to note the extended tees. These are at the second (lengthened to 530 yards—and a mighty fine hole); the fourth (where, in my opinion, the lengthened tee-shot has not helped the hole but rather detracted from it); the eighth (extended to a magnificent testing hole of 510 yards); and the eighteenth (now 515 yards). The other new teeing ground is at the fourteenth, the one weak hole on the course, shortened somewhat, because of the lengthening of the eighth. But this change has not mattered much, for the hole has always been a weak sister. The getaway at Oakland Hills is magnificent with two grand, stretching holes. It would be hard to imagine two finer holes than the 450-yard tenth, followed immediately by the magnificent 400-yard eleventh. Then we must pause to remark about the fine fifteenth. Here again a slight change of teeing ground makes the drive find the fairway differently than of old. No longer may the drive cut the trees on the left but must take to the fairway more on the right and, leaving more of an iron to reach the green, dog-legging to the left. As I see them these are distinct stand-outs in a great collection of holes. And there is just one small matter which must not be forgotten. Wind. It always blows and blows plenty at Oakland Hills. Old Boreas must always be reckoned with there, and he is a great factor.

The distances, official and latest, as they will be carded at this Open, are as follows. All measured to center of greens from the back third of each teeing ground.

Out		Par	In		Par
No. 1-	438	4	No.10 -	450	4
No. 2 -	530	5	No.11 -	400	4
No. 3 -	190	3	No.12 -	550	5
No. 4 -	445	4	No.13 -	138	3
No. 5 -	430	4	No.14 -	453	5
No. 6 -	368	4	No.15 -	440	4
No. 7 -	383	4	No.16 -	360	4
No. 8 -	510	5	No.17 -	193	3
No. 9 -	210	3	No.18 -	515	5
	3,504	36		3,499	36

Total 7,003 Yards—Par 72

In closing, let me again say that Oakland Hills is entirely worthy of this great professional event and there is sure to be a great tournament over a great course. And there is one characteristic of most of the holes, which goes to make them great—the wonderfully fine breaks of the fairway in front of the greens.

In this rather sketchy review of the course for the 1937 U.S. Open, it may be well to add that I think I have never seen a better one for spectators. It will be not at all difficult to handle big galleries here, and there are several locations from which much of the play may be observed without tramping with the herd.

Author's note: As indicated in these pages, when I analyzed the Oakland Hills course, the stalwart hitters were well up to the front in the Open Championship. I would have liked to have seen a bit of the play there but was entirely too busy only a little more than a hundred miles away. If the usual wind was in evidence the scoring was remarkable indeed. Ralph Guldahl's great performance was that of a great golfer, and I hasten to extend my hearty congratulations.

ONE OF THE GREATEST TESTS OF GOLF IN AMERICA: THE OAKLAND HILLS COUNTRY CLUB, AT DETROIT
The venue of the 1937 U.S. Open Championship. Above are some of its wonderful fairways and greens. The upper left picture shows the first fairway from the tee; the upper right the testing one-shot seventeenth; the lower left the fifth and the trap which must be carried from the tee; the lower right the longest hole on the course, the twelfth. In the center is the magnificent clubhouse facing the course and showing the eighteenth (left) and ninth (right) greens.

40   WHEN TRAPS ARE FRIENDLY

DURING the past sixteen months beginning in 1935, since I have been traveling to the remote parts of the country inspecting courses as consultant of the P.G.A., it is a matter of record that I have condemned nearly eight thousand sand traps. I have contended that these have been maintained at considerable cost to nearly four hundred clubs, that they unnecessarily harass the great majority of those who take to the game for pleasure without in the least causing that comparatively small number of par shooters to give them a thought, and usually injecting a thoroughly discordant note and smudging an otherwise beautiful picture of rural landscape.

My arguments against over-trapped courses have already had the ears of many green committees along my route. It is likely that they are sufficiently well known to need no repetition in this article and indeed I have no intention of going back over that trail. Indeed I am now defending some traps, which, although utterly worthless as Hazards, nevertheless serve a good purpose. Let me call these the friendly traps.

First let your attention be called to my sketch. It represents a green, surrounded by rapidly falling grades sloping to remote lies, which obviously would be quite desperate. The drawing shows but the long outside slope on the left of the green. Let it be assumed that the right side is equally severe and that any ball overrunning the green would maliciously go falling down a miniature ravine or perhaps a really poisonous one, and that similar traps are introduced into these other slopes, too. Such situations frequently are common when courses have been built over hilly country, very broken terrain and on wooded tracts. Such traps as my sketch shows are what I choose to call the friendly ones for they do prevent wayward balls from going into trouble, which would be far

"FRIENDLY" SAND TRAPS IN A LONG STEEP SLOPE

133

worse. The wretched player who is trapped may regard the trap as an enemy but, in this case, might he not regard one as a friendly enemy?

The idea of long slopes on the outsides of greens is all right; so right in fact that modern greens are to be constructed in precisely this manner. It is generally conceded that if shots, off-line, which would be taken in by closely placed side pits, were thrown wider away after taking the long roll of a grassed slope, the recovery from a grassed depression would prove more vexing than from sand in these days of ultra-efficient sand irons. But where the finishes of these long slopes are desperately unfair, certainly sand traps or grassed hollows are most desirable.

Traps immediately back of greens are generally taboo nowadays, but if they insure the slightly overplayed ball from worse disaster, we surely cannot condemn them.

So we may contemplate numerous situations in which the trap, ordinarily worthless strategically at a certain place, may be altogether desirable. Sometimes I find them protecting an adjoining teeing-ground, or at least "sort of shooing" play away from it. On other occasions these superfluous hazards help to reduce the element of danger at congested areas, something like traffic police, let us say. Why not regard such as these as friendly traps and be done with it?

GENE SARAZEN PITCHING TO THE EIGHTEENTH GREEN AT FRESH MEADOWS C.C. IN THE 1932 U.S. OPEN
The eventual champion dropped his putt to finish out with a record 66.

Author's Note: *It has been years since I ranked the leading golfers of the United States. Then it was my annual work in contributing to a newspaper column. In arriving at my conclusions, three influences guided me. First, an estimate of the shot-making ability based on my personal observation of the players. Second, the consideration of temperament, that mental quality, developed by experience and an inside knowledge of the game that creates the will and courage to win. Third, the past year's performance of the players in the classic events. But in this last instance, I was influenced to a less extent than by the first two, for after long experience in golf, I realized to what great degree the "breaks" of the game, (or "racing luck") determine these issues. Still the year's successes were recalled in certain placements. It may be interesting here to hark back to 1916 and refer to the syndicated column of that period. In giving my reasons for the ratings of that year, this comment appeared in defense of my selection for the last place. "Little Bobby Jones, of Atlanta, is a really fine player and shows every indication of becoming a tremendously great one, once he is master of himself, which must come with maturity. On his showing in the Georgia Championship and at Merion, I am including him in my ratings, in last place, to be sure, but even in doing so I may be criticized, for I am giving this lad preferences over several others who know more of the game than he."*

41

BACK-STAGE

THE AUDIENCE in the theatre, looking over the footlights, view the play as do most of the gallery following the experts of golf. However, back-stage, there are a few eyes critically regarding the play from an entirely different angle. For many years I have preferred to observe golf shots from back-stage, as it were. Seeing a man whack a golf ball is of little interest to me, and frequently it is a performance that had better be missed. That which concerns me most is where the ball lands and exactly what it does after. In most instances the golf holes I plan are conceived in looking backward from a green's site or from a favorable fairway contour to locate properly the teeing ground. So it has become a habit with me to watch shots coming on rather than going away, and my favorite position is directly back of a green. From this post, I have made some very interesting observations.

For example, while in Philadelphia I looked over the Whitemarsh Valley course, where the 1932 Amateur Championship of that district was in progress. After a while I found a comfortable resting place at the top of a high terrace back of the sixteenth green, which was probably six feet below the end of a one-shotter of good iron length. It was just possible to see the players as they teed off in the valley, directly up a stiff grade all the way to the green. Naturally the shots came up at high trajectory, some landing nicely but very frequently short on the hillside, leaving an entirely blind approach, which usually resulted in a four and often a five. However, out of probably fifty shots there were two which came up greatly overplayed and each rolled partly up the rather steep bank, which was not sufficiently long in grass to hold them there, and back on the green, having gained sufficient momentum to carry them close enough to the pin to warrant visions of a bird two, which in one instance was made. Now all of the contestants knew the hole and they should have remembered that terraced slope directly across the back of the green, a sure safeguard against straight overplay, and yet player after player placed his shot short of the pin and very frequently short of the green itself in a truly awkward spot. No one could have gone wrong on that particular day by slogging one past the flag. Possibly other days find the grass on that slope longer, but in any event it would be far better to be over than short. This is but one of the many things that the man back of the green sees.

But I must digress to pay tribute to the young players coming on in the Philadelphia district where there are certainly a number of very good ones playing the low seventies. Thirty years previously, I participated in this same championship but this field

THE VIEW BEHIND THE EIGHTEENTH
Baltusrol Upper—1936 U.S. Open.

ABOVE THE SECOND GREEN—1936 U.S. OPEN

was four or five strokes faster. So golf has progressed with better courses generally, longer flying balls, better and more effective clubs and more young players.

The year before, another observation from back-green took place. I took up my post directly behind the seventeenth green at Crestmont. N.J., where the Metropolitan Open was being played. This, too, was a one-shotter of usual long iron length. The green is closely guarded and the teeing ground is on a somewhat higher level. It is a good hole, very properly closed in well on the front, and one which is far kinder if over than short. On the day in particular there was a quartering wind from the right against the shot. It is astonishing, but there were twenty professional contestants in succession who missed that green completely before one found it. All were on one side or the other, not one straight and over. This puzzled me and I walked up to the teeing ground to find an explanation. The shot from the teeing ground immediately suggested a spoon up into the

A GOOD VIEW ON THE THIRTEENTH—1936 U.S. OPEN

wind which would have held it faithfully. But not a spoon* came out of the bags. The boys seemed reluctant to take to the short wood, which certainly would have got them home with but little effort. No, they were taking out their No. 3 and sometimes the 4 irons and forcing them, and actually playing for a slight hook, which sometimes worked too much, carrying over to the rough beyond the pits on the left, or not at all, which pushed them over to a similar condition on the right. A high one working into the wind and drifting in to the green was an absolute certainty it would seem, but no one apparently cared to confess a fancied weakness by taking out his spoon. That fine stroke, carrying the ball high from left to right, seems to be going out of fashion, particularly with the steel shafts. But you see Mac Smith playing it

PAUL RUNYAN PUTTING AS "WEE BOBBY" CRUICKSHANK OBSERVES
1936 U.S. Open.

Editor's Note: A spoon is equivalent to a 4 or 5 wood.

constantly and some of the other good ones occasionally. I believe, too, that Smith still uses hickory shafts entirely, and I still adhere to the conviction that the truly great shot makers will do better with them than with the steel shafts in the irons, although the rank and file generally knock them farther. Steel has been a great help to the light hitters.

BACKSTAGE AT BALTUSROL

The "Ghost Champion" at Baltusrol in 1936 was Harry Cooper, the British-born but Texas bred pro who had been dubbed "Lighthorse" because of the speed of his play. When Cooper finished with a total of 284, breaking the U.S. Open record by two strokes, he was hailed by the press as the new Open Champion. His U.S. Open record and apparent victory were shortlived—only twenty minutes, as Tony Manero was still on the course and was mounting a charge.

Starting four strokes behind Cooper and playing with Gene Sarazen, Manero had gone out in 33. When word came over the grapevine that he had birdied the twelfth, the gallery poured back out to the course—just in time to see Manero roll in another birdie putt at the thirteenth and go to five under par for the day.

Horton Smith and Johnny Goodman on the first green.

Manero finished with a 67 and a four round total of 282, two strokes better than Cooper, setting a new U.S. Open record.

During the last hour of play, Sarazen coaxed, calmed and encouraged Manero. Some reporters thought that Sarazen had gone too far in helping Manero, that he had given not just encouragement but advice, and they brought forward a formal complaint to the USGA. After an hour-long closed door meeting, the announcemnet came—Manero's victory would stand.

42 THE UGLY DUCKLING OF THE COURSE

ONE OF THE GREAT problems presented by course reconstruction is the hole measuring from 300 to 325 yards. It is a legacy from the old days of the hard ball, the Gutta Percha, and then, when Bogie was tops and Par was unheard of, this type of hole frequently found its way to innumerable courses, and indeed it was a fairish sort of two-shotter. Then in 1901 the "Bounding Billie," or the first Haskell rubber-cored ball, put in an appearance, and hand in hand with it came greater flights and gradually increasing distances with the passing years, as annually there were improved methods of manufacture producing even farther flying balls.

Undoubtedly this feature has carried golf on to the tremendous popularity which it enjoys today, but certainly for a time it played havoc with courses everywhere. It was not difficult to design new courses to meet the necessities of a longer game, but to transform certain holes on existing courses, that they might measure up to this new condition, often was perplexing.

Immediately the ugly duckling of the old brood of holes strutted forth—the length mentioned in the opening paragraph. In the very early days of the rubber-core few indeed, even under the most favoring conditions ever drove to the very apron of the green of such a hole, but they did get close enough to kick the ball up to the pin with almost anything for a second shot. And, as a matter of fact, the hole got to be known as a "Leveler" for any ordinarily good or even middle-class player would be nicely home with two shots of any description—almost. He could even top his drive badly and with a long iron be right on the green, or level with the opponent who had really hit one from the tee. So it came to pass that the rebuilders of holes devised a plan to check this. They greatly reduced the size of the green, surrounded it with close pits, particularly a most forbidding one directly across the front of the green, and then told the players to drive far enough to be able to hold such a green with a short pitch shot which had plenty of bite. This helped

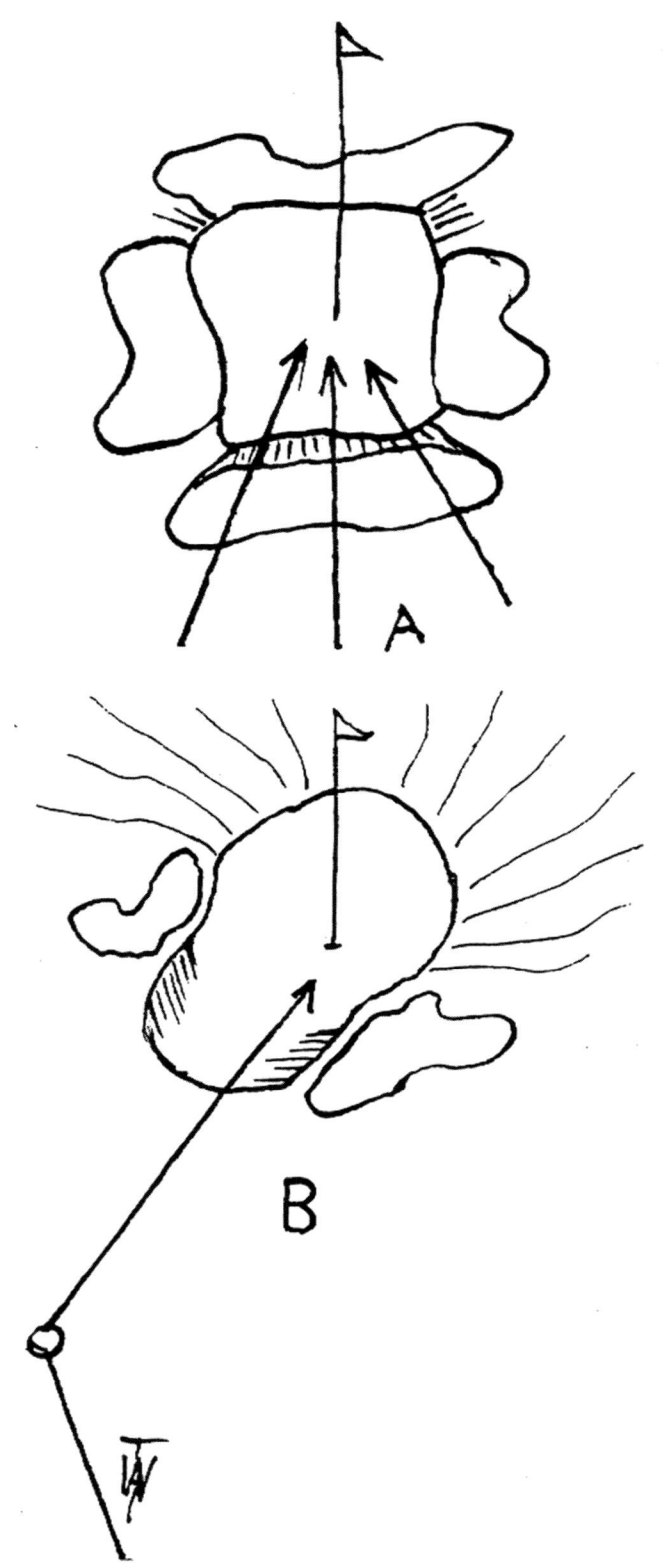

the situation until finally, with balls and clubs too providing greater lengths, some of the long boys began to reach that big front pit from the tee. These were told to use more judgment and, if they were afraid of getting the pit with a driver, to pipe down to a spoon, which was admirable advice.

But all the while the real sufferer was my old friend, the man of the great 90%, who cannot break 90—and his wife and her friends along with her. These good people could not get far enough to carry that front pit at all and when they did they were forced to use such a long club that the ball would not hold the small green but go scooting over to the maw of the sand pit in the back—all of which the designers of the hole hailed with unholy glee, declaring that its excellent qualities were thus proved. But were they right?

In a measure they were, but to a far greater degree they were, and still are as I see it, very wrong, for they were depriving the great majority of the humbler players of golf of the pleasure in the game, which rightfully should be theirs—because they pay for it. But enough of playing more on that string! Those who read this are well aware of my sentiments.

Now let us regard the ugly duckling, as illustrated by Sketch A. Is it not possible to take this same length and without robbing it in the least of its testing qualities take from it the features which make it hideous to so many? I submit Sketch B as an answer. And what is more—it works by ample test and so must not be regarded as mere conjecture.

It will be noticed that Sketch B presents its long axis to the left of the fairway, which makes it necessary to place the drive over on that side, for the Master Trap on the right-front spells trouble for the second shot coming in from the right and incidentally to the narrows of the green toward another trap, which is only a rear hazard if the unfortunate placement of the drive makes it so. As a matter of fact this trap on the left is not actually necessary, for the Master Trap is the true guardian of the gate. It must be borne in mind, too, that the entire character of the hole might be changed by constructing the green with its opening to the right and reversing the whole scheme. The terrain and adjoining holes would influence the selection of this.

Now what is presented to the thought of the player on the teeing ground? Here he must place his drive over on the left half of the fairway to meet with a proper reception for his second, and as far as possible to reduce the length of his pitch-and-run or chipped approach. If one Jimmy Thompson looks out and really wants to go for the green, he may BUT, that mighty blow must be played with greater-than-usual accuracy, which is precisely what I propose to make all very long hitters do. And now let us regard Mr. Humbleman. He has the opportunity of placing his second shot safely to the open side of the green, without the distressing fear of the old Obligatory route over the "Cross Pit," and feels that he may anticipate a careful 5, which after all is the hope of the 90 shooter. And if he is very fortunate with his approach he may get a par 4. We give him the same opportunity of knocking over a par as is given the par man to snare his "bird."

It will be noted that Sketch B requires but two pits at the most, instead of four as shown by A. Usually the outside slopes of the old type greens are very sharp, making necessary constant hand cutting. The outside slopes of B are drawn out and blended to the ratio of one to six. Power machines will cut all slopes such as these. And such maintenance methods save considerable from the budget—which is most desirable, is it not so Brethren?

"!Yea Verily!"

A GREAT SHORT PAR 4
In the Metropolitan District, number twelve on the Upper course of Baltusrol.

44 — Old Ananias Par

THE COMPARISON of Par figures can in no way be regarded as a true representation of the respective merits of golf holes or courses. Yet it is constantly used. For example, let me give the cards of two layouts that you may digest this observation.

Course A

Hole	Yards	Par	Hole	Yards	Par
1	451	5	10	330	4
2	320	4	11	325	4
3	140	3	12	470	5
4	285	4	13	310	4
5	340	4	10	295	4
6	360	4	11	125	3
7	455	5	12	310	4
8	170	3	13	350	4
9	375	4	13	460	5
	2,896	36		2,975	37

5,871 Yards—Par 73

Course B

Hole	Yards	Par	Hole	Yards	Par
1	445	4	10	375	4
2	420	4	11	440	4
3	390	4	12	365	4
4	195	3	13	145	3
5	415	4	10	560	5
6	435	4	11	425	4
7	405	4	12	395	4
8	160	3	13	180	3
9	385	4	13	430	4
	3,250	34		3,315	35

6,565 Yards—Par 69

Here we find one course measuring more than 650 yards more than another yet presenting a par of four strokes less. It may actually play several strokes harder as a matter of fact. Thus, I think, will be demonstrated the fallacy of comparisons according to Par.

Now exactly what governs the present day calculation of Par? We have certain arbitrary yardages fixing the figures. These originated many years ago, a short time after the introduction of the rubber-cored ball, which made its first tournament appearance in 1901 at the National Amateur Championship at Atlantic City, New Jersey. For years score cards carried Bogie figures instead of the modern Par. Colonel Bogie was the mythical golfer who always played immaculate golf with the hard ball. After the longer flying ball had demonstrated that the Colonel was distinctly a back number and certainly a light hitter, the old fellow was buried with scant ceremony and the young and vigorous longer-smiting Par took his place, although, strange as it may seem, Bogie figures still are carried on a few score cards in certain parts.

The present standards of Par were fixed by Leighton Calkins, when he established his handicapping system, and for years it has remained undisturbed. Recently, however, cards have appeared on certain of the more important courses carrying Par 4 figures as high as 475 yards, which is more in keeping with present day standards. With the tremendous improvement of golf clubs and balls this was bound to happen sooner or later. Par players came to establish the new reckonings of the long Par 4s as they played together. "Paying-off" for Bird 4s on 460-yard holes did not seem to have much sense to it. A Bird usually represents an unusually skillful betterment of Par. The Eagle (2 better than Par, as you know of course) may be said to result from either a miracle or a "Screwy Par."

In my visitations to courses all over the country I constantly am reminded by the committeemen that "This is a Par 5 hole," when as a matter of fact only the long established yardage makes it so, for a good player probably would be knocking his second shot home with a Four Iron. Many of the leading players are getting home with long seconds on holes of 500 yards and some of the very long hitters regularly exceed this length. The so-called Par 5 hole of from 450 to 490 yards has been most perplexing to committees in general. They have not been entirely clear in their ideas of the strategy of its design and construction. As a matter of fact we cannot really trap a green for a real three-shot hole (that is three shots to get home) under 525 yards with normal fairway conditions. The most satisfactory bunkering scheme for the long two-shotter is an open green, requiring a very accurate second after a well placed drive to make it necessary for the far-reaching players to gamble a bit—and a moderately sized green trapped with the Master Pit (already described in previous articles) will make the hole interesting to the average golfer, who needs three to get home, and also to the poorer one, who may take four.

In estimating the true merits of any course do not depend on Par as a basis. He may prove very misleading, and is most likely to be just that.

Author's note: At any Open tournament you can stand in the locker-room and see the maulers of the par-wrecking crew come stomping in, sorer than Aunt Sally's bunion because the round has taken a stroke or two over Par figures. What are Pars anyway? Just scan the scores of the professional tournament circuits and you will find that the trouper who gets around seventy-two, after deducting his expenses, doesn't take home enough kale to buy seed for the canary. No, no, little Rollo. If they are not able to batter and better Par they can save money by staying right at home and playing Jackstraws with the family. These lads, who are averaging frequently in the high sixties to win a tournament, when they really get hot will murder any course when it happens to be their day, naturally butchering the pushovers with more brutality. How many dubs would give a right arm for one blissful day when by some miracle he might score within a dozen strokes of the most despised card of these great ones? The value of Par depends entirely on the estimate of Big Shot or Punk.

LAKE HAZARD IS THE CENTER POINT OF THE LAKEWOOD C.C. COURSE

45 THE GIMME GUYS

IT MUST be admitted that the title is not dignified. But it is expressive and if it sinks in by reason of this, may it be held as sufficient excuse. There can be no claim for originality in it. Through the slang of this big country of ours, the "Gimmes" long ago were recognized as those people who boisterously demanded something for themselves, "Give me this or give me that."

Now at the start it must be recalled that, as a builder of golf courses and particularly as course consultant of the P.G.A. for the better part of two years, I have been taking up cudgels for the underdogs of golf—that great majority who rightfully have contended that they be given the consideration that should be accorded those who regard the game as a pleasure and not a penance for sin. We will not return to that topic now for previous articles have rather covered the ground. These humble players have supplicated that they be given opportunity to play shots as best they can without undue humiliation and punishment. We have shown that it is quite possible to design courses which will provide this without, in any sense, robbing the layouts of value as tests for par-shooters and lowering them to the class of "Pushovers" or duffers' Paradises. But now we must give ear to another plaint of the "duffer," consider it well and answer, "Listen lads, after all you must play a bit of golf."

In every locker room of every club in the country are to be found the "Gimme Guys." You hear them, and as a matter of fact, you may be one of them yourself. If this be true let the shoe pinch your tender feet. I refer to the hosts who demand that greens hold "My shots." They infer that any shot of theirs which strikes any green should find a safe resting place there. It never seems to occur to them that at least a small amount of skill should be displayed in knocking a ball to a green, something to make a ball slow up when it hits the carpet, something that their professional coach may show them. No, they insist that the green must be wrong if it does not hold "My shot." These are the most pernicious of the Gimme Guys. They are a greater pain in the neck to green committees than all other pests including grubs and fungus. What has been the result of the demands of these Gimmes? As a general thing the putting greens of these United States of ours are kept saturated with water that does in a measure hold shots, but which is extremely detrimental to the development and maintenance of turf.

The greenkeeper realizes this and tells the chairman of his committee about it. However, we all too frequently find that that chairman is a professional or business man who has been placed in charge of the

---

THE MALEFACTOR

Three gibbets there were on my road of Dream
And from each a grim corpse did sway,
And there hung a sign on which I read,
"Four golfers die here today."

And I looked about for I saw but three
When an old black Carrion crow
Croaked out, "You wonder where's Number four,
Is that what you want to know?"

"Well they hung One for divot neglect,
Number Two for padding his score,
Number Three for bragging about his game,
But hanging's too good for Four."

"For he was one who 'Played on Hard Luck,'
Always whined when he lost a hole,
Who was never beaten by better golf,
A louse-hearted puny fool."

So Careless, Braggart and Cheat were hung,
But they set the other knave free,
To live alone as a leper shunned,
A pitiful thing to see.

conditioning of his course because he happens to be a fine executive in directing the operation of a shoe factory, may we say without casting any reflections at any particular man that we might have in mind. He is a good fellow, and following the line of least resistance, he wants to keep the boys satisfied. I might tell him that doing this to the extent of 100% is something that is beyond the reach of mortal man. The Gimmes cannot be satisfied—but golf courses may be hurt and hurt seriously just because it is attempted. The evils wrought by the locker room Gimmes are more than casually apparent. I see them all over the country. That is why I am devoting this space, necessarily briefly, but I do hope to some measure of success to this condition.

During these months of the spring of 1937, I have worked up through Kentucky, into Eastern Missouri and Iowa. To my utter amazement I find that many courses permit "Winter Rules" to prevail throughout the entire year. Here is but another example of the persistence of the Gimme Guys. It all started by allowing of teeing all balls through the fairway until, let us say April 1, until the frost is well out of the ground. The Gimme Guys were very partial to this convenient way of slapping balls around. After a while the time was extended to April 15, and then to May 1, and so on. Here again we observe the hitting of a golf ball being simplified. (But again we must remonstrate. If the Gimmes are thus encouraged too long, the game will be simplified until it is positively foolish.)

The comment of one green committee chairman in Iowa is worth a thought. He said to me, "Of course I realize that this is not consistent with the traditions of the game, but it does spare our fairway turf."

He was rather of a different frame of mind when I replied something like this, "Whenever a ball is teed through the fairway it is reasonable to suspect that the best available lie is selected, and that lie is on a convenient bit of good turf. That turf is rather sure to be removed immediately. Does it occur to you that the eventual covering of your fairway depends upon the getting together and knitting of those very segregated patches which are ruthlessly destroyed every time one is selected as a good lie? Such a practice is not saving turf but deliberately destroying its very foundation."

A VIEW OF PHILADELPHIA CRICKET CLUB FROM MR. DALLIN'S AIRPLANE

This practice of perpetual "Winter Rules" is alarming as I have observed it throughout a great section. Certainly it is a thoughtless bending of the knee before the demands of the Gimme Guys. One club finds that another is allowing it. Then they all get aboard the train and in company speed to a destination, which is ridiculous and to a far greater degree certainly not golf. I surely hold fast to the doctrine that I have been preaching in every part of the country, to make the game more pleasurable to more people, but as I encounter the inclination to strip it naked of skill for the gratification of the Gimme Guys, too utterly disinclined to attempt an understanding of its fineness, I raise a voice in protest and only wish I could make it louder than is possible in this brief remonstrance.

46   The Long One-Shotter

EXPERTS CALL THIS THE FINEST ONE-STROKE HOLE ON THE COAST
It is the seventh at the San Francisco Golf and Country Club. The two club houses and the two courses of the Olympic Club can be seen in the distance. The players in the foursome shown are Roger D. Lapham of the USGA, George W. Nickel, Vincent Whitney and Gene Tunney.

A NUMBER of years back I was discussing the proper lengths of one-shot or par 3 holes with my old friend, Harry Vardon, and I well recall that he expressed the opinion that 185 yards provided a fine length and, furthermore, he thought that it was a mistake to stretch the length much more than this. Other great players have expressed to me similar views. I agree in the main although I think we would not depart far from the thought if we added ten yards to the length in view of the fact that longer flying balls and more powerful clubs have lengthened shots since the days when Harry was at his peak. May I go on record, therefore, in stating that I have come to the conclusion that 195 yards under normal conditions should be the extreme length of the one-shotter.

Frequently, on nearly every course as a matter of fact, we find the longer shot called for with yardages of 240 yards and even a bit more. Not long ago I was called to examine a municipal course and altogether it was a good one, well above the average. Before starting out over the layout the professional said to me, "We have five par 3 holes."

"True enough," I replied as I scanned the card, "But considering the limitations of the players over a public course such as this, it seems to me that you really have but two one-shotters, for the carded

146

distances reveal that three of these holes measure between 210 and 240 yards."

Now anything over two hundred yards is beyond the range of the great majority of the players over any course, who wang away with their long woods, repeating precisely the same tee-shot that they play on fourteen or fifteen other holes. Two shots of most any description will put them on the green, which is denied them from the tee. And this is an assured fact, even the humblest or most mediocre golfers like to blaze away at a green that they can reach if they hit a good one.

It has been said that no course is any greater than its one-shot holes. These should be stand-outs, altogether imposing and inspiring. Consequently the green itself and its immediate surroundings provide all the character that such a hole has. Nothing other than these has any real value in the case of the hole which should be played with an iron. There may be a pretty little purling brook threading its way across in the foreground, but unless that water shows close to the green itself, preferably on one side or the other rather than directly across the line of play, it is quite useless as a hazard. So we find that the green itself reflects all the greatness of the one-shotter, and when the design of any green that is to take a long wood from the tee is considered, it must of necessity be a rather open and spread-out affair, gradually losing distinctive character as the length of the shot increases.

And so it was when we came to examine intimately the municipal course already referred to. Those three long one-shotters were all drab affairs, altogether the least interesting of the eighteen. We stood back of one of the greens and observed the efforts of numerous players to place a tee-shot on the carpet. Exactly one man from among twenty succeeded in getting home. To be sure these were not expert players but they did represent the golfer in general, who plays for all the pleasure he can get out of the game. All would have derived much more satisfaction from each of those three holes if it had been shorter, not over 195 yards let us say.

I am not contending that on certain occasions, when fields of crack golfers are contesting, that the long one-shotter may not be stretched just a bit. With these occasional events in mind it is perfectly sensible to provide a back teeing-ground, but for steady diet of the family, bring them up close to the table.

THE LOVELY THIRTEENTH AT HERMITAGE (BELMONT) C.C. IN RICHMOND

47   The Tiny Tims Of Golf

PREVIOUSLY we discussed the long one-shotters of our courses, and gave reasons for the limitation of the extreme length of the par 3 hole. Now let us turn to the other extreme and regard the very short ones—the Tiny Tims as I choose to call them. How short may these be?

I recall introducing a very short one when I planned the course at Sands Point, Long Island—the 10th as I remember and it measured a trifle less than a hundred yards. It so happened that it served as a rather necessary connecting link, but with a small green it turned out to be an interesting and, at the same time, testing shot. At the Lakeside Course, Hollywood, California, there is another wee one and if memory serves me this, too, measures around a hundred yards from tee to cup.

Now these are about as short as I would care to see. Anything short of this yardage would be trivial in my estimation and hardly worthy of a place on any course. It is possible that there may be exceptions of course. I would say that from 115 to 125 yards the short pitch hole would be satisfactory—provided it was guarded impressively. And this provision is of the utmost importance. Unless such a green stands forth impressively, despite its Lilliputian proportions, it is utterly wasted. It should be a little David challenging the Goliaths of golf.

Obviously the green should be small, following the precept that the shorter the shot the smaller the target, and here we have a green which should be fairly bristling with hazards, either natural or artificially so. The Tiny Tim is the one situation which causes me to depart from two convictions which have influenced me so long, and these concern the rear trap and the frontal hazard, which presents the obligatory carry.

Regarding the hazard immediately back of the usual green, I strongly incline to the belief that any shot dead on the line should not be punished simply because it is a trifle too courageous. Competent instructors endeavor to impress on their pupils the necessity of playing right up to the pin rather than timidly going for the front of the green and babying the chipped approach. It is for the encouragement of the healthy, brave shot to the flag that I object to the rear hazard. But in the case of Tiny Tim, I must admit that frequently the trap directly back may be

THE SHORT TENTH HOLE (140 YARDS) AT PINE VALLEY
Shown very clearly are the dangers that must be surmounted to reach the green. A player who steps upon this tee for the first time is aware of a sense of dizziness as the chasm, along the edge of which he must play, dawns upon him.

condoned, for here is a very short shot that should be played with something "on the ball" to hold its run.

As for the frontal, obligatory trap, this type of hole certainly causes me to draw away from my usual objection to it. Here the range of carry is fixed and most any class of player, even the most humble, should be able to carry trouble immediately in front of a 125 yard green. It may be remarked that in the case of two-shot holes where the approach, after a decently hit drive, is no longer than this, I frown on the compulsory carry. This is true for the rank and file that do not hit drives even decent enough to enable them to cope successfully with the frontal trap, which must be carried to the green. It is different in the situation of the tee-shot, for here the range is always the same and not at all unreasonable. It is always possible to eliminate the front hazard on any two-shot hole by the Master Trap, swinging partially across from one side or the other to a contoured green, which is only opened to the approach properly if the drive has been placed with precision. That is another subject that already has been discussed in our articles. But at the Tiny Tims a grim and teeth-showing trap is very necessary. Indeed the very short hole is decidedly weak without it. However when we consider even short one-shotters of greater length, let us say 150 yards, the contour of the green and different arrangement of trapping make the compulsory carry quite unnecessary.

It would appear that this recognition of the values of both front and rear traps at the very short holes implies that such a green should be heavily guarded on the sides as well. Most certainly. And the sand should be so arranged as to show vigorously on into the slopes and not confined to the floors of the traps. In brief, Tiny Tim should be a little Tartar, impressive and inspiring as it stands forth. It must be one of the show holes of the course, beautiful as a Siren, yet quite as guilefully dangerous.

The floor of the green should be entirely free of undulations, for luck figures so prominently when pitched balls strike on undulating surfaces. This does not mean that such a green must be monotonously plain—far from it. But the effects of impressive contouring are to be introduced from the outside edges with vigorous flarings to meet the pits. Any semblance of freakishness must be avoided, but for

that matter this rule holds true everywhere. I allude to it however because so often I observe efforts to make the short holes particularly stiff by the introduction of bizarre and ridiculous shapings and contours. Aside from the fact that the floor of the green must insure an honest reception to any properly hit ball and consequently must be barren of undulations, it must be remembered that such a green is smaller than usual and as much cup-cutting space as possible be provided. So many greens of all descriptions actually offer but small areas for cup-cutting because of broken surfaces.

It seems to me that a distribution of par 3 holes as follows would be entirely satisfactory—125 yards, 160, 175, and 195. But these should all be stand-out holes. Remember that no course is any better than its one-shotters.

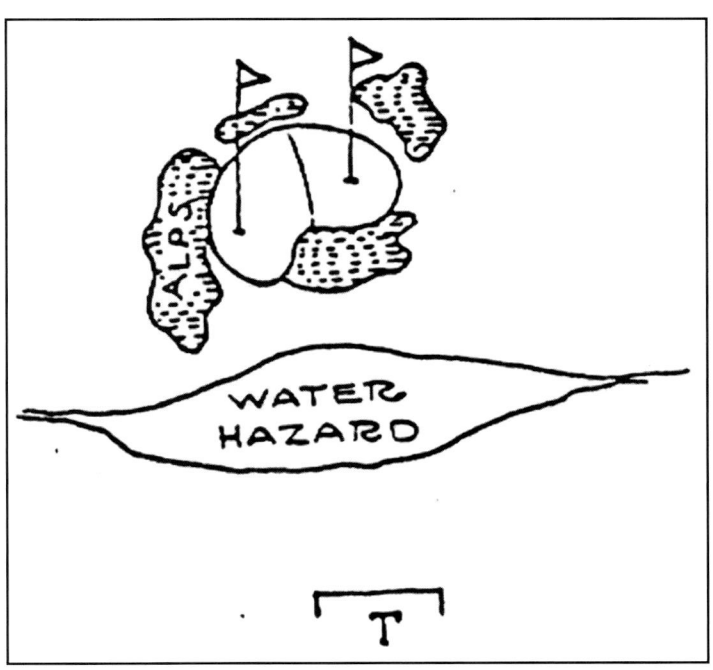

This very short hole is one which was reconstructed at Bedford. The shot which it calls for is a delicate pitch—the wrist shot.

The two flags may appear confusing, but, of course, only one of them is to be found on any occasion. But the bean-shaped green is in two sections, divided by a gentle undulation. That part on the left offers a comparatively easy problem, but when the hole is cut in the other section, a most accurate and controlled pitch is necessary.

The more difficult side of the green is reserved for occasions when a field of experts are to find their strokes tested, and while unusual accuracy is demanded, it must be remembered that the distance is only a trifle more than one hundred yards.

The shape and size of any green should be regulated by the type and length of stroke which is to find it.

48 More Concerning Mr. Par

IN A PREVIOUS chapter there were set forth, briefly, facts concerning the birth of the Par kid in the opening years of the present century and his remarkable and expansive growth during the ensuing years until this moment. As the game of golf lengthened out, as new fangled balls and clubs, not to forget better conditioned courses, enabled players generally to cover more ground, the growth of this Par boy kept pace. The pencils of golf calculators were sharpened when Par was still youthful and a few additions were made to score cards. Birdies and Eagles were rated differently than of old, and then Mr. Par reached manhood and stopped growing. But Golf did nothing of the sort and the length of shots from blows of wood and iron gradually increased. True enough, this was more apparent when the mighty ones of golf foregathered for combat than when the more humble ones trod their devious paths, but everyone began to bag more birds than ever before. In brief, Old Man Par was becoming less difficult to overhaul.

Those who designed courses realized this situation long since, and holes were planned accordingly. But on our score cards, par lengths have remained the same for a number of years now. Par figures have been used as a basis of comparison of courses, yet often enough nothing could be more misleading. For a time, some years back when balls suddenly achieved new flights, it seemed that some sensible legislation might be necessary to restrict this rather alarming tendency. It was prophesied that courses generally would be ruined unless the solons of golf did legislate against greater distance. But after all this drastic measure apparently was quite unnecessary, and sane limitations naturally entered the picture as the ingenuity of dynamite ball inventors neared the peak.

Now all this preamble brings me to the subject of this paper. May we consider the par 5 hole? In this classification we find lengths of 450, 460, 470, 480 yards and more. The par 5 hole is assumed to call for three shots to the green but under normal conditions any first class player would be strongly tempted to chuck his clubs into the lake if he could not get home with a second on any of the four yardages mentioned. The mighty hitters from the tee would probably use a Four or a Three Iron to reach the carpet of any of these, and a Bird 4 or Eagle 3 really is nonsensical nowadays when the big guns are firing. Would you find any of these paying off on this basis when playing among themselves for their own "gelt?" Most assuredly not

Yet we cannot fairly consider the taking of these distances and putting them in the par 4 class, although some of the greatest courses in the country have done precisely this. We must consider the average player to whom these ranges are still par 5s under the best of circumstances. They naturally enough like to have a few pars recorded on their cards, and the more the better for their encouragement so long as they have played decently enough to secure a fair par. No, I think that we should leave our carded distances pretty much as they are. But we assuredly must recognize the necessity of caring for the situation by the design of holes of the lengths we are contemplating.

We can only solve the problem by understanding that there is a great difference between the par 5 which is only a long two-shotter and that which, by reason of its greater length, is planned distinctly to provide for three shots to the green by any player, no matter how potentially long he may be. The 7th at Pine Valley is a splendid example of this type, and other papers have been devoted exclusively to the long par 5, the true three-shotter. But it is of the short par 5 that we speak now.

Let us assume that we are regarding a hole which measures 460 yards, and there is nothing about the terrain or the location of the teeing-ground, or even an estimate of the generally prevalent wind, to cause us to believe that it would play anything other than its yardage—neither longer or shorter. Our conception of the design of the holes, particularly that of the green, for every hole derives its real character from the green itself, must bring to mind two distinct class of players—the par shatterer on one hand and, on the other, that 90% that are striving ever to break 90. Can we conceive a wide open green on the large side to take the second of the average long-hitter or a very tightly bunkered, comparatively small green to take a very accurate third? At this range (460 yards) neither would be entirely adequate in my opinion or according to my custom. The small, tight green would ask too much of our Par friend and the larger, open green not enough of the other.

Theory alone does not influence my reaction to the type I advocate. Practical demonstration alone is responsible. Make this green of medium area, possibly six thousand square feet (certainly not more than seven thousand), and bunker either the left-front or the right-front with a vigorous Master Trap (as has been described in these papers) and with the long axis of the green opening definitely to one side of the fairway or the other, which is quite obvious with the mention of the placement of the Master Trap. This arrangement has proved itself to be entirely satisfactory in its demand on all class of play. The long-hitter, who desires to gamble a bit with his second, must place it with great precision, and the placement of his tee-shot is equally vital. In the case of the more humble golfer who must regard the distance as a par 5 as far as he is concerned, he has to make the placements of his first two shots take him to a suitable position to attack the green from the most favorable angle.

This is entirely in line with my contention that all holes should be so arranged as to make our low-scoring fraternity place their shots with more caution and precision than ever before while, at the same time, we leave the gate even a bit more open for the fellow who is less ambitious, much less skillful, and certainly not as husky.

THE NEW COURSE AT NEWPORT COUNTRY CLUB

Afterword
Following Tillie's Tracks

Acacia • Alameda Muni • Albany • Albany Muni • Albuquerque • Amsterdam Muni • Amwalk • Antioch Muni • Ashbourne • Ashland • Audubon • Aurora • Austin • Austin Muni • Avalon • Avon • Baederwood • Balboa Park Muni • Baltusrol • Bass Rocks • Bear Hill Club • Bear Hill Golf Club • Beaver Dam • Bel-Air • Bellevue • Belvue • Beresford (Peninsula) • Berkely • Berkshire • Berrien Hills • Big Spring • Birmingham • Black Hawk • Bloomfield • Bloomington • Bob-O-Links • Bobby Jones • Bonneville Muni • Bonnie Briar • Brackenridge Park Muni • Brae Burn • Briar Hall • Broadmoor • Brook Hollow • Brooklands • Bryn Mawr • Burlingame • Butte des Morts • Butterfield • Canterbury • Capital City (Tallahasee) • Carolina • Cedar Crest • Cedar Rapids • Chagrin Valley • Charles River • Cherokee Muni • Churchville • Davenport Munis • Davis Islands • Del Paso • Denver • Des Moines • Druid Hills • Drumlins • Duixbury • Dunwoodie • Durand Eastman Muni • East Aurora • East Orange • East Potomac Park • Echo Lake • Edgemere Public • Edgewood • Edison • El Camino • El Rio • Elmhurst • Elyria • Emerald Hills • Essex County • Essex Fells • Eureka • Fairfield • Fairlawn Heights • Fairview • Firecrest • Firestone • Farmington • Forest Hill • Forest Hills • Forest Lake • Fort Douglas • Fort Myers • Fox Chapel • Fox Hills • Franklin Hills • Gadsen • Galveston • Gassy Sprain • Genesee Valley Muni • Glen Echo • Glen Garden • Glen Lakes • Glen Oak • Golden Valley • Green Briar • Green Gables • Green Hill • Griffith Park Muni • Grossingher • Gulf Hills • H.J. Johnson Park Muni • Hacienda • Hackensack • Happy Hollow • Harding Memorial Park Muni • Hawthorne Valley • Henry Staumbaug Muni• Herbert Fisk Johnson Park • Hermitage (Belmont) • Highland Park • Highlawn Park • Hillcrest • Hillview Public • Hollywood • Houston (Gus Wortham) • Hubbard Public • Hudson River • Idle Hour • Indian Hills • Indian Spring • Ingleside Public • Inglewood • Interlachen • Inverness • Irondequoit • Ivanhoe • J.E. Good Muni • Jackson Heights • Jamesville • Keller • Kennett Square • Kenosha • Kilbourn • Kingswood • Kirtland • Knollwood • La Crosse • La Cumbre • La Grange • La Mesa • La Rinconada • Lafayette • Lake Chabot Public • Lake Merced • Lake Shore • Lakeside • Lakeville • Lakewood • Lexington • Lincoln Park • Lincoln Park Muni • Linden • Little River • Llanerch • Longmeadow • Longue Vue • Los Altos • Los Serranos • Louisville • Lu Lu Temple • Manakiki • Manchester • Manor Golf Course • Maple Bluff • Massasoit • Mayfield • Maynard • Meadow Brook • Meadowbrook • Medinah • Melrose • Memorial Park Muni • Memphis • Merchantville • Metacomet • Miami Biltmore • Midlothian • Milburn • Mill Road Farm • Millbrae • Millburn • Minneapolis • Mission Hills • Mobile • Modesto Muni • Mohawk • Monore • Montecito • Monterey Bay • Mount Vernon Muni in City Park • Nakoma • New Haven • Newark • Niagara Falls • Niagara Falls Muni • Nibley Park Muni • Norfolk • North Hills • North Jersey • Northwood • Oak Hills • Oak Park • Oakhurst • Oakland • Oakland Hills • Oakwood • Officer's Mess Puget Sound • Ogden • Oklahoma City • Old Dominion • Old Mission • Old Oaks • Old York Road • Omaha • Omaha Field • Oneida • Orchard Park • Orinda • Osceola Muni • Oshkosh • Owensboro • Ozaukee • Pacific Grove Muni • Palma Ceia • Palos Verdes • Pasadena • Pawtucket • Peoria • Philadelphia • Picadome • Pickwick • Pine Lake • Pontiac • Pittsburgh Field Club • Pontoosuc Lake • Portage • Powelton Club • Presidio • Purpoodoch Willowdale • Quantico • Quincy • Rancho Santa Fe • Ravisloe • Reading • Ridgemoor • Ridgewood • Ridglea • Rio Del Mar • River Crest • River Forest • River Oaks • Riverbuck Muni Course • Riverside • Riverside Municipal • Riverton • Riviera • Rochester • Rockledge • Rocky Point • Round Hill • Sacramento Muni • Salt Lake City • San Diego • San Diego Muni • San Francisco • San Jose • San Marcos Fairway • Sauganash • Seattle • Seneca Muni • Sequoya • Shackamaxon • Shawnee • Shawnee Muni • Sheboygan • Shoreacres • Shreveport • Siwanoy • Sleepy Hollow • Soldiers Memorial Field • South Shore • South View • Southern Hills • Spring Lake • Springdale • St. Andrews • St. Davids • St. Joseph • Stafford • Standard • Stanford University • Stockdale • Stockton Muni • Sunset Hill • Sunset Ridge • Superior Golf Course • Swope Park Muni • Syracuse Yacht • Tavistock • Techny Fields Tekoa • The Park • Timpanogos Muni • Tony Town Tavern • Top O'World • Topeka • Town & Country • Tri-County • Triggs Memorial • Triple A Club • Troy • Tuckaway • Tuxedo • Twin Hills • Twin Orchard • United Shoe Machinery • Vallejo • Valley of Hill Courses • Van Rensselear • Valley • Victory Hills Public • Virginia • Wachusett • Walla Walla • Wallingford • Walpole • Wampanoag • Washington State • Watsonville • Waverley • Wee Burn • West End • Western • Western Turnpike • Westgate Valley • Westmoor • Westmoreland • Westwood • Westwood Hills • Wheatley Hills • White Beeches • White Lakes • Wildwood • Willowbrook • Wilshire • Winchester • Wolferts Roost • Woodbridge Hills • Woodcrest • Woodholme • Woodlawn Public • Woodmere • Woodmont • Woodward • Worcester • Worth Hills • Z Boaz Muni

THE TENTH AT PALOS VERDES CC
Architect's note: *First I located a new green for their present tenth hole, selecting an entirely new site in the trees considerably to the left of the old one. This will add considerably to the length of the hole (something that was very much needed) and at the same time offer a much better approach. I gave full instructions for clearing and grading.*
Editor's note: *The original green can still be seen on the right.*

AT ONE TIME A.W. Tillinghast was the "forgotten genius" of golf course architecture. It was in 1974, when Mr. Frank Hannigan, an executive with the United States Golf Association, published the article that resurrected interest in Tillinghast. And, today, anyone with any knowledge of golf architecture can tell you that A.W. Tillinghast may have been one of the very best. His golf courses are consistently ranked in the top echelon and continue to host the big national championships.

Tillinghast is credited with around 70 original golf course designs, and an equal number of courses for redesign work. The majority of the known Tillinghast courses are in the northeast, within a day's drive of Tillie's former home base of operation—Harrington Park, New Jersey. However, Tillie also got around. Tillinghast courses are found throughout the United States, with a few in Canada. This alone is a noteworthy feat, since Tillie's time designing courses was thirty years, from around 1910 through 1940, a time before interstate highways and commercial air transportation. Tillie's primary mode of travel was by automobile over the highways and byways of those days.

Recent research of Tillinghast's letters has uncovered that the design record of this once forgotten genius spans many more courses than those that have previously been recorded. In fact, Tillie himself, late in his life, wrote, "I have been intimately in touch with the construction of holes of my design on more than a thousand golf courses in every part of the land." Well if this is the case, what additional golf courses have Tillie to credit? And when and how did Tillie impact these courses?

The answer is this: Tillie was a "road warrior." He lived to travel and traveled to lived. Outside of his prime territory of New Jersey, New York, Connecticut, and Pennsylvania, Tillie designed golf courses in California, Florida, Kansas, Illinois, Maryland, Massachusetts, Minnesota, Missouri, North Carolina, South Carolina, Oklahoma, Texas, Virginia and many other states. One of his most famous designs is the San Francisco Golf Club. Over the course of thirty years, Tillie made numerous cross-country automobile trips to California to advise on reconstruction and improvements to this great golf course. You do not have to be a rocket scientist to figure that Tillie did not drive clear across the country just to visit one golf course. Rather he visited hundreds. As most of Tillie's original course designs are known, many more of his redesign and renovation works are not known. This really should not be too surprising, since the records of most golf clubs and courses of that time on most business matters, such as the visits of golf course architects, generally have been lost.

It is a known fact that in the summer of 1935, Tillie commenced a tour of the country's golf courses as a consulting golf course architect for the P.G.A. of America. Tillie was hired by his good friend George Jacobus, who was then president of the P.G.A. of America. Tillie's service was provided free of charge and only to golf courses where P.G.A. members were retained. Tillie's tour lasted two years through the summer of 1937. He visited over 500 golf courses and has generally been credited with the elimination of thousands of sandtraps, which he called "Duffer Headaches," or DHs for short. Tillie's DHs included obsolete bunkers, unnatural mounds (sometimes called chocolate drops) or other antiquated course features that hinder the higher handicap player, and are costly to maintain. In fact, in the middle of his tour Tillie wrote, "It is a matter of record that I have condemned nearly eight thousand sand traps."

However, few people are aware that, Tillie's services were much more than the elimination of obsolete or "useless" sand bunkers. In fact, Tillie had significant design input into hundreds of the golf courses he visited. There are dozens of well known courses with complete golf holes and greens designed by Tillinghast on which golfers play day in and day out thinking they are playing an untouched Donald Ross course, or a course of some other noted designer of the classic era of golf course design.

Tillie also advised on turf conditions. On the municipal course in Worcester, Massachusetts, Tillie wrote, "Their chief problem and those upon which they wanted my direct suggestion, involved the turf on the greens. A condition, which I immediately identified as Dollar Patch, was evident. Already it had been assumed that this was Pythian (requiring liming to correct acidity). I gave them my opinion that fungus was at work and suggested a remedy." Today, similar services are provided day in and day out by the United States Golf Association's Green Section.

Tillie's tour made two complete loops of the United States, with some doubling back in a few spots. His mode of operation was to take temporary residence

ST. DAVIDS BEFORE

ST. DAVIDS AFTER

Architect's note: *The ninth hole represented a compromise with the original plan made necessary when the clubhouse was built. The green was designed to receive a short approach, coming to it from the right, and consequently it is bunkered tightly on the sides. However, it was found necessary to cut down the yardage of the hole (it ranges from 240 to let us say 265 yards from an elevated teeing ground). Consequently it may be driven by the long hitters at times, and the green is not suited to the long shot in any respect. After a careful study of all the conditions I came to the conclusion that the hole would make a better one-shotter to a new green to the right-front of the former green. It is a natural situation and I believe the new hole will play better at the shorter range (a spoon) to a proper green. The loss of yardage will not matter as the course now measures 6,682 yards.*

in a hotel in a major city and make daily visits to courses from there. Tillie coordinated his trips in advance through the local section of the P.G.A., generally with the local P.G.A. section president. Tillie's visits were by invitation only from the host P.G.A. professional. If a non-P.G.A. member pro requested his services, Tillie respectfully declined in each case. He would also let George Jacobus know, as he did in Rochester, NY when he wrote Jacobus of two clubs which he had declined and told him that, "I am going nowhere unless at the request of your members."

In some cities he was greeted with great fanfare and the local newspapers would write a lead story on his visit. But not every one was glad to see Tillie coming. In Massachusetts Tillie was greeted with resentment by the New England Green Keeper's association. In a subsequent meeting with three of the leaders of this association, Tillie convinced them that his motives were pure and each expressed the desire for Tillie to visit their respective clubs.

Tillie reported back to George Jacobus on a daily basis by mail. His letter reports would often describe in detail his recommended design changes to the courses he visited. In the case of new design recommendations and design changes, Tillie would provide each club a written plan and sketches from which to work by. In some cases, Tillie would recommend the services of a local architect to oversee the work. For example, on examining the new course of the Philadelphia C.C. at Spring Mill, Tillie designed a new first hole and reviewed several problems involving major construction. His solution was to recommend the work to William Flynn, a local architect and construction man. Tillie reported back, "Being as helpful as possible as is consistent with the aims and operation of our P.G.A. service." Other architects benefiting from such referrals included Billy Bell in California, John Bredemus in Oklahoma, and Orrin Smith in Connecticut. In fact, Bell would later assert that Tillie's visit "had stimulated his work to a very marked degree."

At the time of his tour, the talented touring professionals were affiliated with a club and many were presidents of their local section. Many of these pros were instrumental in coordinating Tillie's examinations. In Chicago, it was Horton Smith, and Tillie did a complete examination of Horton's home club, Oak Park C.C. In Mobile, Alabama, Tillie examined Tony Penna's winter home: the Osceola public golf course. And in Los Angeles, Olin Dutra's home club, Wilshire C.C., received the same complete treatment.

At the Austin Country Club, Tillie advised Harvey Penick on the location and building of a new green for the eleventh hole, one of 112 yards. Tillie reported that, "I gave him all the information he desired and the new green will be built about twenty yards back of the present." Later that day, Tillie advised Harvey's brother Tom Penick on several additions to the Austin Municipal course.

Tillie's travels were not always easy. Weather was the biggest stumbling block and the roads were not always good. On his way to Houston from New Orleans, flooding from heavy storms made the roads barely passable. He wrote, "The water was over the running-boards. Nothing to do for it but to keep the wheels moving ahead. There was no turning back." In California, on a return trip to check progress he had outlined the year before on the Stockdale course in Bakersfield, Tillie was turned back on treacherous roads in mountain country by heavy rains and mudslides. Many of his visits, primarily in California, were totally rained out.

Although, only in his early sixties at the time of his tour, Tillie became quite sick on several occasions. On March 2, 1937, he wrote Jacobus, "Ever since Washington's Birthday I have been a very sick man. You may recall that a previous report stated that I had been fighting off the flu for sometime. Apparently it caught up with me with a vengeance for on the morning after the holiday, I was confined to bed with an alarming lung congestion. But I am out again although feeling somewhat shaky." On his way through Rochester, Minnesota, he checked into the Mayo clinic for some care by a Dr. Horton, who perhaps was recommended by his son-in-law, a practicing physician at the clinic.

At the Top O' World Golf Club in Bloomer, Wisconsin, Tillie was stood up. On arriving at the course, he reported, "I found absolutely no one on the place. There was no clubhouse, but only a stand at the first Teeing ground, where signs announced that sandwiches were sold. That, too, was empty and locked tight." Despite this, Tillie walked the course noting the general characteristics and deficiencies.

Fairfield C.C.: Hole today and design sketch. "Probably the most important of my findings was an entirely new short fourth. And it is hard to understand how it has escaped notice for the past fifteen years, for it is a natural and peculiarly obvious one; and when I pointed it out, it was hailed by Mr. Vanderbilt as "a stroke of genius." It was nothing more than a practiced eye picking out something which was there for everyone to see."

Tillinghast Design Attributes

So what did a Tillie exam recommend? It generally entailed every hole on the course and would often result in the redesign and remodeling of tees, fairways and greens. In many cases complete new holes were designed. Tillie's recommendations were true to his defined principals of modern golf architecture. The principals are common to all Tillinghast courses, and were clearly spelled out in his reports to George Jacobus. Some of Tillie's principals that stand out in his letter reports follow:

Natural Slopes: "I emphasized the necessity of pulling out the slopes to the ratio of six feet to every foot of elevation (my invariable rule) and of BLENDING all. This word 'Blending' I use a great deal in my explanations and it proves to be a good one for my purposes."

Teeing grounds: These should be graded and blended naturally to meet their surroundings. "I still observe the tendency to preserve pulpit-like, raised teeing grounds." "The larger, natural looking teeing areas are to be found on most of our first class courses today, but I still observe the relics of the dark ages on too many links."

Greenside Guarding Pits: "Sand pits should nestle close-up, with the sand showing up into the slopes."

Green Size: "Let me state here that when I encounter those who are used to extremely large greens I do not try to tear them away from their predilections, except where the great areas rob greens, reached by short shots, of any virtues. It is well known that I always have favored the comparatively smaller and closely guarded green, but I certainly refrained from injecting my personal feelings into the picture where I sense that the contrary method has been favored. I find the courses, where the large greens have been fancied, are cutting them down in size gradually as their futility is recognized."

Duffer's Headaches: "I have contended that these have been maintained at considerable cost to nearly 400 clubs, that they unnecessarily harass the great majority of those who take to the game for pleasure without in the least causing that comparatively small number of par shooters to give them a thought, and usually injecting a thoroughly discordant note and smudging an otherwise beautiful picture of rural landscape." The DHs "catch the poor shots of poor players. These add aggravation and are of no value."

Trees: Tillie incorporated trees to a great extent in his designs. At the Z. Boaz municipal course in Fort Worth he "recommended the gradual planting of trees in clumps to relieve the monotonous flatness of the course." However, Tillie would quickly condemn trees that were out of place and interfered with play: "I sometimes take my very life in my hands when I suggest that a certain tree happens to be spoiling a pretty good hole. The green committee chairman is like as not to glare at me as though I had recommended that he go home and murder his wife."

Tillie developed detailed reports on his design recommendations for each course examined. When construction work was involved, which was often the case, he provided detailed design sketches for the constructors to follow. He would often recommend a local architect and construction firm to perform the work. Tillie would return to the course the following season to check on the progress of his plans. As an example, on his return to San Jose C.C. Tillie reported that his recommendations for a new 7th green and other construction work "had been faithfully followed by Greenkeeper George Satana."

Reflections on his Peers

In reference to other architects of the time, Tillie generally praised the work and capabilities of several of his peers—Donald Ross, George Thomas, Max Behr, Perry Maxwell, Chandler Egan, and Billy Bell. However, on the occasion of his examination of The Valley Club in Santa Barbara, Tillie did slightly knock the bunkering on this Alister Mackenzie and Robert Hunter collaboration: "I complimented Hunter particularly on the masterly manner in which the approaches to the greens were contoured. This is a most noticeable feature of this notably fine collection of holes. However, there were some useless pits, often in the back-flares of greens, and frequently the arrangement of turf and sand in the hazards was trivial and not worthy of the greater part of the work."

As far as DH removal, Tillie most impacted the early American golf courses, designed by the likes of Tom Bendelow, Devereux Emmet, Donald Ross and Walter Travis.

At the Beresford Country Club (which is now called Peninsula), a Donald Ross design, Tillie noted that the course builder had poorly constructed several of the holes which did not resemble the original Ross conceptions. Consequently, Tillie advised on the construction of new sites for the 10th, 12th, and 13th greens. His plans were in no sense a reflection of the original Ross plans, but were "made necessary because those original plans had been sinfully juggled."

Tillie examined many other Donald Ross courses, and from his reports a great respect for his fellow architect can be gleaned. In fact, during his tour in early December of 1935, Tillie turned a bit aside from his scheduled route to drop in on his old friend in Pinehurst, North Carolina. When Tillie knocked at the door of Donald Ross's charming home, Donald greeted him warmly, and after a bit of chat about this and that, the two old golf architects were out the back door and playing the #2 course, where the PGA championship had been scheduled for the upcoming summer. As Tillie and Donald stood on every hole the great architect proudly called to Tillie's attention each subtle feature. Tillie was greatly impressed and later wrote: "Without any doubt Ross regards this as his greatest achievement.

Tillie examined many of America's greatest courses on his tour—the likes of Bel Air, Canterbury, Colonial, Country Club, Firestone, Inverness, Interlocken, Lake Merced, Medinah, Miami Biltmore, Oklahoma City, Pittsburgh Field Club, River Oaks, Round Hill, Shoreacres, Stanford, Waverly, Worcester, and many more. At the request of P.G.A. sectional president Willie Hunter, Tillie went over the entire Riviera C.C. course and prepared a critical report for future reference. Overall Tillie was quite impressed with the George Thomas designed Riviera and stated in the emphatic, "Certainly Riviera is a great course."

Tillie can probably lay claim to the mantle of the first "Open Doctor," to be followed by Robert Trent Jones and his son Rees Jones. In the fall of 1936, at the request of Al Watrous, the P.G.A. professional at Oakland Hills C.C. in Birmingham, Michigan, Tillie examined this great course in preparation for the USGA Men's Open Championship of 1937. Tillie recommended the elimination of several DHs and approved the shifting of five teeing grounds which extended the course's entire length to a trifle over seven thousand yards. Naturally, Tillie thought highly

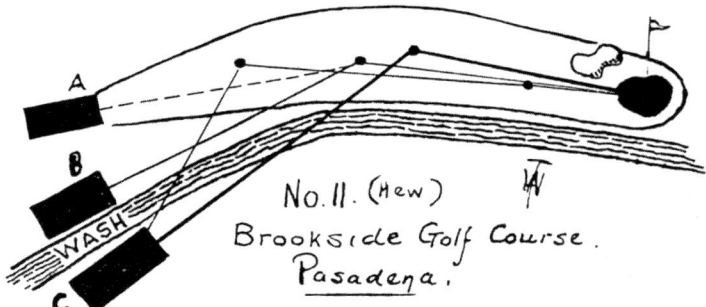

Architect's note: It is interesting, no doubt, to regard the modern touches of general revamping as roughy indicated in my sketch of the 11th hole at Brookside Golf Course in Pasadena. Originally the fairway was open to a drive from a point directly across the wash. This has been abandoned and two entirely new teeing-grounds built close by each side of the wash. An elective carry from each is provided and there is every opportunity to pick off considerable yardage according to the skill and courage of the player. The old teeing ground is indicated at A.

ROCHESTER G.&C.C.
Designed by Tillinghast for his son-in-law, Dr. Phil Brown, and daughter, Elsie.

of Oakland Hills, and would later write, "Make no mistake, here is truly a great course." Tillie also examined the Memphis C.C. in preparation for the Women's National Amateur Championship of 1937.

As may be expected, not all of Tillie's recommendations were implemented. On returning to Bel Air in February of 1937, Tillie expressed some disappointment that his recommendations were totally ignored. He would report, "It has been said that you may lead a horse to water but you may not make him drink." "I can only make recommendations but certainly I show no irritation if they are passed over, as in this case." His solace on the matter, was a strong sentiment among players favoring the recommendations and the hope that eventually they would materialize.

Although Green Committee members would typically accompany Tillie on his examinations, Tillie acknowledged the difficulty of gaining consensus and approval for much needed course improvements. He would report, "the cry of—'It just can't be done here!" has hindered the proper development of courses to a lamentable extent in many sections."

Not every course required improvements or change. Tillie described Lakeside, a Max Behr design in California, as "one of the best courses examined." No changes of any note were recommended. After visiting The Country Club in Pepper Pike Ohio, Tillie declared, "Here is a fine course, exceptionally conditioned, with good greens of Washington strain bent."

On Self Examination

Tillie visited several courses of his own design on his tour: Baltusrol, Brackenridge, Brook Hollow, Cedar Crest, Indian Hills, Niagara Falls, Ridgewood, San Francisco, Shawnee, Swope Park, Winged Foot, and several others.

On his visit to the Hermitage Country Club (now known as Belmont), a design built by Tillie twenty years before, Tillie admitted that he had to take his own medicine and recommended removal of several of his own DHs. He wrote that day, "I candidly criticized a number of hazards, which I had placed myself, just as I have done at many other courses. But it must be remembered that general play has lengthened out considerably in twenty years and that long ago we were much closer to another period of course conception. The pits which I condemned today come under my classification of 'Duffers Headaches' and without hesitation I took my own medicine which I have been prescribing. I will say however that the pits which I closed today were comparatively few in number and in no instance did they represent carries but rather side pits, closer in than we place them now."

In Tulsa, Tillie recommended the fix of some

faulty construction to the Tulsa C.C. and Oaks C.C., courses of his own design. He reported "I made a number of suggestions concerning the rectification of faulty green contours, the result of bad construction work when the course was built by the constructor engaged by the club to interpret my plans. These may be accomplished at little expense."

Tillie was fairly modest in reporting on his own designs. Only once did he express a little "designers pride" in describing San Francisco, "In as much as I planned this lay-out it may not seem entirely proper for me to praise it too much. But it is regarded out here as truly great course."

Tillie's Personality

Much has already been written about the personality traits or flaws of A.W. Tillinghast—his fits of rage, flamboyant lifestyle, lavish spending and drinking binges. From Tillie's letters other more noble personality traits of this genius can be gleaned:

Tireless work ethic: Tillie reported to George Jacobus almost every day on his two year tour and rarely took a day off, with the exception of Christmas, New Years and visits to his daughters, Marion, in Toledo, Ohio, and Elsie, in Rochester, Minnesota.

Family Man: Tillie's wife, Lillian, accompanied him on his cross country travels, and she would remain by Tillie's side until his death in 1942.

Protector of the Game: Tillie had strong beliefs on what was right for the game. On an earlier swing of the West Coast in the winter of 1935, Tillie expressed strong disapproval of a plan to introduce pari-mutuel betting at the Agua Caliente tournament in Mexico. He would later write, "Out here the level heads of golf express regret that the idea has received any encouragement, for certainly it is not in keeping with the traditions of the game and should be regarded as a menace."

Modesty: When asked to rank the best golf courses in California, Tillie replied, "With thanks I must regretfully decline this opportunity to lead with my chin. Although I have formed conclusions I would consider it extremely bad taste for one, so long associated with course designing and construction in the East, to make any comparisons. As I grow older I appreciate the fact that for general publication there are some questions that need a whole lot of letting alone."

Accepting Fate: Tillie would lose his home and fortune to the depression and eventually was forced into personal bankruptcy. Despite this, Tillie never railed his fate in life and always looked forward.

In September 1936, when he lost his house in Harrington Park, there was not a hint of regret when he wrote Jacobus, "Today will see the permanent closing of my old home here and tomorrow I start the drive to the Michigan section."

Letters of Thanks

Gratitude for Tillie's work was expressed in numerous letters to George Jacobus. Typical of the thank you letters was Jack Forester's, the pro at Hackensack, who closed his letter with, "Congratulations to you and the P.G.A. for this fine service." Another wonderful compliment was made by Dixwell Davenport, the Green Chairman at San Francisco G.C., who was also a member of the USGA's Green Section. Davenport told Tillie that in his opinion, "The P.G.A. had put one over the USGA in sponsoring the course service." Well the USGA was not put over for long, for its Green Section developed its own advisory service; and this service has grown tremendously and now has dozens of professionals operating from 10 offices throughout the United States.

TILLIE OUTSIDE THE GATE AT FIVE FARMS

Editor's note: *A.W. Tillinghast's tour for the P.G.A. was researched at the World Golf Hall of Fame in St. Augustine, Florida. The writings of A.W. Tillinghast have been compiled in this book and two prior volumes. For more information, contact The Tillinghast Association at www.tillinghast.net or call 1-888-584-8455.*

Chapter Bibliography

RECOLLECTIONS OF A GOLF ARCHITECT, Golf Illustrated, February, March, April & May 1924

1. *MODERN GOLF CHATS*, The Golf Course, January 1916.
2. *BUILDING GOLF COURSES IN THE SOUTH*, Golfers' Magazine, February 1916; Golf Illustrated, February 1924.
3. *THE CATAPULTERS OF SAN ANTONIO*, Golf Illustrated, Volume 38, 1932-1933
4. *AND THEY BUILT A COURSE BY THE TRINITY RIVER*, Golf Illustrated, November 1934.
5. *OUT TULSA WAY*, Golf Illustrated, Vol 40 #6, 1934; Golf Illustrated, February 1924.
6. *THE NECESSITY FOR A TALE OF WOE COMMITTEE*, The Golfer's Magazine, March 1914.
7. *SPRING LAKE*, Golf Illustrated, Our Green Committee Page, August 1919.
8. *CALIFORNIA COURSES*, Golf Illustrated, Our Green Committee Page, February 1920
9. *ROUGH GOING*, Golf Illustrated, December 1922.
10. *OUR GREEN COMMITTEE PAGE*, Golf Illustrated, July 1917, January 1918, Volumes 9-10 1918-1919, April 1919, July 1919, February 1932.
11. *A HOLE IS JUST AS LONG AS IT PLAYS*, Golf Illustrated, Our Green Committee Page, June 1919.
12. *BOUNDARY HOLES*, Golf Illustrated, December 1918.
13. *DENSE SHRUBBERY*, Golf Illustrated, Our Green Committee Page, September 1919.
14. *AN UNUSUAL DOUBLE DOG-LEG*, Golf Illustrated, Our Green Committee Page, April 1920.
15. *A SHORT PITCHED SHOT*, Golf Illustrated, Our Green Committee Page, November 1918.
16. *THE BOOMERANG HOLE — A GROUND SAVER*, Golf Illustrated, Our Green Committee Page, January 1920.
17. *A WASTED HAZARD*, Golf Illustrated, Our Green Committee Page, March 1920.
18. *THE OPEN AT WINGED FOOT*, Golf Illustrated, June 1929.
19. *A NINE-HOLE COURSE ON 20 OR 30 ACRES*, Golf Illustrated, July 1929.
20. *MAKING THE MOST OF THE TEE*, The American Golfer, May 1932.
21. *TEEING GROUNDS FOR TWO-SHOTTERS*, The American Golfer, August 1932.
22. *SANS SAND PITS*, The American Golfer, January 1933; Golf Illustrated, February 1924.
23. *A DOUBLE GREEN*, The American Golfer, February 1933.
24. *MINIATURE GOLF COURSES*, Golf Illustrated, November 1930; The Professional Golfer of America, December 1936; Golf Illustrated, June 1916.
25. *POPULAR TYPES OF GOLF HOLES*, Golf Illustrated, June 1931.
26. *AN EXCEPTION TO RULE*, Golf Illustrated, June 1933.
27. *BLIND HOLES*, Golf Illustrated, July 1933.
28. *DOWN TO OLD MEXICO FOR GOLF*, Golf Illustrated, December 1933.
29. *WINTER GREENS*, Golf Illustrated, January 1935.
30. *SNAKE HOLES AND GOLF HOLES*, Golf Illustrated, April 1935; Golf Illustrated, February 1924.
31. *THE FIVE FARMS COURSE*, Golf Illustrated, September 1932; The American Golfer, September 1932.
32. *OUT OF THE ADIRONDACKS*, Golf Illustrated, March 1935.
33. *"'WAY DOWN AND 'WAY OUT,"* Golf Illustrated, February 1935.
34. *WHAT THE P.G.A. COURSE SERVICE REALLY MEANS*, The Professional Golfer of America, October 1935.
35. *THE MASTERPIECE OF DONALD ROSS*, The Professional Golfer of America, February 1936.
36. *GLEANINGS FROM THE WAYSIDE*, The Professional Golfer of America, May 1936.
37. *FROM THE GULF TO PUGET SOUND*, The Professional Golfer of America, June 1936.
38. *THINGS I AM OBSERVING*, The Professional Golfer of America, October 1936.
39. *INTIMATE SURVEY OF OAKLAND HILLS*, The Professional Golfer of America, November 1936
40. *WHEN TRAPS ARE FRIENDLY*, The Professional Golfer of America, January 1937.
41. *TEXAS GETTING BENT-MINDED*, The Professional Golfer of America, February 1937.
42. *THE UGLY DUCKLING OF THE COURSE*, The Professional Golfer of America, March 1937.
43. *NOW WHAT ABOUT TREES?* The Professional Golfer of America, April 1937.
44. *OLD ANANIAS PAR*, The Professional Golfer of America, May 1937.
45. *THE GIMME GUYS*, The Professional Golfer of America, June 1937.
46. *THE LONG ONE-SHOTTER*, The Professional Golfer of America, July 1937.
47. *THE TINY TIMS OF GOLF*, The Professional Golfer of America, September 1937.
48. *MORE CONCERNING MR. PAR*, The Professional Golfer of America, October 1937.

Photo Credits

PHOTO CREDITS PHOTO AND SKETCH CREDITS IDENTIFIED BY PAGE (Code: T-Top, C-Center, B-Bottom, R-Right, L-Left)

American Golfer: 6TL, 6LC, 10B, 11T, 11B, 14, 24T, 24BR, 25T, 30B, 32, 44, 71C, 71B, 72CL, 72T, 72CR, 73TL, 73TR, 73C, 74T, 74B, 75C, 78, 80, 82, 84, 106C, 107, 111, 114B, 115T, 115B, 116, 119, 123, 125C, 125B, 130, 134, 137BL, 137TR; Baltimore CC: 59B, 108T; Baltusrol GC: 69T, 94, 136TL, 137TL; Binghamton CC: 17, 38; Brook Hollow GC: 27T; Walter Engel: 135; Elm Ridge CC: 104T; CC of Fairfield: 156T; Fenway CC: 61B; Forest Hill Field Club: 10T; Golden Valley CC: 20, 140; *Golf Illustrated*: 6, 8, 9CL, 9B, 10B, 12, 13T, 13B, 16B, 17TR, 17CR, 17BR, 24BL, 25B, 26T, 27B, 28T, 28B, 29, 33, 35T, 35B, 36T, 36C, 36B, 39, 40T, 40B, 41T, 47, 48T, 48C, 48B, 49T, 49C, 49BL, 49BR, 51, 57T, 57B, 61T, 65, 69B, 70, 73B, 75TR, 75TC, 75TR, 75CL, 75CR, 75B, 76, 79T, 79B, 87, 91, 92, 93, 95, 96T, 96B, 97, 98L, 98R, 99L, 99R, 100T, 100BL, 100BR, 104B, 105, 106B, 108B, 109T, 109BL, 109BR, 110, 112, 113T, 113B, 114T, 114C, 117, 121, 122, 124T, 124B, 125T, 126T, 126B, 127, 128TL, 128TR, 128B, 129L, 129R, 132, 146, 148; *Golfers Magazine*: 6TR, 21, 22T, 23, 26B, 31; *Golfing*: 101, 137BL, 137CR; Hagley Museum and Library, Dallin Collection: 118, 145; Hermitage CC: 59T, 141, 147; Indian Hills CC: 16T; Island Hills GC: 67; Lakewood CC: 15, 143; Edwin Levick: 139; Dan McKean: 156B; Newport CC: 151; *Pacific Coast Golfer*: 156; Palos Verdes CC: 153; *PGA Magazine*: 133; Pietzcker for *Golf Illustrated*: 30T; Ridgewood CC: 85; Rochester G&CC: 158; Rotophotos: 136TR; Scarsdale GC: 41; Strohmeyer: 37, 42, 71T; St. Andrews University Library, Cowie Collection: 86; St. Davids CC: 154; Sunnehanna CC: 63; Wide World Photos: 136B; Wyoming Valley CC: 81.